Young readers responding to poems

WITHDRAWN

Young readers responding to poems

Michael Benton
John Teasey
Ray Bell
Keith Hurst

R

Routledge

London and New York

First published in 1988 by
Routledge
11 New Fetter Lane, London EC4P 4EE
29 West 35th Street, New York, NY 10001

Set in Times 10/11pt.
by Columns of Reading
and printed in Great Britain
by Biddles Ltd, Guildford

Library of Congress Cataloging-in-Publication Data
Young readers responding to poems.
  Bibliography: p.
  Includes index.
  1. Young adult poetry—History and criticism.
2. Reader response criticism.   3. Poetry and children.
I. Benton, Michael, 1939–
PN1085.Y68   1988   801'.951'088055   88-2021

British Library Cataloguing in Publication Data
Young readers responding to poems.
  1. Secondary schools. Curriculum subjects:
  Poetry in English. Teaching
  I. Benton, Michael, 1939–
  821'.007'12

ISBN 0–415–00865–4 (c)
      0–415–01291–0 (p)

Contents

Acknowledgments

There are many friends and colleagues, too numerous to mention by name, who have helped us during the writing of this book. In particular, we would like to thank Geoff Fox and Ros Mitchell for their advice and for their detailed criticism of parts of the manuscript. Above all, we would like to thank the pupils: we hope we have done justice to their responses.

The authors and publishers would also like to record their thanks for permission to reproduce the following poems: the estate of Wilfred Owen and Chatto & Windus, 'Anthem for Doomed Youth' by Wilfred Owen; Andre Deutsch, 'I Share a Bedroom With My Brother' by Michael Rosen; Faber and Faber, 'The Jaguar' and 'The Stag' by Ted Hughes, 'Follower' by Seamus Heaney and 'Days' by Philip Larkin; and Penguin Books for 'Frogs in the Wood' by Brian Patten.

Preface

The task of literature teaching is an enabling one – to encourage children to become 'keen readers'. The ambiguity is deliberate: keen in the sense of enthusiastic and committed, and keen in the sense of intellectually acute and emotionally aware. Holding these twin pressures together provides a tension familiar to most English teachers, for the one indicates the felt need to motivate children to read stories and poems, to enable them to see themselves as readers and to develop a reading habit; whereas the other signals the desire to help children become more subtle and discerning readers. The first demands a generous inclusiveness from teachers and wide, indiscriminate reading from pupils; the second demands that both teachers and taught become more discriminating about the processes they undergo, for literary reading invites nothing less than the concentration of the whole self. How can we achieve this 'double keenness'? The short answer is by developing a methodology of literature teaching that is based upon informed concepts of *reading* and *response* rather than upon the conventional, inherited ideas of *comprehension* and *criticism* which, in the absence of anything else, have passed for the conceptual bases. The two Rs need to replace the two Cs.

Several recent reappraisals of English (e.g. Widdowson 1982, Eagleton 1983) have shown how, once it replaced Classics at the centre of the curriculum earlier this century, English cast about for some theory and method in order to authenticate its position. In literature teaching, criticism and comprehension became the twin pillars and were soon effectively buttressed by the examination system. 'Practical criticism' or 'critical appreciation' became the method with sixth formers and undergraduates; comprehension exercises became the lot of schoolchildren. The essential and peculiar discipline of literature – the use of language as 'symbolic form' (Langer, 1953), that is, where words operate not only as a system of referential symbols but are also shaped into aesthetic forms – was perverted. The uniqueness of subject English, the imaginative engagement with the symbolic forms of stories and poems, was despoiled.

Against this background, the aims of this book are all invested with the feeling that literature must be rescued from the teacher's *explication du texte* and given back, as it were, to readers. In order to reorientate teaching methods it is necessary to investigate what readers actually do when reading poems and in order to carry out such enquiries it is necessary to devise appropriate research methods. The particular aims of this book are, therefore, threefold: first, to describe our substantive findings about the nature of children's responses to poems; second, to develop and refine methods of enquiry that will be of use to others interested in the field; and third, to derive the implications for teaching and learning in the poetry classroom.

Our professional stance as teacher-researchers working with children who were mostly known to us as our own pupils, ensured the inter-relationship of these three aims throughout the enquiries. The concept of response, the means of exploring it, and the continuous striving for good practice in poetry teaching each acted upon the others. Quite properly, in the illuminative research we were engaged in, each was only fully definable by reference to the other two. For the phenomenon we were dealing with – young readers responding to poems – was a construct, supported by other contextual elements, comprising three main components: the concept of 'response', the means of monitoring, and the pedagogical assumptions that the participants brought.

Accordingly, our *substantive concerns* are to explore the nature of young readers' responses to poems by close attention to the ways individuals and groups negotiate with texts; to theorise the process of responding and to discover how readers move from an initial apprehending of a poem as a blur of words to the comprehending of it as a felt experience. Our *methodological concerns* are to study the effects of different monitoring procedures, in particular the use of spoken and written language as ways of constructing the reality of poems in both individual and group work; and to explore how varied sequences of such activities might elicit more developed and refined responses. From a research angle, the insights gained allow a more sophisticated description of 'reader response' to be formulated; from a teaching angle, they suggest improvements that can be made in classroom method. Indeed, our *pedagogical concerns* to develop a methodology based on 'keen' reading are our prime motivation. A main outcome is to suggest classroom practices that will interest and motivate children to read poetry with enthusiasm based on the knowledge that their individual responses are not only valid but valued as the main subject-matter of poetry lessons.

The five parts of the book exist in a federal relationship rather than develop as a linear argument. Chapter 1 discusses the theoretical ideas and practical approaches that have influenced our work and outlines the main conceptual and methodological problems in exploring responses to poetry. Chapter 2 studies the individual reader's processes of responding in close detail, and illustrates the movement of responses in and around poems. Chapter 3 explores the effects of different approaches to monitoring responses and develops a pattern of the stages of response. Chapter 4 focuses upon how groups make meaning from poem texts and illustrates how young readers construct a poem in three 'frames' as story, poet and form. Finally, Chapter 5 draws together what can be concluded from these three enquiries about the elements of response to poetry and offers a response-centred methodology; it suggests issues for further research and makes recommendations for classroom practice.

Chapter 1

Exploring Response

Michael Benton

A From Richards to Rosenblatt

The sub-heading focuses attention on the two most significant scholars in studies of response to poetry, yet it may mislead, for, as Louise Rosenblatt, herself, has pointed out, a mere two years separates her own earliest publication from the major work of I.A. Richards.[1] Both writers have been acknowledged as 'pioneers':[2] Richards for his analysis of the inadequacies of his students' readings of poems and for his famous 'ten difficulties'; Rosenblatt for her illumination of the way in which interpretation results directly from the relationships between the reader and the text and for the pedagogical implications of this transactional theory. In the fifty years that separate *Practical Criticism* (1929) and *The Reader, The Text, The Poem* (1978), both the literary and educational climates have changed but such is the hold that Richards' ideas have had on poetry teaching that although Rosenblatt's *Literature as Exploration* first appeared in 1938, it is not until the last decade that either her transactional theory of the literary work has been fully appreciated or the climate of literary education has been ready to receive it. It is only in recent years, too, that Louise Rosenblatt has fully developed her ideas (1978; 1985) so that it is now an especially propitious time to reappraise and realign the theory and practices of poetry teaching. These first two sections review the main educational enquiries and some of the key ideas in reader-response theory and criticism in so far as they relate to poetry teaching. Protracted discussion of either is inappropriate here and also unnecessary since all the sources are readily available for those wishing to pursue detailed arguments or evidence further (see Bibliography p. 229). A summary of the background influences from these two main directions will help to set the later studies in context and, it is hoped, provide a starting-point for others interested in working in this area.

1

Michael Benton

(i) Re-reading Richards

The problem of I.A. Richards (as with many seminal writers) is that
the density and subtlety of his arguments, the tacit acknowledgment
of the paradoxical nature of creative activity, and the inadequacy of
language (however precisely and elegantly used) to account for
psychological phenomena all combine to produce a text that, as
Humpty Dumpty might have said, can mean what you want it to
mean. It is a problem compounded by the fact that, while Richards'
pedagogical instincts and principles are sound, his literary assumptions in *Practical Criticism* about the 'correct' reading of a poem are
suspect; and the problem is complicated further because, fifteen
years later in *How To Read A Page*, Richards describes the notion
that there is a 'proper meaning' to a poem as the 'scholastic ghost'.[3]
It is best to begin, therefore, by setting out what Richards was
attempting in *Practical Criticism*.

Richards' celebrated list of the ten 'principal difficulties that may
be encountered by one reader or another in the presence of almost
any poem'[4] has been the main influence on the criticism and
teaching of poetry for the past fifty years. His avowed aims were
methodological and educational: to develop a new kind of
documentation through what is, in effect, a large scale case-study;
and to make individual reading and class teaching more efficient in
'developing discrimination and the power to understand what we
hear and read'.[5]

The evidence for Richards' study is derived from the written
statements of undergraduates drawn largely from public school
backgrounds. His concern is with their exercise of literary judgment.
His premise is that the literary texts he put before them contained a
verifiable essence: a 'correct' understanding of a poem is assumed to
be possible and 'correct' judgments therefore become the aim of
critics, teachers and students. Richards' emphasis is upon error,
upon how far and in what ways readers deviate from an implied,
normative reading of a poem.

It is unfortunate, to say the least, that the most influential thinker
about the teaching of poetry should have cast his ideas in the
negative form of 'difficulties' and, unwittingly, encouraged the
attitude that reading poetry is a problem-solving exercise directed
towards a single solution. The major misconception of traditional
teaching methodology is that far too often it implies that poems are
puzzles to which the teacher holds the key, so that what have
become emphasised in classroom discussions are the relative
weaknesses of the children's readings and the paucity and inadequacy of their responses. This aspect of the Richards legacy, derived

from the miserable performances of his students as they attempted to evaluate untitled, unattributed and previously unseen poems, has contributed directly to the widespread lack of confidence among both teachers and taught when dealing with poetry.

The central problem for poetry teachers is to clarify the relationships between response, criticism and evaluation. Richards saw this and, moreover, affirmed unequivocally that the first and most important job of the teacher is to facilitate an 'improvement in communication'. It is an enabling role; the teacher must first make the poem accessible to its readers:

> When we have solved, completely, the communication problem, when we have got, perfectly, the experience, *the mental condition* relevant to the poem, we have still to judge it, still to decide upon its worth. . . . Our prime endeavour must be to get the relevant mental condition and then see what happens.[6]

Richards operates, as he says elsewhere, upon the basis that ' . . . the two pillars upon which a theory of criticism must rest are an account of value and an account of communication'.[7] While the process of *evaluating* is clearly an element in the act of responding to poems (as Richards' students' writings amply show), *evaluation* is best delayed until the reader has fully engaged with the experience of the poem. Richards clearly stresses the importance of the reader's 'capacity to get the experience' of the poem and claims specifically in relation to teaching that 'value cannot be demonstrated except through the communication of what is valuable.[8] Terry Eagleton would, no doubt, approve both the sentiment and the pithiness. For, simultaneously, Richards is both separating 'value' from 'text' thus suggesting (as Eagleton does) that value in literature is a transitive term – value for somebody in a particular situation;[9] and also respecting the individual's power to assert and communicate his or her response. All of this demonstrates that, from a pedagogical standpoint, Richards is a powerful advocate of the now widely canvassed view that poetry must be experienced before it can be analysed. What his ten difficulties demonstrate is that the perspective he takes upon the *process* of that experience is to regard it as a necessary but ultimately distracting means to the higher end of establishing the correct judgement of a poem. For Richards, value is all, as even his analysis of reading a poem in *Principles of Literary Criticism* (1924), chapter 16, demonstrates. From his literary critical standpoint, therefore, those features that teachers and researchers concerned in the area of response to literature find to be major sources of interest, are for Richards the sources of critical traps. Richards' pedagogical clear-sightedness is constrained by his literary critical blinkers. He honours the importance of individual responses but then wants to fit them into a fixed, consensual reading.

Reappraising Richards' ten difficulties is an awkward task but a manageable and necessary one if we are to do justice to his innovatory studies and to reinterpret them in the light of subsequent work on readers' responses in both criticism and education. It is especially necessary when we are considering *the process of responding* of young, relatively inexperienced, school readers rather than the considered responses of university undergraduates. What follows then is a re-reading of Richards' ten difficulties in the light of the shift of emphasis, indicated in our Preface, from the two Cs to the two Rs. It is not an attack, it is more an adjustment. Clearly, it would be foolish to criticise Richards for not doing something he did not set out to do. The fact remains however that the pedagogical priorities that have flowed from his 'difficulties of criticism' have elevated the concept of 'criticism' and created an assumption of 'difficulty', to the detriment of poetry teaching in schools, colleges and universities.

(a)   First must come the difficulty of *making out the plain sense* of poetry . . . readers . . . *fail to understand it*, both as a statement and as an expression. They fail to construe it just as a schoolboy fails to construe a piece of Caesar.[10]

Poetry is, significantly, likened to a dead language bristling with difficulties and inducing failure, as the hapless reader struggles with a translation of the text into his own idiom, always knowing that the correct version is beyond his reach. What needs to be acknowledged is that the process of making sense, of coming to understand a poem, involves mis-reading, error, lines half-understood and ideas only partially glimpsed. The supposed 'plain sense' of a poem, in anything more than its bare syntax, may be anything but plain. Ambiguity, as Empson illustrated two years later, is endemic to poetry; and, indeed, he takes Richards gently to task for suggesting that 'the process of apprehension, both of the poem and of its analysis' can be separated into a list of categories, what Richards calls his 'four kinds of meaning' – Sense, Feeling, Tone and Intention:[11] 'Detailed analysis of this kind might be excellent as psychology', says Empson, 'but it would hardly be literary criticism'[12] The difficulty with Richards' difficulties is that he is bringing a sharp, refined, analytic instrument to bear upon the complex, ambiguous, fluid experiences of reading poems. The feeling persists that it is rather like using a scalpel to anatomise water.

(b)   Next are . . . the difficulties of *sensuous apprehension*. Words
      in sequence have a form to the mind's ear and the mind's
      tongue and larynx, even when silently read.[13]

Re-reading this 'difficulty' with children in mind, the sense of
Richards as a print-bound analyst is strong. If young readers are
given the idea that their natural affinity with sound and rhythm
(derived from their play and from TV jingles) is only useful in so far
as it illuminates the silent reading of printed texts, then they will be
unlikely to draw on their full potential for 'sensuous apprehension'.
To achieve this, poems have to be performed, readers have to be given
the freedom to recreate them, texts need to be regarded as scripts. It
is no use castigating readers for their lack of 'sensuous apprehension'
if the invitation does not allow them a chance to show it.

(c)   Next may come those difficulties that are connected with the
      place of *imagery*, principally visual imagery, in poetic
      reading'[14]

The mental imagery that accompanies reading is seen as erratic,
idiosyncratic, unstable and 'a troublesome source of critical
deviations'. The phenomenon is, indeed, as variable as Richards
describes but the fact remains that, for the overwhelming majority
of readers, mental imagery is a means to the end of making sense of
literature as well as a source of pleasure in itself. It constitutes, in
fact, part of our 'sensuous apprehension' of a poem and, as Iser
(1978) and others have argued, mental imagery is the principal way
in which readers process text. If, as Richards grudgingly concedes,
'poets . . . may be suspected of exceptional imaging capacity . . .',
then it is hardly surprising that their products evoke a corresponding
capacity in their readers. What worries Richards, of course, is that
such infinite variety – far from being a source of individual pleasure
and shared fascination among readers – threatens the authority of
the single, correct reading. While real readers have been liberated
in these post-structuralist times, the figure of Richards still lurks in
the consciousness of many poetry teachers muttering about
troublesome critical deviations.

(d)   '*Mnemonic irrelevances*'[15] which create 'misleading effects' are
deemed problematic because they make it difficult to define what is
relevant during reading. Again, modern developments in reading
theory and literary theory stand such a view on its head since a
dominant concept in both is that the mnemonic baggage that the
reader brings to a text in his literary and life experiences forms, at
the very least, an undeniable context for his reading. A reader does
not start as a *tabula rasa* any more than a writer does. Memory is a

5

fundamental source of creative activity for both. Writers know this. Stephen Spender points out that

> . . . memory is the faculty of poetry, because the imagination itself is an exercise of memory. There is nothing we imagine which we do not already know. And our ability to imagine is our ability to remember what we have already once experienced and to apply it to some different situation.[16]

Readers need reassuring that their imaginative recreation of a poem from a text is a blend of what is known with what is new.

Richards acknowledges that 'relevance is not an easy notion to define or apply . . .' and later he says of the intrusion of a train of associations into the reading of a poem that 'everything depends upon how essential the bond of thought or feeling may be that links it with the poem'[17]. Given his distrust of mental imagery, Richards wants everything demonstrably tied to the 'four kinds of meaning' prescribed earlier (see (a) above). Taxonomies of comprehension[18] as well as later psychological approaches to reading literature[19] have all emphasised the importance of those aspects of the reading experience that are not so tied. The reader's 'retelling' or 'literal comprehension' of the situation and substance of a poem may well encompass Richards' four kinds of meaning; and, at the other extreme, the reader's 'fantasizing' responses, where perhaps a mere phrase or word provides the catalyst for gossip or day-dream, may well be judged to be irrelevant associations. Yet, in between, lies the important area of 'assimilative comprehension' where readers often parallel events in their own lives or instances in other literature with the ones depicted in the poem. These analogies are valid and relevant ways of understanding and of making the experience of the poem personal by fitting it into the aggregate of all one's experiences. To rewrite Richards, they have a mnemonic relevance with educative effects!

(e) 'More puzzling and more interesting are the critical traps that surround . . . *Stock Responses*.'[20] Richards warns against 'views and emotions already fully prepared in the reader's mind, so that what happens appears to be more of the reader's doing than the poet's'. Again the implication is that the 'good' reader's 'correct' response originates somewhere other than the matrix from which stock responses come. The issue of 'stock responses' becomes as marginal as that of 'correct responses' as soon as we operate a pedagogy that signals to readers that their individual responses are both valid and valued. After all, in secondary schools, the commonest stock response to poetry is the dismissive groan! Negative responses need to be accepted and unravelled just as much as positive ones. In fact, in those classes which are based on the primacy of individual response this stock response to poetry is hard to sustain; and the pre-packed reaction to a poem that Richards describes tends to disappear rapidly as students learn to trust their own judgement rather than taking refuge in stereotypical behaviour or guessing at the 'correct judgement' supposedly embodied in the teacher's views.

(f) and (g) *Sentimentality and Inhibition*[21] are portrayed as the Scylla and Charybdis between whose weight a balanced response to a poem may be crushed; 'balanced' because here Richards extends the normative principle explicitly into the affective domain. He says of sentimentality that 'it is a question of the due measure of response'; it is recognised by 'over-facility in certain emotional directions', just as inhibition may result from a poem requiring us to respond to something we find painful and all we can do is to take evasive action to avoid the feelings or aggressive action to overcome them.

The concept of 'personal style' in reading (Holland, 1968, 1973, 1975) is the one to set alongside Richards' notion of 'a due measure of response' with its eighteenth-century feel of reasonable moderation about it. For modern post-Freudian critics argue that, during reading, readers rehearse their own psychological processes bringing to bear upon a poem all those aspects of their personality, temperament and general disposition that they bring to every other aspect of their lives. They develop a style in reading literature that tends to stay the same irrespective of the texts they read. Whether stemming the emotional gush or loosening the emotional corset so that readers can all join hands in a 'due measure of response', seems less important than enabling every reader to gain a sense of his or her personal style – to realise the use they make of mental imagery, the degree of interrogation they give a poem, the strategies they adopt in reading and interpreting, the types of poems that they tend to respond to – in short, becoming aware of themselves as readers.

(h)   '*Doctrinal Adhesions* present another troublesome problem.'[22] Richards is here concerned with the relation of the 'truth-value' (his term) of the views expressed in a poem to the work of the poem itself. Readers, he argues, may accord a poem *emotional* and/or *intellectual* belief.[23] Our happiest reading experiences (and the poems we like and return to) are when both are in harmony. Emotional belief is characterised by the satisfaction of our feelings, desires, interests, attitudes, tendencies to action and so on. Intellectual belief is located in our sense of the structure of ideas and the coherence of a poem 'to bring *all* our ideas into as perfect and ordered system as possible'.[23]

With young readers especially, the capacity to disentangle their emotional belief – say, their distaste for the religious views contained in a poem – and an oppositional intellectual belief – say, their liking for the skill with which those views are expressed – is a

7

fairly late development. The emotional belief tends to dictate the response. A more common occurrence, therefore, is a preference for poems which chime with their own emotional states in respect of, for example, family relationships, or attitudes to war or discrimination, while showing simultaneously a disarming willingness to suspend their intellectual belief by resisting scrutiny of the coherence and subtlety (or lack of it) with which the ideas and emotions are presented. The younger the readers the more likely it is that they will respond directly to the subject matter and to the feelings and ideas behind the words, however subtly or clumsily the surface is wrought, or however cleverly the intellectual structure is developed. Unless the poem specifically invites it, comment on the formal qualities will come fairly low on the agenda. It is not that they are unaware of form, rather that they *assume* its effects. First, young readers want to know what a poem is about and who the person is who is saying these things. With poems, as with anything else, children have an enviable directness which may sometimes be at odds with our teacherly priorities of language and form.

(i) '*Technical Presuppositions*' represent a different order of difficulty as Richards says. 'Whenever we attempt to judge poetry from outside by technical details we are putting means before ends. . . .'[24]

One problem here is that the surface features of poems do loom large (see p. 18). 'Poems should rhyme' is usually considered by teachers to be the commonest presupposition voiced by young readers; yet it is just as likely that it reflects a positive awareness of sound and pattern in a poem as it does any insensitivity to the more profound effects of the language of feeling. Young readers' preoccupation with such technical details may be more fairly seen as the continuity they sense between the chants of playground games or the rhymes of television commercials and printed poetry, than as the superficial response which puts means before ends.

(j) 'Finally, *general critical preconceptions* . . . intervene endlessly . . . between the reader and the poem'[25]. They interfere, Richards later elaborates, '. . . in two different ways. By blinding the reader to what else is in the poem, so that he *forces* his predilection, if he can, upon the poem. . . . Secondly, by blurring and disabling his judgement.'[26]

Richards seems to be asking the reader to arrive naked before a poem, stripped of all preconceptions, baring his critical faculties in the exercise of pure judgement. The logic of this is that our aim should be to cultivate some hybrid of the 'qualified reader' and the 'ideal and perfect reader' that Richards favours in *Principles of Literary Criticism*, chapter 30,[27] who is capable of erasing all the personal elements in his reading, and of utilising his fine training in order to deal with each new poem as though it were the first.

Real readers behave differently. They *do* bring their literary and life experiences with them, preconceptions and all; judgements are partial and provisional. While not wishing to defend the reader who violates the reading experience in the way Richards describes, there is little point in setting up the 'ideal reader' at the other extreme. Critics too, like readers, carry their predilections with them. They intervene most noticeably between the reader and the poem when they promote the illusion of a single 'correct' reading above all the real ones, and moreover, when they do so in the belief that their job is '. . . to bring the level of popular appreciation nearer to the consensus of best qualified opinion'.[28]

In re-reading Richards' ten difficulties we have made a double shift of perspective: first, to focus on school-age readers; and second, to allow such readers room for response rather than to require critical judgements on demand. Richards' diagnosis that the two main issues are communication and value remains valid but his over-riding concern with the latter has often become translated in the school context to requests from teachers for premature value judgements of poems. Before the advent of Louise Rosenblatt's ideas of 'evocation' and 'response', the theorising of poetry-reading was becalmed, not least because of the innovatory brilliance of Richards' work. Slowly, literary criticism has disentangled such interconnected processes as the reader's construing of the text, his apprehension of meaning, his exercise of judgment and so on, always looking back to Richards, but increasingly advocating a middle position for the reader, somewhere between that of the 'literary archaeologists' who believe in digging for the single, hidden meaning in the words on the page and that of the 'literary anarchists' who argue that meaning is the province of individual idiosyncrasy and that any response goes. A text being read is the manifestation of a truth existing neither as an external artefact nor as an internalised meaning but as a virtual experience between the two. Responding must be responsible to both the reader and the poem. The middle ground is where the reader now stands and his position has been illuminated in recent years both by literary theory and criticism and by educational enquiry.

(ii)   Reader in the middle

We have developed elaborate vocabularies for classifying and anatomizing literary works; we scarcely know how to talk about their powers and effects. We have an immense accumulation of knowledge about authors, periods, movements and individual

9

texts; we know almost nothing about the process of reading and the interaction of man and book.[29]

It is in such terms that, writing in 1970, Walter Slatoff identifies both the preoccupations and the areas of neglect in literary studies during this century. Prior to the mid-1960s, with a few notable exceptions, Richards (1929), Empson (1930), Lewis (1961) for example, most critics took the process of reading for granted and concentrated their effects upon evaluating the product before them as a 'given' object, supposedly unmediated by how it was read. While praising the acumen that yielded unique critical insights, few critics had any time for the distinction between criticism and interpretation that Wilson Knight advocated. In his Introduction to the revised edition of *The Wheel of Fire* (1949), Leavis was grudging in his acknowledgment of the worth of Wilson Knight's concept of interpretation; yet, all that Wilson Knight was arguing for was that the critic, as reader or spectator of a play, should trust his own responses and reconstitute them in his writing about literature. With reference to Shakespeare (and in his own preface he said his approach could be 'applied widely to literature'), Wilson Knight warned against the practice of thinking critically before we have first received uncritically the whole of the poet's vision. Criticism is seen as a refinement of our initial responses by means of interpretation. Hence, we are counselled to

> interpret our original imaginative experience into the slower consciousness of logic and intellect, preserving something of that childlike faith which we possess, or should possess, in the theatre. It is exactly this translation from one order of consciousness to another that interpretation claims to perform. Uncritically, and passively, it receives the whole of the poet's vision; it then proceeds to re-express this experience in its own terms.[30]

Despite his eminence, Wilson Knight has always stood outside the currents of mainstream literary criticism. Part of the reason for this maverick stance is his insistence that the initial responses that comprise 'our original imaginative experience' of a literary work are the starting-point for all criticism.

In the last two decades the emphasis has changed, approximating more closely to Wilson Knight's view and often calling on Richards or Empson to authenticate a particular approach. Belatedly, criticism has realised what it means to exorcise Richards' 'scholastic ghost'. It means the acknowledgment of the primacy of the individual reader's imaginative remaking of a text. This shift is nowhere more apparent than in Iser's *The Act of Reading* (1978) in which he inveighs against the traditional idea of the 'hidden meaning' of a work in favour of a view that sees the meaning of a book in the 'interaction between the textual signals and the reader's acts of comprehension'.[31] During the 1960s the debate between advocates of these absolutist and relativist positions developed, as Iser records, in books such as Susan Sontag's *Against Interpretation* (1966) and E.D. Hirsch's *Validity in Interpretation* (1967). One of the more modest contributions was that of F.H. Langman who argued a middle position in his examination of the concept of the reader in criticism. Since literature finds a language for private experience and thus enables it to become part of public, shared understanding, inevitably some part of our experience and our understanding of language will always remain private. Hence, he claims that it is pointless for critics to deny the possibility of differing interpretations. The critic has the difficult task of enlarging the common understanding of a work (via synthesising readings, pointing out misreadings, etc.) while, at the same time, acknowledging that the work means something unique to each of its readers.

During the 1970s the focus of the debate moved on to the nature of the reader's response. Iser heralds the shift in this sentence:

> So long as the focal point of interest was the author's intention, or the contemporary, psychological, social or historical meaning of the text, or the way in which it was constructed, it scarcely seemed to occur to critics that the text could only have a meaning when it was read.[32]

'Response studies' thus became respectable, and the paucity of research in this area much lamented.[33]

In education, earlier enquiries into readers' responses (Squire, 1964; Purves and Rippere, 1968) gained a wider audience and increasing respect. Two summaries of past work in this area were published (Purves and Beach, 1972; D'Arcy, 1973), one in America the other in England and, by the 1980s, some studies began to appear of children's responses to poetry (Wade, 1981; Dixon and Brown, 1984; Atkinson, 1985; P. Benton, 1986; Dias, 1986).

In literary theory and criticism the reader was fast supplanting the 'objective text' as the focus of interest and, by the turn of the decade, two major collections of essays on reader-response criticism were published (Tompkins, 1980; Suleiman and Crosman, 1980), so that, by the mid-1980s, as one commentator puts it, '. . . this area of criticism threatens to engulf all the [other] approaches'.[34]

Finally, one bid has been made so far to establish the ground rules for enquiries into readers' responses. *Researching Response to Literature and the Teaching of Literature*, (Cooper (ed.), 1985) is a collection of articles which explores the question: What theories should guide our study of readers and what methodologies will

11

enable us to learn more about readers? Its approach is eclectic. It attempts to draw upon both educational and literary sources, to theorise the concept of 'response' and to cover the main techniques of enquiry. Of particular interest in the present context are the three articles by Purves, Kintgen and Rosenblatt, the last of which (as will be argued presently) forms a valuable summary of the ideas of the writer who, more than anyone since Richards, has illuminated the area of response to literature.

Where, then, do these recent developments in literary and educational studies leave us? Looking back to Richards, it is easy to see how his seminal work, with its twin concerns of pedagogy and criticism, led to two contrary emphases.

In one sense Richards privileged the text, and the American New Critics[35], particularly, seized upon the evidence of *Practical Criticism* to insist that close analysis of the words on the page was the principal job of critic and teacher. In modern structuralism, the terminology has changed but the orientation is similar. Hence, in the context of an attack on the view of poetry as the expression of individual experience and of the reader as one who 'recreates or relives this experience which is communicated to him or her', Antony Easthope writes:

> Poetry is not to be read for truth or falsity of reference. . . . The poet as historical author is typically dead or absent; what we have as the poem is the message itself, *writing*. . . . Poetry consists *only* of artifice. . . . We never have the 'presence' of a poet; what we have is language, fiction, artifice, means of representation, poem.[36]

Yet, in another sense, Richards privileged the reader, and no enquiry into responses to poems can be conducted without reference to his initial studies. In modern reader-response criticism, the terminology has also changed and the reader is often given freedoms that infuriate text-oriented critics. Hence, Stanley Fish writes:

> Interpretation is not the art of construing but the art of constructing. Interpreters do not decode poems: they make them.[37]

Or, even more provocatively:

> It is the structure of the reader's experience rather than any structures available on the page that should be the object of description.[38]

As Laurence Lerner has pointed out recently, perhaps the most important division in contemporary literary studies is between those who see literature as a more or less self-contained system, and those who see it as interacting with real, extra-literary experience (that of the author, or of the reader, or the social reality of the author's or the reader's world).[39]

While there are lessons for the teacher in all aspects of modern literary theory, the second part of this division describes the inevitable context in which he or she operates. Reader-response theory, in particular, is of special importance to literature teachers. It offers a new perspective on the moral values of reading literature by asserting the importance of the individual's 'reading' of a text. The responsibility for making meaning lies with the reader; the teaching/learning emphasis shifts away from critical authority and received knowledge towards the development of personal responses, their refinement through sharing these responses with others, and their evaluation through that Stanley Fish calls the authority of the interpretive community of the classroom.

The variety of strands in reader-response theory and criticism has already been indicated. It is relatively easy to explore its continental origins through Holub (1984) and its more recent manifestations through the two excellent collections of articles by Tompkins (1980) and Suleiman and Crosman (1980). What is important for literature teachers is to gain a sense of how best to define and develop response to literature in such a way that neither text nor reader is 'over-privileged'. The work of Louise Rosenblatt achieves this balance.

(iii) Rosenblatt's transactional theory

The transactional view, while insisting on the importance of the reader's contribution, does not discount the text and accepts a concern for the validity of interpretation.[40]

Rosenblatt, like Richards, has a profound concern for both literature *and* learning. *Literature as Exploration* (1938) was a book before its time. Its particular contribution now (it was reissued in 1970) lies not so much in the freshness of its insights as in its commitment to a theoretical position that stresses the reader's active role, the validity and uniqueness of his responses and, incidentally, the need for literature teachers to rethink their methodology. The word 'exploration' in the title is designed to suggest that the experience of literature is a form of intense personal activity and, because the reader is seen as being of at least equal importance as the book itself, Rosenblatt is led to a description of the literary experience which says that 'the literary work exists in the live circuit set up between reader and text; the reader infuses intellectual and emotional meanings into the pattern of verbal symbols, and these symbols channel his thoughts and feelings'.[41] This tension between the reader's freedom and textual constraint is one that Rosenblatt sees as central to the reading process. She describes the interaction of what the text offers with what the reader brings as follows:

> What, then happens in the reading of a literary work? Through the medium of words, the text brings into the reader's consciousness certain concepts, certain sensuous experiences, certain images of things, people, actions, scenes. The special meanings and, more particularly, the submerged associations that these words and images have for the individual reader will largely determine what the work communicates to him. The reader brings to the work personality traits, memories of past events, present needs and preoccupations, a particular mood of the moment, and a particular physical condition. These and many other elements in a never-to-be duplicated combination determine his response to the particular contribution of the text.[42]

The emphasis here is distinctive: whereas mainstream criticism admits the reader as an active student of the text, a sensitive interpreter of his reading, Rosenblatt gives him an altogether more human face. Each 'reading' is to be understood in the context of the whole literary and life experience of an individual. A reader's personality, needs, interests and so on are significant mediators in his response. This fuller role for the participatory reader rescues him from the image of intellectual cipher that is implied, for example, by Wayne Booth[43] and others without consigning him to the analyst's couch as the transformational theorists[44] are tempted to do; and it derives directly from Rosenblatt's belief that literature stands in a unique relationship with knowledge. Literature does not provide information as much as experience. 'New understanding is conveyed . . . dynamically and personally . . .' for, she adds succinctly, 'Literature provides a *living-through*, not simply *knowledge about*'.[45] This experience of 'living through' is necessarily a creative one in which the reader's response, like the writer's activity before it, is moulded by selective factors. This selection makes each 'reading' uniquely personal and leads her to the conclusion that ' . . . the literary experience must be phrased as a *transaction* between the reader and the text.'[46]

Traditionally, of course, critics have operated comparatively: literary experience has been an implicit element in reading. Rosenblatt lays a new emphasis upon the life experience of the individual, for, she claims, this is the source of the most significant guiding factors during reading. Past literary experiences are important in helping the reader to situate a story or poem within certain conventions but these have usually been emphasised to the exclusion of the more important elements derived from general life experience. This linkage with life in the reader's primary world, rather than with the virtual life of other secondary worlds, is seen as a vital prerequisite of reading literature.[47]

This emphasis is as near as Rosenblatt comes to the psycho-analytic school. Any hint that, in stressing the importance of the individual's life experience, there lies an invitation to fantasise is stifled by her insistence that the text acts as a regulator upon the reader's imaginative activity. The balance between freedom and constraint is caught in her clearest formulation about recreative reading:

> Every time a reader experiences a work of art, it is in a sense created anew. *Fundamentally, the process of understanding implies a re-creation of it, an attempt to grasp completely the structured sensations and concepts through which the author seeks to convey the quality of his sense of life. Each must make a new synthesis of these elements with his own nature, but it is essential that he evoke those components of experience to which the text actually refers.*[48] (Rosenblatt's italics)

Rosenblatt's later work deepens this concept of recreative reading. In *The Reader, The Text, The Poem* (1978) several basic definitions and concepts are discussed which, in varying degrees, have influenced the three studies described in Chapters 2, 3 and 4 of this book.

First, we need to note Rosenblatt's distinction between the reader who brings his accumulated literary and life experiences to bear upon the act of reading, the *text* which is simply the words on the page, and the *poem* which is created only when reader and text interact. With definitions thus delimited, texts and readers are plentiful but a poem is a relatively rare happening. Rosenblatt summarises this transactional stance:

> The poem . . . must be thought of as an event in time. It is not an object or an ideal entity. It happens during a coming-together, a compenetration, of a reader and a text. The reader brings to the text his past experience and present personality. Under the magnetism of the ordered symbols of the text, he marshalls his resources and crystallizes out from the stuff of memory, thought, and feeling a new order, a new experience, which he sees as the poem.[49]

She goes on to use a now familiar analogy: the re-enactment of the text of a poem is like a musical performance. The text is the score and the concept of 'poem', as an event in time, is an experience shaped by the reader/performer under the guidance of the text. The transactional theory thus rejects a preoccupation with the author's text where the reader is seen as receiving an imprint of the 'poem'. It also rejects the opposite extreme from which other theorists like Bleich (1978) and Holland (1975) see the 'text' as an empty vessel waiting to be filled by the reader. Instead, as the musical metaphor suggests, it views reading a poem as an aesthetic transaction which combines both openness and constraint.

Second, in contrast to Richards' inquiry in which his students gave their considered written responses to a text over the course of several days, Rosenblatt was more interested in having her students use jottings 'to discover the paths by which (they) approached even a tentative first interpretation'.[50] She was not concerned initially with evaluating responses but focused on the ongoing processes involved. By asking readers to note their first responses, Rosenblatt was deliberately inviting the readers to make articulate the stages that are often ignored or forgotten by the time a 'satisfactory' reading has been arrived at. Logging these early procedures led directly to the definitions of reader, text and poem, noted above, that underpin the transactional theory, and also to the active relationship between them. She describes this relationship in terms of two major functions of words in a poetic text. First, the text acts as a *stimulus* activating elements of the reader's literary and life experience. Second, the text serves as a *blueprint*, a guide for the reader to select, reject and order his own response. The text thus has both generative and regulatory functions. Both can be seen in the activities of the individuals and groups, as they shuttle back and forth in and around a poem, recorded in later chapters of this book.

Third, Rosenblatt gives clear priority to the essentially *aesthetic* nature of reading literature. Her distinction between the aesthetic reading of poems and stories and informational reading (what she calls 'efferent') turns upon what the reader actually *does* during the transaction with the text. In aesthetic reading the text is not an object but an event, a lived-through process or experience. In efferent reading readers are more concerned with what they can take away, with the information or ideas they can gather. This distinction is discussed further presently (see p. 18). For the moment, it is important to emphasise this aesthetic dimension for, as Rosenblatt implies, it is all too easy to neglect the lived-through experience of literature. There are plentiful examples in modern literary theory and in reading theory of approaches and techniques which reduce the reading process to a ready-made system of analysis. Sadly, there are many instances, too, where classroom method reduces what should be the experience of literature to the arid inquisition of yet another text-book. In theory and practice, in literary and educational studies, there is the constant danger of dealing with aesthetic experiences in efferent ways. As Rosenblatt says: '. . . keeping the aesthetic transaction central (has) important implications for questions raised and methods used in both teaching and research.'[51]

Fourth, Rosenblatt both keeps the aesthetic central and deepens the concept of the process of responding by discriminating between *evocation* and *response*. This is not a sharp distinction but a way of indicating that literary experience has to be evoked before a response can be articulated. The evocation is 'what we sense as the structured experience corresponding to the text';[52] our response is usually cast in terms of reactions to the language, imagery, form, feeling, associations with our own lives, and the value we come to place on the poem. Yet even as we are evoking a poem we are reacting to it (see p. 18), which is why it is so easy to restrict our classroom focus to the elements of response and to neglect the evocation – how the 'poem' came into being in the readers' imaginations. Chapter 2, in particular, illustrates the process of evocation.

It should now be apparent that Louise Rosenblatt's transactional theory, particularly as it is developed in her recent work (1978; 1985), is the most pervasive influence on these present studies. Her stance is one that honours the unique importance of each text and each reader; it draws upon a profound knowledge of both literature and learning; and it is concerned to further teacher-researcher enquiries into aesthetic experience in the conviction that good teaching means continuous reflection upon the processes involved and good educational research means active involvement in the processes of teaching and learning.

B The Aesthetic Perspective

Following Rosenblatt, this section attempts to capture the aesthetic phenomenon of evoking and responding to poems. It is an elusive goal best approached not by sequential argument but by 'keeping the aesthetic transaction' of poem-reading, as it were, 'central' and describing it from a number of vantage points. The ten statements developed below are responses to this phenomenon with all the potential for expansion, overlap and contradiction that this implies. Thus, Rosenblatt's pedagogic principle underpins this section. A further aim is to distinguish the unique nature of reading poetry from that of reading prose fiction. A further hope is that ten positive statements are also a better basis for teaching than 'ten difficulties'.
1. *The reader is invited to 'look at' a poem yet to 'dwell within' it*

Poem texts are ostentatious; they are also obstinately miscellaneous. Poetry-reading is different from story-reading. For, even though novels invite regular circling back and round, the infinite variety displayed by poem texts signals that the initial responses when compared with those provoked by the predictable, linear ways stories are presented, are likely to be more diverse. Instead of the eye tracking back and forth along regular lines of print to engage with a fiction, it is invited to a more varied exercise where the disposition of the words on the page is of greater significance than in the rectangular blocks of story text. The sense of artifice is more immediate. We are aware of looking at something which is drawing attention to itself by the way in which it is presented. The conscious effort of construction that this sort of 'onlooking' (to use D.W. Harding's word) entails accounts for the heightened spatial awareness we experience when reading most poems. The spaces around the words on the page are ones we inhabit mentally as readers to 'look at' the text, as it were, from various viewpoints; rather as, when looking at a piece of sculpture, we often feel impelled to move around the object thus tacitly acknowledging that the space in which it is placed affects our perception and contributes to our understanding. Granted we initially have to read a poem text forwards; nonetheless, our ways-in to its meaning will be many and varied and will depend in part upon the vantage points we adopt and the sort of approaches we make during reading.

Yet, the poem only yields a meaning if we also 'dwell within' it imaginatively. We may look at a Henry Moore or a Picasso and not be able to interact with the work; similarly, a poem text may remain just a collection of words. The indwelling value of the poem becomes available to the reader only if his act of reading includes those features that are integral to the nature of the art form. Typically, this requires the reader to be alert to sound and rhythm, to hear the tune on the page as a tune within his own consciousness as he reads.

It is this mental performance of the text that allows him access to the poem and to the possibility of dwelling within an imaginative experience; to become an 'insider' rather than an 'outsider'. It is harder to achieve this status with poetry than with story. The fact that most poems draw attention to themselves makes it more difficult for a reader to become immersed. He may become easily lost in the secondary world of a story; it is harder to get lost in a poem text since its surface features are continually reminding him of how this particular one should be read.

2. *The reader's stance is both 'efferent' and 'aesthetic'*

The stance the reader adopts in respect of the text dictates whether the poem will be created. The journey metaphor – invoked to describe literary reading by writers from Coleridge to Calvino[53] –

implies that, at the point of embarkation, what the reader brings is as important as what the text offers; and part of the emotional and mental luggage the reader carries with him is his sense of the sort of journey he anticipates. With a poem he starts with an expectation that this reading experience is to be different from that of a typical novel.

In the last decade studies in the development of literacy have focused, among other things, upon function. Knowing what writing is for and, in particular, developing the growing sophistication of the skill from 'expressive' beginnings into 'transactional' or 'poetic' purposes (in Britton's terms),[54] has been identified as a significant element in learning to write. The complementary process lies in coming to know how a text demands to be read. Rosenblatt provides a corresponding schema to Britton's: the initial development from decoding to fluency in reading is accompanied by a growing differentiation of the 'efferent' or 'aesthetic' purposes to be served. In 'efferent' reading the reader's concern is with what he will carry away from the act; his orientation is utilitarian, his focus is directed towards the information that lies *beyond* the reading event. By contrast, in 'aesthetic' reading the reader's concern is with the feelings and ideas being produced by his deciphering; his orientation is to savour what he is living through at the time, his focus is on the experience itself *during* the reading event. Both schemas smack of caricature; both Britton and Rosenblatt put up the notion of a continuum to shield their concepts from this charge. To categorise an act of reading with one of two labels is clearly facile. What actually happens as we take a mental walk around a poem (to extend our earlier metaphor) is that we adopt a 'shifting stance'; images, ideas, associations and feelings dart and flicker in the mind as we move to and fro between the 'efferent' and the 'aesthetic'. For, even when we are free from critical or pedagogic pressure to show a definite 'yield' from our reading of a poem (in the form of notes or essays), the linguistically condensed nature of poetry is such that the reading process has to be 'efferent' enough for us to carry away a meaning as well as 'aesthetic' enough to give us pleasure.

3. *The reader both produces the poem from the text yet reacts to what he produces*

Reading is active and reactive together. With a poem the reader experiences this 'double-take' with peculiar power. He may look at Blake's lines,

Tyger! Tyger! burning bright,
In the forest of the night;
What immortal hand or eye,
Could frame thy fearful symmetry?[55]

and as he constructs a provisional meaning from the words this meaning echoes against his background of literary and life experience, words knock against each other in unfamiliar ways, and the reader begins to discover what Lawrence called the true power of poetry – a 'new effort of attention' that breaks fresh perceptions of the familiar and the routine.

The first stage of a 'double-take' is a glance, the second a long sustained look. The reading of a poem is a series of literary 'double-takes', where the reader engages both in the swift interpreting of the words and the reflective interpreting of his responses to the words. The way words are deployed in poems demands this effort to 'attend twice at once' in Ryle's phrase which because of its impossibility, typically leaves the reader in limbo, somewhere between the deconstruction of verbal artifice and the development of personal response. It is an uncomfortable position for the inexperienced reader. There is none of the sustained invitation into the secondary world of fiction. The reader is put on the spot. A double demand is being made – to read the words and to read his own sensibilities. The next statement adds a gloss upon this phenomenon.

4. *The reader's social relationship may be not only with an implied author but also with the real poet*
Far from joining in a ghostly dialogue with an implied author, a narrator and a cast of characters in a story, the reader of a poem knows a demand is being made upon him directly and uncompromisingly by the single voice of the poet. True, in some long narrative poems and dramatic monologues, the reader may feel in the company of angels and devils, mariners and spirits, dukes and duchesses, saints and clergy; likewise, he may feel privy to a host of conversations among ordinary folk that, for example, characterise ballad poetry from medieval times to the present day. Nonetheless, the social contract between reader and author is different from that of the novel. Typically, the novel presents characters to explore the development of motives and feelings in a series of situations; even long narrative poems do not aspire to such detailed exploration. In poetry, characters stand for certain qualities the poet wants to symbolise; they are metaphorical – versions of a single voice, not the voices of carefully developed people. The poet may choose to play the ventriloquist in some of his poems but, if he goes *beyond* throwing his own voice, the very form of poetry becomes transmuted into poetic drama. In fact, in most poetry, Wordsworth's description of this social relationship as 'a man speaking to men' can be taken at face value. With lyric poems especially, the reader's construct of the implied poet may lead to a growing awareness of the real one. This ambiguous social relationship is itself often

implied in the way thinking and feeling are expressed in the voice that addresses the reader.

5. *The reader exercises both an intelligence of thinking and an intelligence of feeling*

Poems are places where thinking and feeling remain unified. Thought may subdue feeling; feeling may overwhelm thought but, simultaneously as it sustains the artifice of every poem, the same 'cool web of language winds us in . . .'[56] Working with words takes the heat out of experience for both poet and reader. The act of reading a poem lies between the turmoil of the individual consciousness and the immediacy of the workaday world. And as the reader takes time out for this experience he brings his whole self to bear upon it. He cannot do otherwise if the text demands it powerfully enough. Thoughts are imbued with feelings – uncompromising, ambivalent, contradictory, elusive; feelings are constrained by thinking – directed and rational, autistic and free-ranging. The meaning he constructs from the words on the page will be an amalgam from such sources. Moreover, unlike other types of reading, unless the reader receives intelligences from both antennae – allowing thought and feeling to operate upon each other – then the poem will not be evoked.

6. *The reader reads with both ear and eye*

The distinction here is not simply the functional one between speaking a poem aloud or reading it silently. Rather it is to stress that whenever we read a poem our performance has aural and visual dimensions simultaneously. If we read well, we cannot stop ourselves sounding the words in the head; there is, as has been said above, a tune on the page to be played and a design in the mind to be explicated. The voice of the 'inner speech' that we hear as we are reading a poem comes to us through both ear and eye. Frye makes the point:

> In every poem we can hear at least two distinct rhythms. One is the recurring rhythm . . . a complex of accent, metre and sound-pattern. The other is the semantic rhythm of sense . . .[57]

And in developing this notion in respect of lyric poetry he coins the terms 'babble' and 'doodle' to indicate 'the two elements of subconscious association' which operate during reading.

'In babble,' he tells us, 'rhyme, assonance, alliteration and puns develop out of sound associations'. The sound patterns that Ruth Weir recorded of her two-and-a-half year old son Anthony's pre-sleep monologues[58] illustrate the fundamental quality of language and meaning which poetry exploits – namely, that sounds, and the shaping we give them through rhythm, precede 'sense'.

By contrast 'doodle' describes 'the first rough sketches of verbal

21

design in the creative process' and indicates the increasing tendency, after Caxton, to address the ear through the eye. The impulse to put words into patterns, as seen in the proliferation of verse forms, is a symptom of the visual dimension of poetry. Frye sees riddles as the primitive signposts to 'the whole process of reducing language to visible form'.

The language of poetry speaks to both ear and eye; it combines the abstract art of the aural and the solid presence of the visual. At the extremes are repetitive chants without texts and 'concrete poems' without music; but most poems lie between. Reading them with the ear, words are performed and celebrated in pursuit of the *experience* of meaning; reading them with the eye, words become windows through which we see *extractable* meanings. Poetry thus holds its reader in a double spell: we find both 'a charm in syllables that rhyme'[59] and a riddle in the verbal patterns on the page.

7. *Capturing the 'poem' means playing with words within the discipline of form*

The central paradox of all creative activity is that it grows from both freedom and constraint, the play of the imagination operating, in this case, in the rule-governed medium of language. Creative reading of poems means reading like a writer – being alert to how words combine in unusual patterns, to ambiguity; being open to nonsense and the ability of language to turn our view of the world upside down. But, as well as enjoying the medium for itself (which, if left to itself, would produce only the randomness of a writer's notebook) there is the complementary pressure towards form – a shaping which, with the novel, is signified by the desire for 'closure'; given the spatial qualities of poem texts, their shaping is more a matter of 'enclosure'. The poets' art lies in their skill at capture; it is a subtle skill, as their metaphors show, exercised through a 'net of words' or in the 'cool web of language'. Only when the poem has been thus caught and enclosed within the formal discipline of the text on the page does the verbal play achieve any artistic significance. Reading like a writer means realising how far the constraints of language and form produce expressive freedom.

8. *Reading a poem is an event in time and an artefact in space*

For a poem to be evoked through the interaction of the reader and the text, it must come into existence in two dimensions. 'A poem should not mean/But be' concluded MacLeish[60], insisting that a poem is not a record of experience but the experience *itself*. Its infinitive is to be, not merely to communicate. Of course, a poem *does* communicate but it achieves a 'double discourse'. It speaks in words laid out in linear sequence, it comes into being through time; we read a poem forwards. Yet it speaks also in words laid out in patterns, it comes into being through its spatial relationships; we read a poem as a design.

This two-dimensional existence gives a poem a peculiar status – not that, as we have seen, of the secondary world of fiction, but rather that of a separate, self-contained image; as clear and telling as the reflection in a mirror but equally as inviolable and apart. A poem relates intimately to the actual world, catching facets of its substance in this looking-glass image, tantalising us with the boundary line between the real and the reflected, yet by its nature keeping to its own plane of existence. So, whether we read of Blake's Tyger 'burning bright' or of Burns's love as a 'red, red rose'; of Hughes's 'hawk roosting' or of Larkin's 'whitsun weddings' – the tiger, the lover, the hawk and the brides remain as looking-glass pictures. They reflect aspects of the actual world and they may well appear to be the more 'real', but they only exist within the medium of the poem. This peculiar status of poetry experience is what Ted Hughes celebrates in 'The Thought-Fox'[61] where the imagined fox 'enters the dark hole of the head', its vivid presence remains in suspended animation in the reader's mind, and the separateness of its existence is established as Hughes concludes 'The page is printed'. Hughes himself has commented upon the capturing of this animal that is 'both a fox and not a fox'. The virtual existence is attained because 'the words have made a body for it and given it somewhere to walk'.[62]

9. *A reader reads both the parts and the whole together*
In his discussion of how poetry, fiction, scientific and historical prose communicate both truth and pleasure, Coleridge concludes that a poem is 'a species of composition' which proposes 'for its *immediate* object pleasure, not truth'; and further, that it is unique in 'proposing to itself such delight from the *whole*, as is compatible with a distinct gratification from each component *part*.[63] Coleridge thus points to a phenomenon integral to the evocation of a poem – the reader's pleasure in a poem derives from his awareness of a qualitative and necessary unity. It is qualitative because the reader's valuing of the poem will depend upon how well its constituent parts cohere; and it is necessary because his acceptance of this 'species of composition' as a poem at all is conditional upon his sense that every element (metre, rhyme, diction, imagery . . .) is interdependently related.

The process of reading a poem, in itself, reflects the gratification Coleridge describes. We read through and then re-read; we move to and fro about the poem, savouring some lines, asking questions about others; we look for development in feeling, idea or image, but, above all (or, better, unifying all), we read with the assumption that the composition has been well-wrought. Because poetry is such a condensed and precise form of language, any blemish – an inappropriate word, a jarring rhythm – undermines the integrity of the whole. In reading a poem we anticipate an inevitable sense of the appropriate.

10. *A reader uses both the 'auditory imagination' and the 'narrative imagination'*

Poetry-reading involves a unique blend of these two fundamental aspects of imagination. The appeal of sound and rhythm, as we have seen (p. 21), is peculiar to poems. It is the recurring evidence of what Eliot called the 'auditory imagination (which) is the feeling for syllable and rhythm penetrating far below the conscious levels of thought and feeling, invigorating every word . . . .'.[64] It is readily evident in young children's play, as the Opies demonstrated. Repetition of key words, the liking for particular word sounds and rhyming patterns, tongue-twisters and the like are all sound effects that children enjoy. Similarly, they bring an innate sense of rhythm to poetry. The younger the readers the greater the preference for a strongly-marked rhythm and a clearly accented beat.

The appeal of imagery and story are no less important in poems. Just as Eliot's phrase 'auditory imagination' incorporates the elements of sound and rhythm, so the notion of the 'narrative imagination' includes the elements of imagery and story. Our pictorial sense may be exercised in response to form and lay-out or in the picturing that we find the words evoking as we read. Just as we are proliferators of images, so we are of stories. The mind's natural propensity to link pictures into sequences leads to the ordering and shaping of experiences in order to represent them to ourselves more coherently. The story of a 'poem' is the shape we give its evocation as it comes into being for us during reading.

C Monitoring Responses

(i) The ethnographic approach

'Response' has become an umbrella term to cover a variety of interrelated processes that occur during and after reading. Rather as D.W. Harding elaborated the term 'identification'[65], we need to open it out and be explicit about why this is the preferred term and what is meant by it.

'Response' is preferred for several reasons. It has a long history and situates our studies in the Anglo-American tradition begun by Richards and carried on in the work of Squire, Rosenblatt, Purves and others. It is also a broader concept than is suggested simply by 'reading', for it encompasses everything from the initial evocation of a poem to responses that may be recorded in different modes on later occasions. Also, it places the reader centrally; 'response' signals that what the reader brings is part of the construction of the literary experience.

Theorising what is meant by the concept of response is more complicated. We have already met Rosenblatt's discrimination between 'evocation' and 'response'. Others, too, working in this field have often made similar or related distinctions: Josipovici distinguishes between 'activity' and 'meaning',[66] Applebee between 'process' and 'meaning',[67] and Iser between 'effect' and 'explanation'.[68] However, all are agreed that response and the interpretation of response in words are not mutually exclusive activities. Part of the experience of reading is the reflection it generates, and often this reflection takes the form of interpretive comment to ourselves or others. Iser argues that the reader cannot hold himself aloof as a detached observer for, as we have seen, meaning exists in the interaction between the text and the reader's efforts at comprehension. Text and reader are seen as merging into a single entity (described subtly in Wallace Stevens's poem 'The House Was Quiet . . .'),[69] such that 'meaning is no longer an object to be defined but is an effect to be experienced'. The assymmetrical relationship between effect and explanation is the problem that Iser identifies as being at the heart of any discussion of the reading process. He catches the paradox thus:

> Meaning as effect is a perplexing phenomenon, and such
> perplexity cannot be removed by explanations – on the contrary,
> it invalidates them. The effectiveness of the work depends on the
> participation of the reader, but explanations arise from . . .
> detachment . . .[70]

Clearly, there is an element of catch-22 about Iser's argument. For the researcher needing to theorise the concept of response as his practical work gets underway, some working definitions are necessary.

Two basic distinctions need to be made about the notion of 'response'. First, we must discriminate between the process of responding (what happens when we are actually reading) and immediate or considered responses after the process is over. Second, we must differentiate between primary responses, 'natural' activities that we can never fully know, and stated responses which are 'artifically' elicted in speech, writing, or drawing. Further, it is prudent to keep in mind Ryle's (1960) point that much of what purports to be introspection is, in fact, retrospection. So if we ask readers to tell us what is going on inside their heads during reading, we must be clear about the difference between their 'looking in' and their 'subsequent reporting'. Introspecting is generally considered to involve looking inwards and thereby gaining a self-awareness of private thinking procedures; introspective reporting, however, is a form of recalling which is influenced by the effects of interpreting and reconstruction. The most useful enquiries for English teachers to carry out are those which focus upon the process of responding since these relate directly to the dialogue between teacher and children when they are discussing a piece of literature in the classroom. Such enquiries that set out to monitor the stated responses of children using introspective methods may be usefully characterized by the term *introspective recall*, since this emphasises both the 'looking in' and the positive effort at recollection.

There are particular problems associated with introspective approaches which, as Elizabeth Valentine (1978) has noted, cluster under the related headings of inaccessibility and distortion. In respect to the first, we have to acknowledge the limited nature of the information available; the richness of much of our psychic life is not accessible via conscious introspection. Moreover, even if we accept the partial nature of the data, we are still left with the difficulty of translating into words what can be recalled.

The mediation of language is an inadequate and cumbersome way of representing the speed and variety of psychic life. Compensatory measures that we might take to overcome this first set of problems lead directly to the second set associated with distortion. In particular, introspective recall invites readers to think in slow motion, to think more explicitly than normal, and to concentrate on just the major items. However, these evident difficulties are not different in kind from those that beset other modes of enquiry which depend upon inference. Much research tends to value the tidily explained above the dimly apprehended. Yet, in order to study the processes of reader response, we must inevitably work with uncertain data. Fleeting images, half-formed notions, inadequately articulated meanings are the yield of introspective recall. It is important to explore these data with all their imperfections, to resist approaches which, by design, exclude material of potential interest and significance, and to strive to improve the techniques of introspective recall in just the same ways as we would with any other mode of enquiry. For all research approaches are ultimately judged by the same criteria of appropriateness, plausibility, and consistency.

The use of introspective recall to monitor readers' response has many of the benefits of the ethnographic approach which itself is increasingly recognised as an appropriate mode of enquiry in classroom research. Rosenblatt indicates that it is especially congenial when exploring problems involving the transactional view of literature.[71] Ethnography takes many forms and is increasingly susceptible to fashionable appropriation. The term is now commonly used to characterise the work of teacher-researchers whose research problems are formulated before their own eyes, as it were, in the course of their teaching; who collect data from the classroom and develop concepts and theories to explain what they find. This working definition means that particular studies may be some distance from the essentially descriptive, theory-building stance of 'classical' ethnography. It will become evident that the enquiries described in Chapters 2 and 3 wear the ethnographic label more easily than the one in Chapter 4. However, at the risk of offending the purists, it is reasonable to claim that teacher-researchers are 'doing ethnography' when they are using observation and interview as their main methods of investigation, recognising the significance of their own role as actors in the situation and, through attending closely to the descriptions they generate, attempting to theorise the phenomena they observe.

Ethnography is characterised by distinctive methodological emphases. It uses the techniques of the anthropologist rather than those of the natural scientist. It is concerned to build up detailed descriptions of particular phenomena, through field notes, recordings, interviews and the like. It is interested in understanding the perspectives of those under study and of observing their activities in normal surroundings, rather than resorting to second-hand accounts or 'artificially' created situations.

In reader-response studies there are several characteristics of the ethnographic approach that are particularly important. First, *reflexivity:* the stance of teacher-researcher signals that the enquirer (like the reader he is enquiring into) is 'in the middle'. The role is one of 'participant observation' and, as such, acknowledges that we are part of the phenomena we are studying. As Hammersley and Atkinson point out: 'This is not a matter of methodological commitment, it is an existential fact'.[72] Ethnographies involve the presence of the enquirer for extended periods of time with a narrow focus upon one classroom or one group of children. They recognise the effect of such presence on the evocations of and responses to poems. The 'common-sense' knowledge that the teacher-researcher has of the situation and the professional judgements that he makes are both rendered problematic by the reflexive scrutiny that is involved.

Second, there is the significance of the *context*. Responses to literature are the expressions not only of a particular group of readers but also of the particular setting. At its most inclusive this reflects – like a series of concentric circles around the child reading a poem – earlier experiences of literature teaching, the dynamics of the particular classroom, the influence of books and reading at school and at home, the status of literature in the curriculum, the ethos of the school and its role in the wider community. While ethnographies of readers' responses cannot expect to deal in explicit detail with the implications of this broad context, they must be alert to its influences. The effects of the particular settings permeate the enquiries and are recognised as important factors rather than deliberately excluded by the research design or ignored as irrelevant features. Clearly, the study of particular readers' responses in particular settings raises questions about the transferability of the findings and the amount of generalising weight they will bear. Yet, these are issues to be aware of rather than problems to be overcome. For it is an over-simplified view of classroom research that polarises the 'artificial' conditions that obtain, say, when interviewing readers outside their usual lessons according to a prespecified list of questions or when coding their responses against some prescribed schedule, with supposedly 'normal' conditions that exist in the context of routine lessons when the teacher is also the researcher. In both settings the readers are likely to feel 'special' and their performances invested with an unusual significance. Moreover, where reading and responding to literature are con-cerned, what constitutes an 'artificial' or a 'normal' setting is debatable. If we want to discover how readers read, the classroom could be seen as a highly artificial setting; at home or on the bus may be more normal. Reader-response enquiries quite properly define their contexts more widely than the classroom, not only because 'readings' within the classroom are influenced by the broader cultural surroundings, but because a good deal of reading and responding actually goes on *outside* the classroom.

Third, ethnographies of readers' activities with literary texts are valuable in *theorising the process of response*. The teacher-researcher starts from description not preconception in respect of the responses he studies. Elements of response emerge from the data; they are not identified as the result of applying preconceived categories. The development of theory as itself an organic process becomes a fundamental concern. The theoretical statements that we can make about the process of responding to poems are derived from the particular methodology employed by the teacher-researcher. Conversely, the enquirer is consciously exploring the effects of changes in methodology upon the plausibility and validity of general statements about reading poems. The conventional way we express the relationship between theory and practice is better resequenced as one between practice and theory. Each, of course, acts upon the other; but the ethnographer's stance is to observe, record, describe, scrutinize and look for patterns in readers' responses from which theoretical statements can be generated. He is able to theorise response in ways that provide '. . . much more evidence of the plausibility of different lines of analysis than (are) available to the "armchair theorist", or even the survey researcher . . .'[73]

Fourth, a valuable feature of the ethnographic approach is its *flexibility*. The general advantages of this method which, as Hammersley and Atkinson point out, do not entail extensive pre-field work design, are especially evident in reader-response enquiries. This is not to say that preparatory work is not essential – it is, as will be seen presently – but the preliminaries are concerned with focusing the readers and putting them at their ease rather than with fixing the course of the work unalterably. Both in general in this approach and, in particular, with ethnographies of readers responding to poems,

> the strategy and even direction of the research can be changed relatively easily, in line with changing assessments of what is required by the process of theory construction. As a result, ideas can be quickly tried out and, if promising, followed up.[74]

That ethnography is such a flexible and responsive mode of enquiry is especially important when studying the processes of responding to literature of young readers.

Studies of children's responses to poetry have taken various forms. At one extreme are the broadly-based surveys such as Yarlott and Harpin's account of '1000 Responses to English Literature'[75] and the more narrowly focused questionnaire studies about pupils' and teachers' experience of and attitudes towards poetry in school carried out by Tony Oakley[76], Peter Benton[77] and by the APU.[78] As Peter Benton has pointed out:

> The Secondary Survey provided for the first time clear evidence of a massive rejection on the part of secondary pupils of much that goes on in the name of teaching poetry.[79]

Such surveys provide a significant backdrop against which to set smaller scale inquiries; they form an important part of the teacher-researcher's context.

Relatively few enquiries have looked closely at what actually happens to poetry in the classroom and many of those that have tend to use content analysis adapted from studies of fiction reading. For example, Wade (1981) uses a modified version of Squire's (1964) categories to compare how a supervised and an unsupervised group of children discuss a poem; and Atkinson (1985) studies the developmental aspect of response through the application of Purves and Rippere's (1968) categories to her pupils' written accounts.

Different again is the work of Dixon and Brown (1985) which sets out to document and analyse the written protocols of seventeen-year-old students after the manner of I.A. Richards and with the added dimension of detailed comments on the students' writing from a panel of teachers from schools, colleges and universities. Despite the richness of the material and the careful scrutiny and reflection it is afforded, there is a worrying flaw in the methodology. In order to identify what counts as a 'response', the panel were not given the questions or tasks the students had been set but simply extracts from their writings or untitled essays. Hence, responses to the text were deemed separable from responses to the questions about it. To detach the interpretations of the responses from the conditions which produced them is a curiously self-defeating feature of an otherwise laudable attempt to analyse one sort of manifestation of considered responses to literature.

At the other extreme from the surveys and of different character from descriptions that rely on content analysis, are studies that take an exploratory or illuminative stance and which, by accident or design, adopt features of the ethnographic approach. Three recent enquiries by Kintgen, Peter Benton, and Dias have useful affinities with aspects of the present studies.

Kintgen's concern is, in Rosenblatt's terms, with evocation rather than response. He asked sixteen graduate students and colleagues 'to verbalize into a cassette recorder whatever they did while they tried to understand a poem.'[80] He wanted to know how expert readers 'converted a series of marks on the page into a unified mental conception' and chose to monitor their comments via tape-recording the process of what he calls 'subjective simultaneous introspection'.[81] The argument that his procedure offers '. . . the greatest possibility that the basic thought processes will appear undistorted' makes too great a claim, despite its hesitancy, for, as we have already suggested, distortion is inevitable. Nevertheless, Kintgen's analyses of his readers' transcripts are interestingly handled from two main directions: differences in syntactic perception and a description of the elementary perceptual processes his readers demonstrate. Although he does not present his findings in this way, the first approach is text-oriented, the second reader-oriented. The first generates a number of questions arising from the conclusion that 'linguistic analysis may . . . provide a description of the syntax of the poem, but it does not describe how readers perceive that syntax.'[82] Readers, it seems, are just as likely to decide, in a general way, what a poem means and make the syntax fit that conception, as they are to allow the syntactic construction of the poem to direct their reading. The second claims to identify a tentative list of twenty elementary processes, three modalities (statements, questions, hypotheses), and a catch-all category (interpret) which derive from the study of the transcripts. The important thing here is not the category divisions *per se* but the exploratory character of the enquiry and the willingness to construct profiles of readers' responses which are provisional, non-dogmatic descriptions of literary perception; Kintgen's study is appropriately tentative. Several of his suggested ways of developing and improving such enquiries are, in fact, ones that are engaged with in later chapters of this book. These include working with articulate and cooperative readers and striving to refine the introspective method of monitoring responses; exploring how responses to poetry develop over a period of time; describing how individuals negotiate several different poems in order to identify aspects of 'personal style'; and monitoring group discussions of poems. In these and other respects our Chapter 2, 3 and 4 aim to give a detailed and sophisticated account of how readers read poems.

A further dimension of Peter Benton's work, one which complements the survey mentioned above, is his enquiry into how groups of secondary school children discuss poetry. Chapters 3 and 4 of his book provide valuable evidence of both the commitment and the insights pupils can achieve in unsupervised discussions. Building particularly upon the work of Barnes, these chapters demonstrate the ways in which small group work can be especially beneficial in poetry teaching without being blind to some of its limitations. The principle upon which the responses were elicited was the straightforward pedagogical one that free speech requires a firm framework. Groups need to feel secure and task-oriented in order to make full use of the talk-time they are offered. Hence, for example, when one group had heard Ted Hughes's *The Warm and the Cold* read aloud, they were asked to

> Talk about the poem in any way they pleased but at some point to consider (i) what the poem was about (ii) how it said what it was saying (iii) any things they liked or disliked about it (iv) why they felt as they did about it. It was made clear that these were not tasks to be taken in order and that they could organise the discussion in any way they chose. The group was left unsupervised. . . . No time limit was given.[83]

Later this procedure is characterised as 'lightly structured, self-directed discussion' and is seen as a key activity in improving pupils' attitudes towards poetry. The particular affinity of this work to the present studies is its teacher-researcher stance and the implicit recognition that the principles and practices of good teaching and good research share much in common. The group discussions described in Chapters 3 and 4 of our book illustrate the effects of varying degrees of teacher control and task direction. (cf. p. 95ff; p. 129ff and p. 157ff.)

Dias, too, focuses on the oral responses of secondary school pupils – 28 fourteen- and fifteen-year-olds in the middle ability range – in two comprehensive schools in Quebec and England. His work is salutary both methodologically and in the way he analyses his findings. He has developed the use of *responding-aloud protocols* or RAPs.[84] Essentially, these require individual pupils to think aloud as they attempt to make sense of a poem with the help, if needed, of a non-directive interviewer. Preparatory group discussions were employed to build up confidence for the individual sessions. The RAP transcripts (two per pupil) were then analysed to see how the pupils had negotiated meaning. Dias's enquiries are, it appears, work-in-progress and it is perhaps surprising to be offered more of his conclusions than of his evidence. Moreover, there seems to be uncertainty about whether the RAPs tell us about 'patterns of reading' (p.50) or 'kinds of readers' (p. 46). Having claimed that the protocols reveal four kinds of reader – paraphrasers, thematisers, allegorisers and problem-solvers – thus raising the issue of developing a typology of readers, he retreats from his own labels and insists that his findings cannot be generalised in this way. Dias's work raises more questions than it acknowledges but, though there is a strong sense of premature categorisation, his enquiries have some useful pointers to the care and sensitivity with which it is necessary to handle monitoring procedures.

All the issues touched on in these recent studies, and more, are addressed by the enquiries reported later in this book. Through close scrutiny of our evidence we have attempted to theorise individual readings and group discussion, to keep our methods of working under continuous review, and to conceptualise aspects of the response process, where appropriate, in diagrammatic form (see Chapter 2 *passim* and p. 177). Our studies all developed from the approach summarised in an earlier article (Benton, 1984), one which was rapidly outgrown as the enquiries proceeded. Our main modifications were methodological and it is to the practical matters of monitoring children's responses to poems that we now need to turn.

(ii) Practical Matters

Chapters 2 and 3 are each extracts from small-scale investigations carried out by a teacher-researcher working alone. They have a narrow focus on the interaction of a small number of teenage pupils, usually between four and six boys and girls, and particular poems. It is important to limit the scope of such enquiries to keep the amount of data manageable, to make it feasible to integrate the work with other normal teaching commitments, and to encourage in-depth analysis of the responses. It is important to signal, too, that such enquiries are relatively easy for the classroom teacher to pursue.

Given the orientation of our enquiries, the kind of poetry which was chosen was largely that which required reflective reading. The selection of texts in the first two studies was, in part, a matter of negotiation between the teacher and the children; in the third study, the poems to be taught were jointly short-listed by the researcher and his teacher assistants. Involving teachers and readers in selecting some of the poems to be responded to increased the commitment to the task and ensured that the texts had appeal to the children as well as making a demand upon them.

The selection of readers was no less important. The common wish to monitor a whole class was relatively easy to resist since for the teacher working alone, it soon became apprent that the amount of data would lead to superficiality even if it could be controlled. We focused, therefore, on small numbers of readers, sometimes a mix of boys and girls, at others, single sex friendship groups. The schools in which the enquiries were carried out were all mixed comprehensive schools. There was no point in attempting a spread of social backgrounds among such a small number of children. We opted, instead, for reasonably articulate, willing children who enjoyed reading and talking about literature on the principle that, if we can discover what committed readers do, we may then find pointers, if not panaceas, towards helping not only them but also their less enthusiastic classmates.

One issue to be borne in mind in the selection of readers was the particular focus of the enquiry – whether to monitor individual responses, pair work, group discussions and/or some combination of these in sequence or in parallel. We felt that there was much to be said for working *initially* with the children as a group in the preparatory stages, even if the teacher's intention was to carry out enquiries with single readers. This built up confidence, gave the readers a sense of common purpose and felt fairly like the group work that was part of their normal English lessons – which, of course, in some instances, it was.

The decision about whether to monitor individuals or groups was fundamental to the enquiries. Arguably, the one-to-one contact between researcher and reader would produce the most sensitive and detailed reporting, particularly if – as recorded in Chapters 2 and 3 – the researcher could set things up in such a way that the contact upon which we eavesdrop is that between the reader and the text. Clearly, such a focus is one that lends itself to the collection of case studies around a common text. However, poetry invites group talk, as we have seen in the studies mentioned above. One of the problems addressed in Chapter 4 is how to maintain the focus upon the process of shared interpreting without becoming preoccupied with matters of group dynamics. In all these respects the study of literary responses is intimately bound up with the deployment of the readers. This is as relevant to teaching as it is to research.

The design of any enquiry into individual readers' responses has to allow for preparatory activities that will orientate the readers towards the nature of introspective recall whether this involves monitoring their own responses through making notes around a text or getting used to talking by themselves into a tape recorder. Recording their own image-making, feelings, associations and the like in stream of consciousness style is not something that children are generally familiar with in relation to *reading*, even though Ted Hughes recommended something similar in relation to *writing* more than twenty years ago.[85] The advent of reading logs or journals in some schools has helped children to think more like writers and to become more self-aware as readers. (Susan Hackman's *Responding in Writing* (1987) is an excellent account of what can be achieved in this area.) These devices are particularly useful in loosening up writing and in encouraging children to use it to record their thinking and feeling in the course of their reading. Our experience has been that this informal use of writing is welcomed by children. Activities such as taping and logging responses signal that reading has shared elements as well as highly individual ones, that the researcher is interested in *all* responses without evaluating them, and that describing the 'world in the head' is an enjoyable and valid way of talking about literature.

From the role of the readers to that of the researcher – a role, as indicated earlier, that is a central issue in ethnographic enquiry. Practical questions about the different means of monitoring are inextricably caught up with the teacher-researcher's role in relation to the children. For example, the decision as to whether a particular reading experience will be 'audio-visual' (researcher reads, live or taped, and children follow in the text), or silent, cannot be isolated from role questions: is the researcher to be a member of the group? an interviewer of individual children? a remote controller (i.e., absent, having given oral/written directions to the children)? or some combination of these roles? Clearly, these matters lie at the heart of all enquiries into children's responses to literature. Essentially, we found three sets of issues existing in a creative tension during our enquiries:

(a) the need to recognize and be responsive to the directions taken in individual introspective accounts and group discussions;
(b) the need to adopt a non-directive, facilitatory role; and
(c) the need to devise means of monitoring responses that were both manageable and interesting for the children and productive for the researcher.

In this latter respect, and given our prime concern with the process of responding, we tended to favour playing to the children's linguistic strength by using tape recorders, acknowledging that the writing down of anything more formalised than initial jottings was likely to intervene too massively between the world in the head and the articulation of responses.

It is worth re-emphasising two points about these procedures that were hinted at in general terms earlier. First, readers' efforts to articulate their mental processes during reading are poorly served by tape-recording and note-making. Not only is language an inadequate instrument for capturing the richness and elusiveness of mental activity but it operates primarily in a linear, one-dimensional fashion and is not good at recording things that happen simultaneously. Even so, these means are the best available and we have tried to exploit them to the full. Secondly, we are well aware that exploratory enquiries such as these can become self-fulfilling prophecies just as easily as other research modes, such as questionnaires or controlled experiments. All readers, whatever the mode of enquiry, have assumptions and expectations about what they are doing. Throughout, we have tried to keep alert to the two complementary aspects of this problem, namely, that how the readers respond will depend upon the signals the teacher-researcher gives, and that what he, in turn, discovers in their responses will be, to some extent, what he expects to find.

Chapter 2

Close Readings

John Teasey

A From pilot study to main enquiry

(i) The pilot study

In a recent spring term, I was engaged in a study with five fourth year pupils to assess the effectiveness of two teaching strategies intended to promote a personal response to literature: first, a period of private reflection during which the readers recorded their initial responses to a poem, followed by a small-group discussion of 'any lines that stand out, the form of the poem, any feelings the poem has created, and what you think has caught the writer's attention.' At the time, I found it difficult to make sense of the data derived from the study, largely because – as I now realise – I thought I knew what I meant by a 'personal response' to literature. It had, after all, been an article of faith for over twenty happy years spent in the classroom.

During the study, the pupils had been most moved by Causley's 'Song of a Dying Gunner'. The prompt sheet, with its open-ended questions, was put to one side. *Their* agenda for the discussion was very different: first, they shared their private responses; then, the talk turned to an animated exploration of the personal associations aroused by their reading of the poem. It was during an argument as to what thoughts really would pass through the mind of a dying person that I felt sufficiently uneasy to intervene, to move the talk on to a 'proper' consideration of language and form:

> *Teacher* (in a slightly exasperated tone) But don't you want to talk about the language of the poem?
> *Elizabeth* (with feeling) It's irrelevant to what's inside the poem and to what's inside the poet when he's writing the poem and what's inside us when we're reading the poem . . . the words you should go to afterwards.
> *Ian*: (drily) Feelings is the bit that strikes you most and it's the

piece you can talk about . . . in this poem it's the underlying current that drags everything along.
Elizabeth: The whole is more important than the individual words . . . you don't so much want the identity of the person, as to be able to get inside the feelings and understand why he feels like this.

It was equally clear that a 'proper', orderly explication of the text would have been an inappropriate activity at this point. In order to grasp at 'the whole', the readers were moving around inside the text, deferring consideration of what was felt to be insignificant, whether understood or not, and attending to what appeared to be important. They were also deriving obvious pleasure and benefit from reading aloud, to themselves and to each other, sections of the text under consideration, an activity not accorded priority in my normal classroom practice.

With hindsight, the tensions reflected in the study between teacher and taught reflect the ambiguity within the word 'response'. It may refer to how an individual responds at the time of reading; it more commonly refers to that kind of response which is the product of a discriminating mind trained in the literary-critical discipline. It is this second meaning which seems to have informed my intervention during the group discussion, and which Eagleton argues still informs most classroom practice:

> The fact remains that English students . . . today are Leavisites whether they know it or not. . . . That current is as deep-seated as our conviction that the earth moves around the sun.[1]

Of the followers of *Scrutiny* he writes:

> Its adherents would go out to the schools and universities to do battle there, nurturing through the study of literature the kind of rich, complex, mature, discriminating, morally serious responses which would equip individuals to survive in a mechanised society of trashy romances, alienated labour, banal advertisements and vulgarising mass media.[2]

Such high ideals have not always translated well into classroom practice. Mulford's caricature may perhaps be recognisable:

> Only someone with my degree of intelligence and sensitivity can properly appreciate these works, and since you don't appreciate them, for the time being at least you are denied occasions for the exercise of intelligence and sensitivity. If you are potentially one of that minority of readers of intelligence and sensitivity, then you are going to have to rely on me as one of those with custodial access to the one, right total meaning.[3]

In that classroom, the pupil will have to learn to profess someone else's response. It is also likely that the experience of poetry will be destroyed, for the sake of its analysis.

The reading experience set in motion by the teaching strategies adopted in the pilot study was, however, powerful enough to deflect a well-intentioned if inept intervention on my part, and appeared to be as rich and complex as any carefully nurtured response. As Figure 2.1 makes clear, somehow what was 'inside' (the readers) had to do with what was 'inside the poem' and 'inside the poet'. Instinctively they knew what is often forgotten in the classroom, that the text becomes poem only when the reader interacts with the experiences that lie behind the words on the page.

The Reader	*The Poem*	*The Writer*
'what's inside us when we're reading'	'what's inside the poem'	'what's inside the poet when he's writing the poem'

The Reading Experience

'feelings is the bit that strikes you. . .
the whole is more important than the
individual words. . you want to be able to
get inside the feelings and understand
why he feels like this'

Reading Strategies

'the readers had moved around inside
the text. . attending selectively. . . .
reading aloud sections of it'

Questions arising from the pilot study

1 What is the relationship between the reader, the poem and the writer?
2 What is the nature of the reading experience?
3 What is the purpose of the reading experience?
4 How do 'good' readers read poetry?
5 What are the implications for the classroom of the answers to these questions?

Figure 2.1 The activity of reading as suggested by the pilot study

The starting-point for the design of any methodology intended to promote a personal response to literature must surely be an understanding of the activity of reading itself. By not introducing the readers to the notion of introspective recall, I had missed the opportunity of obtaining an insight into that elusive world.

(ii) The main enquiry

The five readers who had participated in the pilot study readily agreed to take part in the enquiry. A last-minute change in holiday arrangements, however, meant that Ian's place was taken by Kristina, a former pupil, who was going up to Art College.

The task for the week was as follows: the five readers, drawing on the resources of the departmental stock cupboard, were asked to compile an anthology of twenty of their favourite poems. Half of the poems were to be agreed upon by the group and half would reflect the individual choices of the readers. In addition to monitoring their own responses to some of the poems, they were asked to explain briefly why they had chosen particular poems, and how they would organise the twenty poems into an anthology. At the end of the enquiry, each reader would express a final response to a single poem, in whatever manner thought most satisfying.

The broad focus of the enquiry reveals how little I knew about the nature of aesthetic reading, but also my concern to devise a task which, while satisfying the research objective of eliciting accurate data about reading, would also be a satisfying experience for the readers.

They were all accustomed to entering in literature journals their thoughts about the books they were reading; the enquiry was to explore what was happening as they were reading. The significance of this distinction had become clear during the pilot study. Attending to the activity of reading, and thus focusing on their own responses, seems of particular importance for a full experience of poetry, given its richness and density.

Through a study of their responses, I hoped to gain a better understanding of the nature of reading. Understanding on the part of the teacher, and self-awareness on the part of the readers, are both essential to good classroom practice.

The experience of the pilot study suggested a number of measures to be adopted. First, the texts selected by the readers would be re-typed and placed centrally on A4 paper. This would allow the pupils to write around the text of the poem, in accordance with the model of reading already observed. Second, to encourage the readers to record as fully as possible all that was taking place as they read, they would be asked to jot down their responses, around the text, numbering them as they occurred. Third, they would reflect on their own responses, on tape and in writing. This had a two-fold purpose: as a learning strategy which compelled the reader to build on his or her own experience; and as an attempt to catch any information about the reading process which had escaped the net of the second measure. Last, the opening session would include an introspective recall exercise, so that everyone was clear about precisely what was required. Their discussion would be taped, and, if appropriate, I would join in at the end to follow-up any points of interest.

As the inquiry was to take place in school during a week in August, there was unlimited access to texts, typewriters, tape recorders and private reading areas.

Figure 2.2 sets out the provisional timetable drawn up for the week; Figure 2.3 is the timetable which was actually worked.

Monday	(a) Outline of week
	(b) Introspective recall exercise
	(c) Preparing and setting up materials
Tuesday	Group choices A, B and C
Wednesday	Group choices D and E
	Personal choices, Readers A and B
Thursday	Personal choices, Readers C, D and E
Friday	(a) 'I like this poem because . . .'
	(b) Final Response
	(c) Compiling anthology

Figure 2.2   Provisional timetable

Monday	Session One	1	Outlining the week's activities
		2	Introspective Recall Exercise
	Session Two	3	Preparing materials
Tuesday	Session Three	4	Sharing choices
		5(a)	'Frogs in the Wood': personal responses
		5(b)	Follow-up, written or taped
		6	Sharing responses
	Session Four	7	'History Lesson': personal responses
		8	Sharing responses
Wednesday	Session Five	9	Sharing choices
		10	'Home is so Sad': personal responses
		11	Sharing responses
	Session Six	12	'Mirror': personal responses, *Elizabeth and Kristina*

		13	Sharing responses
		14	Cloze activity, *Colin, Sara and Sasha*
		15	Michael Rosen: group discussion
Thursday	Session Seven	16(a)	'First Ice': personal response, *Elizabeth*
		16(b)	Follow-up, taped
		17	'Days': personal response, *Elizabeth*
		18	'First Ice': personal response, *Kristina*
		19(a)	'Days': personal response, *Kristina*
		19(b)	Follow-up taped
		20(a)	'The Stag': personal response, *Colin*
		20(b)	Follow-up, written
		21(a)	'HMS Glory': personal response *Colin*
		21(b)	Follow-up, written
		22(a)	'The Lockless Door': personal response, *Sara*
		22(b)	Follow-up, written
		23	'Paralytic': personal response, *Sara*
		24(a)	'Cut Grass': personal response, *Sasha*
		24(b)	Follow-up, taped
		25	'Prayer before Birth': personal response, Sasha
Friday	Session Eight	26	'Mirror': final response, Elizabeth
		27	'First Ice': final response, *Kristina*
		28	Charles Causley: final response, *Colin*
		29	'Home is so Sad': final response, *Sara*
		30	'Frogs in the Wood': final response, *Sasha*
	Session Nine	31	Compiling the anthology
		32	Completing 'I like this poem because . . .'

Figure 2.3   The worked timetable

B   The Poem as Event

Something else is alive
Beside the clock's loneliness
And this blank page . . .

As teachers, we offer our pupils a variety of poetry texts. But if we
are to accept the distinction made by Rosenblatt, as described in
Chapter 1, between texts and poems, then we must admit that
poems are creatures rarely to be found coming to life within the
confines of a classroom. Indeed, belief in the existence of such
creatures is more an act of faith on our part, than a considered
response to irrefutable evidence.

Yet during the week of the enquiry I feel confident that two such
creatures, each 'coming about its own business', were captured in
the nets of the initial responses of two of the readers. On these two
occasions I had the feeling of attending rarely glimpsed moments of
creation.

(i)   Elizabeth evokes 'Frogs in the Wood' by Brian Patten

Our first activity on Monday had been, as planned, the introspective
recall exercise, to establish a shared understanding of what was
meant by personal response: all that was experienced by the reader
during the act of reading. The rest of the morning was spent
browsing through a large collection of poetry books, a period of
time characterised by stretches of silence interspersed with, 'Listen
to this one'. After lunch, those texts of interests to one or more of
the readers were typed up and photocopied, and by the end of the
day we had agreed on a dozen poetry texts to be taken home, to be
read by everyone.

The next morning, it quickly became obvious that Brian Patten's
'Frogs in the Wood' had caught the interest of most of the readers,
Elizabeth being the least enthusiastic. The readers were then asked
to jot down their initial responses (IRs) around the text, and to
comment on these responses in a written or taped follow-up.
Elizabeth's initial responses are set out in Figure 2.4, and given in
diagrammatic form in Figure 2.5.

At the end - everywhere I've lived I've had my own private little place where I can be alone - sometimes inside the house sometimes outside where I go to think or just to be alone
- after first reading of
last verse

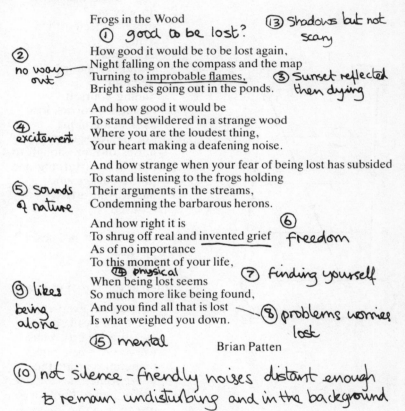

Frogs in the Wood

① good to be lost?

⑬ Shadows but not scary

② no way out

How good it would be to be lost again,
Night falling on the compass and the map
Turning to improbable flames,
Bright ashes going out in the ponds.

③ Sunset reflected then dying

④ excitement

And how good it would be
To stand bewildered in a strange wood
Where you are the loudest thing,
Your heart making a deafening noise.

⑤ Sounds of nature

And how strange when your fear of being lost has subsided
To stand listening to the frogs holding
Their arguments in the streams,
Condemning the barbarous herons.

And how right it is
To shrug off real and invented grief
As of no importance
To this moment of your life,

⑥ freedom

⑭ physical
When being lost seems

⑦ finding yourself

⑨ likes being alone

So much more like being found,
And you find all that is lost
Is what weighed you down.

⑧ problems worries lost

⑮ mental

Brian Patten

⑩ not silence - friendly noises distant enough to remain undisturbing and in the background

⑪ happy-surprised-relieved   ⑫ light-airy

Figure 2.4   Elizabeth's initial responses to 'Frogs in the Wood'

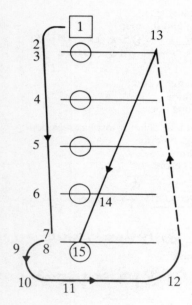

Initial Responses

Elizabeth 'Frogs in the Wood' *Eliz, IRs 1–15*

1 good to be lost
2 no way out?
3 sunset reflected then dying
4 excitement
5 sounds of nature
6 freedom
7 finding yourself
8 problems worries lost
9 likes being alone
10 not silence – friendly noises distant enough to remain undisturbing and in the background
11 happy – surprised – relieved
12 light airy
13 shadows but not scary
14 physical
15 mental

written at the top of the page:

> At the end, everywhere I've lived I've had my own private little place where I can be alone. Sometimes inside the house sometimes outside where I go to think or just to be alone. After first reading of the last verse

Figure 2.5 The movement of Elizabeth's responses to 'Frogs in the Wood'

Elizabeth immediately picks up the unusual assertion to the opening line: '(1) good to be lost?' Then follows a careful reading down through the text, showing the awareness of the patterning by ringing the initial word of each stanza. The difficulty of 'improbable flames' is noted but not resolved. By the time she reaches the final stanza, the clustering of jottings suggests that the meaning is becoming clear: '(7) finding yourself'; (8) problems worries lost'. At this point her responses alter in nature. In (10) she reflects at length on the significance of the noises in the strange wood. Her first query, as to how it could be good to be lost, is answered in part by the realisation that 'the friendly noises (are) distant enough to remain undisturbing'. She then notes the feelings aroused by the text/poem, and/or contained within it: '(11) happy – surprised – relieved' and '(12) light – airy'. At this point occurs the most striking jotting of all, a lengthy note, written 'after first reading of the last verse' describing 'my own private little place where I can be alone'. Elizabeth returns to the opening stanza, (13), where the significance of the light and shade can be reinterpreted as 'not scary', and she closes, (14) and (15), by noting the two senses in which 'lost' is used in the final stanza.

Her responses have developed thus: initially, a close attention to texual cues in responses (1) to (9); then, (10) to (12), a much more explicitly worded account of the feelings aroused by/within the text/poem, at the same time as a narration of a personal association, analogous to the experience developed within the text/poem; then, (13), a brief re-reading, and clarification of the concluding stanza.

Figure 2.5 representing the movement of the responses diagrammatically, makes clear the rhythm of her reading within the text and emphasises the significance of jottings (9) to (12). They have been placed at a distance from the text, just as she has been able to stand back sufficiently to interpret the cues she is decoding. The pattern becomes even more interesting when viewed in the light of her taped reflections on her own responses.

Elizabeth: 'Frogs in the Wood'

Taped follow-up	Commentary
1 I didn't really want to do this poem 'cos I didn't like it at first, but I do like it now 'cos it's a happy poem really, it's a sort of surprise . . . kind of relieved sort of a poem.	*1–3* E. expands IRs (11) and (12). Her comment shows that the first reading had revealed the emotional life within the text/poem, and her own experience of this.
4 The title isn't really what it's about, 'Frogs in the Wood'. It's about being alone and finding out that when you're alone all your problems and worries not only seem not to be so big but sometimes go away altogether.	*4–7* She confidently states the idea behind the text poem, a coherent understanding hinted at in IRs (7) and (8). She now turns to address the IRs in sequence.
7 Um, the first line was funny, I thought, what's this, because it says, 'How good it would be to be lost again', and I wondered how it could be good to be lost, you always associate being lost with being panic-stricken and being by yourself. I went through after that first line I thought that the rest of the lines would be sort of funny like that so I went through the first verse anyway, line by line.	*7–13* Because she had been struck by the unusual assertion of the opening line, she was alerted to a very careful reading, 'through the first verse anyway, line by line': the implication is that such a reading is for Elizabeth unusual.
13 The second line is, 'Night falling on the compass and the map'. I get the image of a sort of a shadow falling over a compass and a map and what it means is that he this person really and truly is lost because he can't get out now, 'cos he can't see his compass or his maps, so he's in there for good.	*13–17* The image referred to appears not to have occurred on first reading; it is an image she 'gets' rather than 'got'. The second line was immediately understood, as IR(2) makes clear.

46

18   I don't know what an 'improbable flame' is, I've no idea so I missed that line and went to the next one . . .

19   . . . where I got my first real image, it says, 'Bright ashes going out in the ponds'. And I can see a pond surrounded by trees I think, I'm not sure, but the sunset is reflected in it being the bright ashes, it's little sort of golden flecks in the pond, and then they die out like they're being extinguished.

24   But by the time I'd finished the first verse I was curious about what would happen so I went sort of through it then . . .

26   . . . and each, the middle three verses all start with 'and' and I noticed that which made it sort of flow better.

28   He, he's, excited to be in this wood and to not know what's really going on and he likes to be the loudest thing, he says, 'And how good it would be to be the loudest thing', he says, and be able to hear your heart beat and hearing no noise around you, I guess.

18–19   In the light of 7–13 above, we must assume that her response to this textual difficulty is the normal one – not to interrupt the impetus of her reading.

19–24   For the first time, the taped comments add new information to the IRs. This particular line caused the other readers difficulty, but she appears to have pictured the line, the image indistinct around the edges, the 'golden flecks' at the centre.

25–26   This comment signals a faster reading, not merely because she has understood the opening stanza, but also because her curiosity has been aroused about the feelings of the man in the woods.

26–28   But her 'reading' is not so headlong that she fails to make meaning from the form in which Patten has cast his words.

28–32   Patten had used the word 'bewildered'; Elizabeth uses the word 'excited'. This is not a mis-reading, as it predicts the direction the text/poem takes. It does suggest that the focus of her attention is on what the man is experiencing, and that she has held on to her first reaction to the opening line.

32   And then he says, 'And how strange when your your fear of being lost has subsided.' So you're not, you're not so uptight and tense because you're lost, so you feel easy and can relax and sort of become part of your surroundings and he's hearing the sounds of nature which is where the title comes from 'Frogs in the Wood.'

To stand listening to the frogs holding
    Their arguments in the streams,
Condemning the barbarous herons.

That's not really anything to do with the poem, it's just the fact that he's so relaxed, and he's in a setting where he doesn't belong, but he's not out of place, he's still part of his setting and he can become a part of it and listen to it.

32–44   Because she is identifying with the man's situation, she understands a stanza which the other readers found perplexing. She has switched from 'he' to 'you' in lines 33 and 34, of significance when read with the hindsight afforded by a reading of the final passage when she talks of her own experience. She also makes increasing use of reading the text aloud, to experience and to gain a greater understanding of the text/poem.

45   And the next verse is shorter than the others, it's still got four lines but the lines are shorter:

And how right it is
To shrug off real and invented grief
As of no importance to this moment of your life.

He's taking life as one moment . . it's almost like he's stopped, suspended in time and time is only one moment. What is invented grief? Grief that he has invented for himself, because society demands it of him? I don't know. Could be grief, might not necessarily be grief as I understand it, it could be, um,

45–46   The urgency in her voice echoes the movement of the text/poem to a climax. She still responds to the patterning, which is noted but not explained. Nor does she allow her difficulty with 'invented grief' to delay her reading. She 'shrugs it off' as she notes the speaker shrugs off his grief.

sadness, but it's invented either by society around him or it's invented within him. But either way he shrugs it off.

57 In the last verse,
  When being lost seems
  So much more like being found,
  And you find that all that is lost
  Is what weighed you down.

That's that's when the poem became personal for me because, um, he's saying, 'when being lost', he's talking about the physical sense of being in a place where you don't know where you are, 'seems so much more like being found', he's not being found physically, he's talking about finding himself mentally. 'And you find all that is lost/Is what weighed you down.' What is lost then are his problems and his worries and his doubts and things, 'is what weighed you down'. He's found that having lost them or them gone into the background for a while, it's made him a happier person.

At this point the tape recorder was switched off, and Elizabeth listened to what she had said. She concludes her reflections as follows:

72 So this is a happy poem because I can relate to the man, I mean, the personal experience that comes to mind with me came to me after the first reading of the last verse, is a place where you can be alone in.

57–71   When Elizabeth had been jotting around the text, it was noticed that responses 13, 14 and 15 had occurred after she had returned to the initial stanza. Here she incorporates these into her account of the final stanza, where understanding seems complete – the experience has left the man in the wood, and Elizabeth, happier. But most tantalising of all is her unexplained assertion that 'that's when the poem became personal for me'. It is from this point that the word 'poem' can be used instead of 'text'. Fortunately, having listened to herself, she carries on, and makes explicit what had been happening to her as she read.

72–77   The lengthy note added to the text, in the top left hand corner, is explained; when she reached the final stanza, there is 'a personal experience that comes to mind', of a place which had the same

Every place I've lived in I've had my own little private place where I can be alone. Sometimes it's in the house, sometimes it's outside . . .

77 . . . but I can just go there to think or not to think, you know, sometimes it's better not to think when you're by yourself. You can be by yourself and not have to think, whereas when you're with other people they force you to think. That's, that's why this poem is happy because it is true that you lose a lot of your problems when you're by yourself. Everything sort of, it's funny, really, because everything comes down to you, and the fact that it does means it's easier to solve. You've got no . . . You've got nothing in your way.

84 I don't know what problems this man has but he obviously has got some problem. I don't know, I think he's, that this is something that has happened before, he's gone to a place where he's been alone but he's not now, he's imagining to be there and wanting to be there, he says 'how good it would be' and 'how strange it would be' and 'how right it is.' Perhaps he's learned the secret in the last two verses of doing it relaxing, not being alone.

91 This poem leaves me feeling happy. I don't know what the others will have made of it, but I think I would like now not to say any more about it but to find the others and find out what they think about it, before I can sort of really close it.

significance for her as the woods for the speaker in the poem.

77–84 She reflects on how she feels in this private place, and on the strange truth that problems are sometimes solved by not thinking about them. Her experience of 'Frog in the Woods' has brought to life a personal experience, which she is evaluating.

84–91 She assumes the man in the wood to be the poet, and speculates on why he wrote the poem. She imagines what he must be feeling to want to be by himself, and his life seems as real to her as her own.

91–94 The poem has been experienced; her natural urge is to share this experience with her friends before 'closing' it.

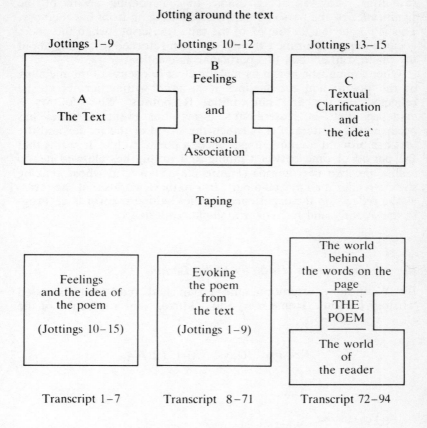

Figure 2.6 The pattern of Elizabeth's responses, initially, as jottings around the text, then, as reflections on tape.

The critical moment in the reading, on the evidence of Elizabeth's initial jottings and subsequent reflections, occurred after the first reading of the last stanza, when 'the poem became personal for me' (line 62). This can be clearly seen when the two activities are compared in Figure 2.6.

When jotting around the text, Elizabeth had moved IRs (10) to (12) away from the main body of the text. At this point in time, when, on the evidence of her jottings, she was attending to her own responses, she was at the same time becoming aware of the significance of the personal experience emerging from her memory. This is made clear in line 62 of the tape transcript, 'when the poem became personal for me', though she then returned to talking about the poem, rather than this particular association.

When taping, she began by making clear her sense of the meaning of the poem, and the feelings it aroused within her. Next she reflected on the first nine Initial Responses. What follows is evidence that, in Rosenblatt's terms, 'an event in time' has occurred. The interaction between the world of the reader and the text has brought a unique experience, a poem, to life. It seems that the period of time between taping and jotting has allowed her to realise the two new worlds (Figure 2.6), above, in whose making she, as reader, had played a part. It is to these worlds that she turns, as she reflects on the experience that lies behind the words of 'Frogs in the Wood', and to her own, similar experience.

(ii) Kristina evokes 'Days' by Philip Larkin

By Wednesday afternoon, the group had read and discussed 'History Lesson', 'Home is so Sad', 'Mirror' and a selection of the

Kristina 'Days' Kris. IR 1–4

Days

④ childlike attitude, no questioning, simplistic

What are days for?
Days are where we live. ① like a house/family
They come, they wake us
Time and time over. ② opposite = ??
They are to be happy in:
Where can we live but days?
Ah, solving that question ③ pro/anti
Brings the priest and the doctor questioning our
In their long coats existence~?
Running over the fields.

Philip Larkin

Figure 2.7 The movement of Kristina's initial responses to 'Days'

work of Michael Rosen, in addition to 'Frogs in the Wood'. They now decided to spend Thursday jotting around texts of their own choice and following up these responses, without afterwards presenting the texts/poems to the group, as had been intended. But they had the interest and the confidence to work on their own, and I was happy to alter the programme. I was also hopeful that I would once again obtain data similar to that which arose from our third session of the week.

Elizabeth began Thursday by reading, on Kristina's suggestion, 'First Ice'. She then turned to 'Days', but her responses showed no poem was evoked from the text. At lunch, I asked Kristina to read 'Days' at home that evening. A first glance at her initial responses (Figure 2.7) suggests that they conceal rather than reveal the imminent arrival of yet another creature 'coming about its own business'. It is the taped follow-up which allows us to attend a second event in time, and to understand her initial, questioning jottings. By eavesdropping on her taped account of her responses we can follow her progress through no fewer than six readings of the poem.

Something more near
Though deeper within darkness
Is entering the loneliness:

Elizabeth appears to have evoked 'Frogs in the Wood' quickly and easily. My sense of attending this 'event in time', therefore, derives less from detailed evidence of a creature slowly 'coming about its own business' than from what the organisation of her taped follow-up reveals about the purpose of her reading.

Kristina's evocation of 'Days', on the other hand, was the result of a persistent and painstaking reading, the very slowness of which enables us to glimpse the process of reading. She brings to the text, understandably, an understanding of 'days' and 'doctors' quite different from that of Larkin. The tape-recording allows us to overhear her attempts to resolve the tension, which is at once a source of difficulty and of delight. Figure 2.8 sets out the interaction between reader and text; it is during this transactional relationship, Rosenblatt argues, that a text can become a poem. It is not an object, but can be thought of as an event in time.

The window is starless still; the clock ticks,
The page is printed.

Kristina: 'Days'

Taped follow-up	Commentary
1 This is the first time I've ever read this poem, unlike 'First Ice' which I'd read several times before attempting the recording. 'Days' is a poem which is new to me on making this tape . . .	1–3 It is evidence from the first engagement with the text which is likely to be most revealing of the process of reading.
3 . . . Days . . . I think . . . it's an unusual way of seeing days he . . . it's almost a physical state isn't it he's . . . 'Days are where we live. They come, they wake us'. 'They are to be happy in:' . . .	3–6 Larkin demands 'a new effort of attention' to which Kristina responds, savouring his opening lines.
6 . . . he's, it's like a kind of little safe house, or a mother, or something like that, something you live in, something you're surrounded by, where else can we live . . .	6–8 Her first jotting, (IR1, in Figure 2.7) expresses what the first stanza has evoked in her. The importance of this response can be heard in her performance of the text during the reading. She acknowledges its imprecision: 'a kind of . . . house, or a mother, or something . . .'. She will hold on to this understanding until subsequent reading demands its revision and/or clarification.
8 . . . I mean, he's saying quite black and white, days are to be happy in, and the opposite, you can't be happy in . . . where can we live but there, that seems straightforward enough . . .	8–11 Kristina had signalled her uncertainty about IR2 by adding '??'. She will eventually conclude (lines 97/98, below) that 'it's quite a succinct little poem about mortality'. Here, her reference to 'the

11 . . . and then, the last verse brings up pictures of priests and doctors and all the experts trampling across, busy, rushing around, 'Brings the priest and the doctor/ In their long coats / *Running* over the fields', it's a rather sort of undignified image, they're sort of running around trying to catch something . . . it's like trying to catch a butterfly, they can't, they're running around clumsy . . . bustling, trying to get something which can't be had . . . 'In their long coats', that suggests they're tripping over their tails, in their desperation to try and find this, running over the fields. . .

First Reading: Lines 3–19

20 The first part is just making, just a straightforward statement, 'Where can we live but days?', there's no, there's nothing to contradict it, we're alive from day to day, what else is there to do . . .

opposite' is a surprisingly early indication of her awareness of what lies behind the lines. What she has apprehended she has still to comprehend.

11–19 She senses that there is a contrast between the two stanzas, and that there is, within the last stanza, something unsatisfactory about how we 'solve the question' of 'Days'. In her reading she stresses the word 'running'. Her 'pictures' of the movements of the priest and the doctor are set against the feeling of the first stanza, with its 'little safe house'; they are 'trampling', 'busy', 'rushing around', 'undignified', tripping over their tails, 'in desperation'. The futility of the arrival of these 'experts' is also, at this point in time, seen in physical terms: because 'they are trying to get something which can't be had', 'it's like trying to catch a butterfly'.

Subsequent readings of the text – and there is evidence of six readings, of which lines 3–19 are the first – will enable her to work from this first 'holding form', as she makes the poem, guided by the text.

20–22 This time there is no reference to home or family. She appears to be trying to clarify her first interpretation of the text.

22 . . . and the second half you get this image of professionals, supposed experts, running around and around, chasing their tails, uh, makes them seem rather silly, like a . . . he's saying how ironic it is, they're busying themselves with something which doesn't need solving . . .

27 What are days for?
Days are where we live.
They come, they wake us
Time and time over.
They are to be happy in:
Where can we live but days?

Ah, solving that question
Brings the priest and the doctor
In their long coats
Running over the fields.

37 'Running over the fields', it's like they've come a long way, running over the fields, it's maybe, um, they're running at you from a distance. . . from their distant knowledge almost. (15 secs)

Second Reading: Lines 20–39.

40 I'm just reading it through again . . . 'What are days for?/ Days are where we live'. . . that first stanza brings to mind very much a . . an image of a

22–26 Having pictured the arrival of the priest and the doctor on her first reading, she can now explain its significance within the text: 'he's saying how ironic it is, they're busying themselves with something that doesn't need solving'.

27–36 Lines 20–26 are like director's notes to guide her performance of the text. Listening to the words was also an important strategy for Elizabeth.

37–39 She ends this second reading by speculating on the significance of 'over the fields', a phrase to which she appears to have paid little attention before. Her understanding of the priest and doctor as 'experts' informs this speculation.

40–49 She returns to her initial association, but is more specific. Our feelings about days she compares to a child's feelings about its mother, whose presence child being cared for by a mother. 'They come, they wake us / Time and time over./They are to be happy in;' or happy with, 'Where can we live but days?', what is there but mother, that kind of thing, um, I don't know, that's the strongest association I get, a baby, a little child . . . and there's this constant, reassuring presence and the closest thing I can think to that is a mother, a loving family mother, um, . . what is there but days, where can we live but days . .

is described as 'constant and reassuring'. This is the first mention of constancy, and her thoughts suggest the demands the text is making upon her as reader to bring into a proper alignment her world and the world of the text/poem.

49 . . . and then these men who come and complicate it . . . the experts . . . when really they don't know . . . it's like a priest and a doctor interfering with family life, or days, or life, or anything like that, just come along and complicate it and confuse things, I think he's very anti, well, I don't know, he sees the futility of seeking answers where there doesn't have to be one, I mean, a priest, a priest is a person who's supposed to have a great faith and not question things and yet . . they're seeking . . . they're seeking a life beyond days and the doctor . . wants to know what happens when people are in a coma, when people die . . what goes through their minds, what physical processes do they go through . . . 'Where can we live but days?' (15 secs.)

50–59 A similar process is under way in the second stanza. Having thought of the priest and doctor in general terms as 'experts', she now defines her own use of the term. Her description of the priest is more convincing than that of the doctor; but neither description answers completely the demands of this text/poem. Yet her grasp is becoming more sure. On her first reading, she concentrated on the physical aspects of the experts' arrival; in the second, she commented on the irony of their actions; now, she can locate their actions within the context of the whole text/poem: 'he [Larkin] sees the futility of seeking answers'. A glancing reference to IR3, 'he's very anti', is not pursued.

Third Reading: Lines 40–59

57

59 . . . it's a question that needs a lot of thinking about . . . I'm still trying to work out the point of the poem . . . I think he's quite . . . he's quite . . . he can see how good it is to be content with what there is and to accept that that's all there is, but then again, that's quite a child-like attitude to life, like with mummy; mummy will be there, mummy will come and wake us up, and look after us every night and every day . . .

59–66 A poem is beginning to emerge from the text, as Kristina continues to align her world and that of the text/poem. From the general notion of a home, to the reassuring presence of a mother; she now sees that our attitude to days is child-like, in that we 'accept that that's all there is'. Mummy, like days, will 'come and wake us up'; like children, we assume that days will look after us, as mummy does. IR4 now makes sense: 'childlike attitude, no questioning, simplistic.' We have been fortunate to understand how she arrived at that response.

66 . . .um, but the ones with the training, the priest and the doctor, they're, um . . . they want to know why, like he, Philip Larkin, he doesn't say whether that's a good thing, or a bad thing, but the image of these people running around is rather undignified and I think that he can see that it is futile, and yet people are going to ask these sort of questions anyway, and the more intelligent or well-trained or questioning they are, the more they're going to fuss around trying to find the answers (15 secs) . . .

66–73 When she first read the second stanza, she pictured the undignified movements of the priest and the doctor. The irony of what they were doing then suggested the futility of seeking answers to impossible questions. She thought about the fact that they were experts. Now, she makes the connection that had been eluding her: the futility is emphasised by the fact that it is 'intelligent' people who are behaving in this 'undignified' way. 'And yet people are going to ask these sort of questions anyway, as inevitably as day follows day. Again, IR3 is glanced at, in the reference to Philip Larkin.

Fourth Reading: Lines 59–73

73   Apart from her performance of the text (lines 26–36 above), this is the third occasion on which the length of silence suggests that Kristina is re-reading the whole text.

74–77   She moves beyond IR4, for days, unlike mothers, don't 'need to assert (themselves) as a presence'. She does, however, hold on to the notion of constancy which emerged on the third reading.

77–79   On her fourth reading she realised that the sense of futility was heightened by the fact that the priest and the doctor were trying to 'solve the question'. She is now free to think of them as 'mortals' rather than as 'experts' . . .

79–81   . . . and to imagine what they must be feeling. From observing their movements, she has moved to an understanding of how they would feel within the world of the text/poem.

81–87   Suddenly, the significance of the word 'brings' becomes clear.

73   (15 secs) What are . . .

74   days for (5 secs) they're a constant, they're elusive at the same time, they just come, they just happen, they're just there, it doesn't explain itself, it doesn't need to assert itself, as a presnece, it's just . . . a thing which is there . . .

77   . . . and these mortals, these priests and doctors who probably by the fact that they are mortal want to know what there is beyond days for the human life . . .

79   . . . I should think they're quite depressed about it, they feel quite concerned about what happens beyond days, in their long coats, running over the fields . . .

81   . . . I wonder why solving that question *brings* the priest and the doctor . . . perhaps its on a death-bed, or something like that, they come trekking over the fields to say their last rites, and to give medical aid where they can. Once somebody's lived out their length of days, the priest comes along to give them the last rites, and the doctor tries to sort of prolong the days artificially.

87 It's rather silly, in this context it seems rather silly anyway . . .

88 . . . of course, people want to live as long as they can, but I think Philip Larkin here is submitting that there is a fate, and that we have a time to live, and when that time is up we should accept it, perhaps, perhaps that's what he's saying . . .

91 but I think, he doesn't have a point to this poem, he's stating something, he's not saying, well, people shouldn't try and save people's lives, or people shouldn't give last rites, or anything like that . . .

94 . . . he's well he's just pointing out our mortality, we live in our days, and then they're gone . . .

95 . . . it's quite a powerful poem . . .

96 . . . it's nice that they chose it . . it's very simple language, but it is quite a succinct little poem about . . . mortality (20 secs)

Fifth Reading: 73–98

98 . . . I mean, he doesn't give any hint of people being depressed, 'Days are where we live./They come, they wake us/Time and time over./They are to

87–88 This 'context' is the poem which is emerging from the text.

88–91 As the poem emerges, so the meaning becomes clear.

91–94 IR3 is addressed directly: 'point', of course, is point of view.

94–95 An event in time . . .

95 . . . which Kristina has experienced.

96–98 She thinks of others with a similar experience to share.

98–108 With a firm grasp of the whole poem, Kristina returns to the opening stanza, and realises how the fact that it 'doesn't give any hint' of what is to follow days makes the final effect of the poem so 'powerful': 'it's just like one long childhood of happiness and then when it's over people . . . want to prolong it.'

be happy in:' so, of course, while we have our life, we are happy, and then it's gone, and that's it, that's the implication of the first verse . . . 'Where can we live but days?' where can we live . . . it's odd that he puts it in this very strong physical sense, but it's good, it works . . . it gives no hint of people wanting to end their days prematurely, people wishing that certain days did not exist because they were unhappy in those times, it's just like one long childhood of happiness, um . . . and then, when it's over people get all fussed and then want to prolong it . . . anyway, I like it.

Sixth Reading: 98–108

Stanza 1	Stanza 2
First It's an unusual way of seeing days . . . it's like a kind of little safe house or a mother, or something like that . . .	*Running*, it's a rather sort of undignified image, they're sort of running around trying to catch something . . . it's like trying to catch a butterfly
Second . . . the first verse is just asking, just a straightforward statement, where can we live but days . . .	supposed experts . . . he's saying how ironic it is, they're busying themselves with something which doesn't need solving . . . they're running at you from their distant knowledge almost
Third that first stanza brings to mind very much an image of a child being cared for by its mother . . . there's a constant reassuring presence	the experts come along and complicate it and confuse it . . he sees the futility of seeking answers where there doesn't have to be one . . . yet they're seeking a life beyond days
Fourth . . . I think he can see how good it is to be content with what there is, to accept that that's all there is, but that is quite a child-like attitude to life . . .	yet people are going to ask these sort of questions anyway, and the more intelligent and well-trained they are, the more they are trying to find the answers
Fifth . . . days are a constant, they're elusive at the same time, they just come, they just happen, they're just there . . .	these mortals, I should think they feel quite concerned about what happens beyond days . . . why does solving that *bring* the doctor . . . he's just pointing out our mortality . . . it's quite a powerful poem . . .

Sixth while we have our life, we are happy, and then it's gone, and that's it . . . where can we live but days? . . . it's odd that he puts it in this very strong physical sense, but it's good, it works . . . it's just like one long childhood of happiness, and then, when it's over, people get all fussed and then want to prolong it. . . anyway, I like it . . .

Figure 2.8   Kristina's reading of 'Days' as a self-ordering and self-correcting process

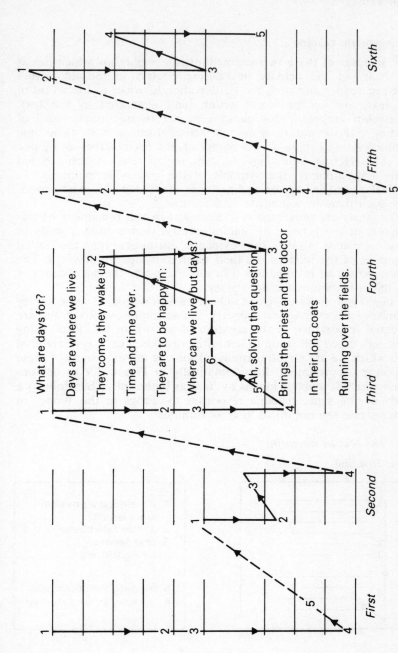

Figure 2.9 Kristina's taped responses to 'Days' by Philip Larkin

What are days for?

Days are where we live.

They come, they wake us

Time and time over.

They are to be happy in:

Where can we live but days?

Ah, solving that question

Brings the priest and the doctor

In their long coats

Running over the fields.

C Aesthetic reading

The analyses of these two events illustrate a paradox which lies at the heart of the activity of reading poetry: in the interaction between reader and text, the reader attends twice, to the world of the text, and to the world within him, generated by the text. Rosenblatt embraces this paradox in her transactional model of reading with the notion of the text acting at one and the same time as blueprint and stimulus. As blueprint, the text: 'serves as a guide for the selecting, rejecting and ordering of what is being called forth.' As stimulus, the symbols of the text will: 'point to . . . particular associations or feeling-tones created by his past experience with them in actual life or literature.'[4]

The analyses, presented and discussed in the remainder of this chapter, of the activity of reading poetry, derive from a study of those accounts where the evidence includes both the initial responses of the readers and their written or taped follow-ups. The latter proved an invaluable aid in understanding the significance of the initial responses for the readers.

I begin with two examples to illustrate how words release contrary impulses whenever we read poetry. These impulses coexist and are of equal importance in the creation of a work of art. First, using Kristina's taped follow-up to her initial responses to 'Days', material with which we are already familiar, I look at the *movement* of these responses, represented diagrammatically in Figure 2.9 to demonstrate what Rosenblatt means by 'text as blueprint'. Then follows a study of the same reader's responses to 'Frogs in the Wood' to demonstrate the notion of 'text as stimulus'.

(i) The text as blueprint

First Reading

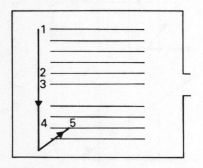

1 it's almost a physical
  state isn't it?
2 a little safe house
3 that seems
  straightforward

5 tripping over their tails
4 running around clumsy

Figure 2.10

Her first response, (1), is to Larkin's unusual assertion that 'Days are where we live'. It will not be until the third reading that she begins to appreciate the significance of this line within the whole poem. At this stage, her response informs her interpretation, (2), of part of the first stanza. Next, (3), she asserts that the question, 'where can we live but days?' is 'straightforward', yet her reworking of this line is, in fact, one of the keys to her successful evocation of the poem. She closes, (4) and (5), by commenting on the physical details of the priest and doctor. She will, on third reading, attribute less significance to these details, and, on her fifth reading, refocus her attention completely to the force of the word 'brings'.

Second Reading

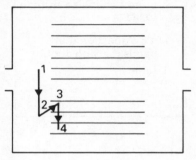

1 just a straightforward statement

3 reads stanza aloud
2 supposed experts

4 running at you

Figure 2.11

That she now re-enters the text at the end of the first stanza, (1), suggests that she is less convinced than she insists that Larkin's question is 'straightforward'. She attends more closely, (2) and (4), to the opening of the second stanza, after (3) reading it aloud.

Third Reading

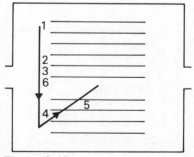

1 reads stanza aloud

2 constant reassuring presence
3 reads line aloud
6 reads line aloud

5 futility
4 the experts

Figure 2.12

John Teasey

The text, however, demands that she returns to the first stanza, which she reads aloud, (1). She alters her initial response to 'Days are where we live', (2), and reads aloud (3) the 'straightforward' line. She repeats this activity, (6), to close the reading, having first confirmed the significance of the opening of the second stanza, (4) and (5).

Fourth Reading

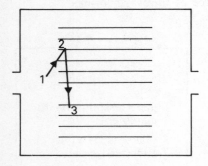

2 quite a child-like attitude to life

1 it's a question that needs thinking about

3 futile

Figure 2.13

She returns yet again, (1), to the question which demands 'it needs thinking about', before confirming her understanding of the first stanza (2) and the opening of the second stanza, (3).

Fifth Reading

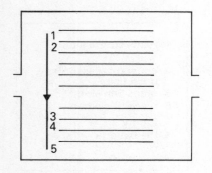

1 reads stanza aloud
2 they're constant, they're elusive

3 these mortals
4 why 'brings'?

5 a succinct little poem about mortality

Figure 2.14

Unexpectedly, it is during her fifth reading that the poem emerges; unexpectedly, because there is no evidence of her having 'talked out' the difficulty she has acknowledged herself at the end of the first stanza. She begins, (1), by reading the stanza aloud, modifies, (2) and (3), her understanding of 'Days are where we live' and the significance of the priests and doctors, and, (4), for the first time, focuses on the word 'brings'. She closes her penultimate reading by making clear that the journey from apprehension to comprehension is complete, (5).

Final Reading

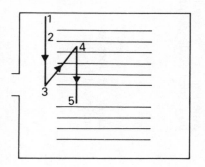

1 he doesn't give any hint
   of people being depressed
2 reads the stanza aloud
4 one long childhood of
   happiness

3 it's odd, but it's good, it
   works
5 people get all fussed
   and then want to
   prolong it

Figure 2.15

She closes her readings by, (1), hinting at how her view of days differs from that of Larkin. Then, (2), she reads the first stanza aloud, and dwells on the three lines, (3), (4) and (5), which had been held most frequently in the forefront of her attention.

(ii)   The text as stimulus

Of ten responses (see Figures 2.16 and 2.17), only two (3) and (5), relate directly to the text. Kristina notes and, presumably, interprets to her satisfaction two phrases which cause the other readers difficulty: 'improbable flames' and 'invented grief'.

The remaining eight responses are 'memories of self' generated by the text as stimulus – in particular, by the opening and closing stanzas. Her taped follow-up (Kris. TF1–34) helps us to understand their significance.

Kristina: 'Frogs in the Wood'

Taped follow-up	Commentary

Taped follow-up

1 On first reading, I did not associate the poem with my own experience. I thought a lost or a frightened child or animal.

4 As I understood the poem better,

5 I recalled incidents in the past, particularly on reading:

> You are the loudest thing
> Your heart making a deafening noise

That brought to mind hearing my own heartbeats around my head and ears, it did not strike me that the heart was deafening to anyone else, but that it was deafening to myself.

13 I did not picture the poem as looking at myself; no figure was present. Instead I saw the scene through my own eyes.

I saw the stream as below my standpoint. I was standing some way above the scene and frogs and herons and a stream. They are distant and do not realise that I am there.

Commentary

1–3 She does not gloss 'e.g. fairground' (IR1), a setting irrelevant to the text, but perhaps of relevance to the reader?

4 We must assume that by now Kristina has read through the text. The dotted line in Figure 2.17 indicates that the reader is about to re-enter the text, which she does at IR3 – perhaps where she had experienced difficulty initially.

5–12 IR4 makes it clear that she is thinking of childhood. One of her 'vivid memories' is of the experience of hearing her own heartbeats. There is no textual evidence that the speaker is a child.

13–19 It does seem that she has entered a world provoked by the text . . .

20 As the poem turns toward the stream, the concentration on the self subsides;

22 however, in the fourth and fifth stanzas, my mind recalled more recent incidents in which grief/disappointment were shrugged off.

25 The first half brought to mind childhood, isolation (e.g. being locked in my bedroom and screaming).

28 The second half reminded me of times when I had the capacity to discard sorrow which means the recent past as a young adult. As a child, love is craved and is important and when that source is gone, it is calamitous, but as an adult, you are more self-contained, and do not demand so much.

20 . . . if only momentarily.

22–24 The closing stanza evokes 'more recent' memories (IR7) . . .

25–27 . . . whereas the opening stanzas evoke childhood memories. Her first response had been to think of any lost and frightened child; here is a very particular memory (IR9).
More childhood memories return, (IR10), as she closes her reading.
28–33 She evaluates her own more recent memories, as she reflects on why what is 'calamitous' to a child is less so to an adult.

Her grasp of the text, at this stage in the reading, relies heavily on the personal experience described from line 25 to the end.

Figure 2.16   Kristina's initial responses to 'Frogs in the Wood'

(iii)   Diagrammatic studies of the process of responding

Representing the way in which the reader moves in and around a text diagrammatically draws our attention to a number of important features.

In 'Days', only once does Kristina read sequentially. This is on her fifth reading, as the poem is emerging. In her earlier readings, she moves backwards and forwards through the text. Even her first reading is selective: it serves to provide a 'holding form', from which she can proceed in her evocation of the poem. The pattern of her subsequent readings is wave-like. The larger movements of the first,

Kristina 'Frogs in the Wood' *Kris. IR1–10*

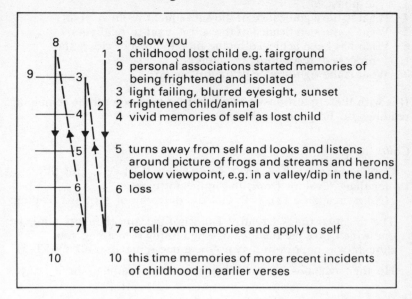

8   8 below you
1   1 childhood lost child e.g. fairground
9   9 personal associations started memories of
      being frightened and isolated
3   3 light failing, blurred eyesight, sunset
2   2 frightened child/animal
4   4 vivid memories of self as lost child

5   5 turns away from self and looks and listens
      around picture of frogs and streams and herons
      below viewpoint, e.g. in a valley/dip in the land.
6   6 loss

7   7 recall own memories and apply to self

10 10 this time memories of more recent incidents
      of childhood in earlier verses

Figure 2.17   The movement of Kristina's responses to 'Frogs in the Wood'

third and fifth readings are interrupted by the gentle swell of the second and fourth readings, where she attends to a small segment of the text only. And it is on these two readings only that she re-enters the text on her 'straightforward' question, 'Where can we live but days?'. This line is read aloud on a number of occasions. The need for its reinterpretation is signalled, but the explanation, so central to her evocation of the poem, is never articulated. Indeed, each revision of her understanding of the text follows not upon an explanation or a discussion of the difficulty, but upon a reading aloud of the text – and not necessarily a reading aloud of that part of the text which contains the difficulty that is subsequently resolved.

These observations, which confirm the tentative conclusions drawn during the pilot study, suggest that the following questions would provide a useful framework for analysis.

1   What is the significance of the first response?
2   What is the significance of the first unbroken series of responses?

3   What has been achieved by this initial response and/or series of responses?
4   What is the significance of the subsequent re-entry point?
5   What is the significance of the subsequent re-reading(s)?
6   What has been achieved by the time the reader closes the process of responding privately?
7   What is the significance of the follow-up?

It is with these questions in mind that we turn now to the remaining readings of 'Frogs in the Wood'.

Colin

Colin's written follow-up, below (Colin WF1–35), also fills out, rather than develops from, the initial jottings.

His first response (1), is in fact the outcome of his third reading:

> The first two times I read it I did not get any thoughts until the end which gave me the idea of when losing something you thought was important may not be a bad thing after all. (WF1–5)

He then explains how, during his fourth reading, three images

Colin   'Frogs in the Wood'   *IR1–8*

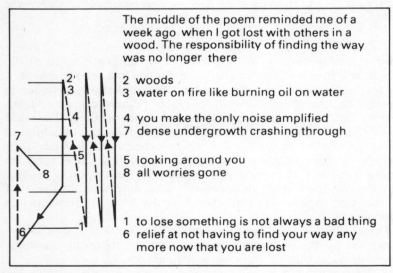

The middle of the poem reminded me of a week ago when I got lost with others in a wood. The responsibility of finding the way was no longer there

2 woods
3 water on fire like burning oil on water

4 you make the only noise amplified
7 dense undergrowth crashing through

5 looking around you
8 all worries gone

1 to lose something is not always a bad thing
6 relief at not having to find your way any more now that you are lost

Figure 2.18 The movement of Colin's responses to 'Frogs in the Wood'

Colin Bathe
Frogs in the Wood

The first two times I read it I did not
get any thoughts until the end which gave
me the idea of when losing something you
thought was important may not be a bad
thing after all. The third reading of the   5
first verse gave me the idea of woods
with a small pond in the centre with
small flames licking the serface. The
second verse gave me a very clear black
and white picture of me crashing though   10
a / forest bent double. This being the
coniferous
only noise that could be heard. When you
stopped there was deadly silence which
you didn't want to disturb by starting
moving again. The third verse gave me   15
a clear colour picture of a shallow part
of a medium size pond. Frogs croaking
away in the water lilies, birds singing
in the small oak trees. The forth verse
was still giving me troubles so I skipped   20
it and went onto the last verse which
gave me no picture just a great sence
of relief. I then added a few more
details to the pictures I felt on the other
verses which are included. Then went   25
back to the forth verse. This gave me
no picture again just a sence of
relaxation with all of your worries gone.
        The second verse of the poem
reminded me of a time when I got lost   30
in a wood at night when I was checking
another persons map reading. I was in a
sence releaved that I did not have to
concentrate again until we found a place
that we could find on the map.   35

occurred, in response to the first three stanzas, and to which (2)–(5) refer.

> woods with a small pond in the centre with small flames licking the serface. (WF6–8)

> gave me a very clear black and white picture of me crashing through a coniferous forest bent double . . . (WF9–11)

> a clear colour picture of the shallow part of a medium sized pond. Frogs croaking away on the water lilies, birds singing in the small oak trees. (WF16–19)

This reading ends when 'the forth verse was still giving me troubles so I skipped it and went onto the last verse. Which gave me no picture just a great sence of relief.' (WF19–23)

On his final reading he returns to the middle stanza (7), and rereads the fourth stanza which 'gave me no picture again, just a sence of relaxation with all of your worries gone.' (WF26–28)

Sara

Sara's first response suggests that she is summarising the little that the text has yielded on her first reading, that (1), 'something has changed that he can't describe'. This minimal understanding is confirmed by the next three responses; all that she does know is that

Sara *'Frogs in the Wood'* *IR1–9*

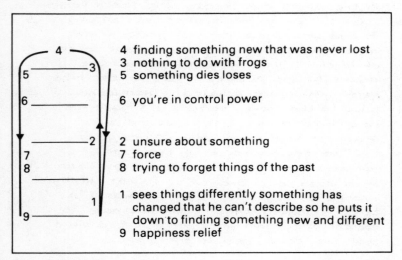

4 finding something new that was never lost
3 nothing to do with frogs
5 something dies loses

6 you're in control power

2 unsure about something
7 force
8 trying to forget things of the past

1 sees things differently something has changed that he can't describe so he puts it down to finding something new and different
9 happiness relief

Figure 2.19 The movement of Sara's responses to 'Frogs in the Wood'

Frogs in the Wood   Sara W. F. 1-29

1. The title doesn't make much sense
2. Reading through the poem no image appears, only a blank black space.
3. The last verse is the strongest, it sums up the poem and gives it its meaning.   (5)
4. The 3rd verse is unsure and unstable it is about something confused
5. At this point I decided the poem had nothing to do with frogs or woods. This was almost immediately clear   (10)
6. Frogs in the wood finding something out, atthough never lost, wasn't there.
7. There is something about the first part of the poem something fades away and dies. Its sad but nothing to do with the death of a person   (15)
8. Towards the middle I noticed a sense of force beginning to show gaining strength.
9. Happiness at the end mixed with relief
10. The feelings of the poem begin to show, no detail and a picture or image is hard to find as feelings do not create a picture. (20)
11. The poem has a strong message and feeling about it
12. Personally it made me think of death, this is really a   (25) morbid thought but the last verse about being lost creates a feeling of death, losing yourself, your feelings and thoughts also reminds me of the poem. Your not really lost but you think and feel it

the text has (3), 'nothing to do with frogs'. But, though she has, in Richards' term, construed very little, she has responded to the emotional development within the text. In the first stanza, (5), she feels 'something dies loses' and by the final stanza, (9), she notes 'happiness relief'.

Whereas Kristina and Elizabeth, in their taped follow-ups, were able to build on their initial responses, Sara's written follow-up, above (Sara WF1–29) serves largely as a gloss on her original jottings. It does nevertheless make clear that however little she might be able to explain, the text has had a significant effect on her.

> The last verse is the strongest, it sums up the poem and gives it its meaning. (WF4–5)

> There's something about the first part of the poem something fades away and dies. It's sad but nothing to do with the death of a person. (WF13–15)

> Towards the middle I noticed a sense of force beginning to show, gaining strength. (WF16–17)

> The poem has a strong message and feeling about it. (WF23–24)

> Personally it made me think of death, this is a really morbid thought but the last verse about being lost creates the feeling of death . . . (WF25–27)

Sasha

Sasha's first response takes the form of a surreal image of 'a heart beating loudly . . . with a red glow being given off'. Her subsequent responses to the text are equally surprising. Her second response she says 'happened so suddenly, this black and white idea just appeared in my head where it was really quite scary, like a horror movie' (Sasha TF9–11), and she pictures the herons and frogs, (3) and (4), as the government and the striking miners: 'the herons were the leaders and yet maybe the frogs had control over them.' (TF14/15)

Unlike Colin and Sara, Sasha had not sustained her initial reading through to the final stanza. 'I started by reading the first couple of verses but it didn't really make much sense, and then I read it over again and started to work out the second verse.' (TF1–3) This may account for the speculative tone of (5): 'maybe finding out something that before you never knew'. Patten uses 'lost' in two senses in the final stanza; Sasha introduces a second sense of 'found', as she writes: 'You've found out something about yourself.' (TF19)

She returns to the opening stanza and describes two more

Sasha 'Frogs in the Wood' *Sasha IR1–9*

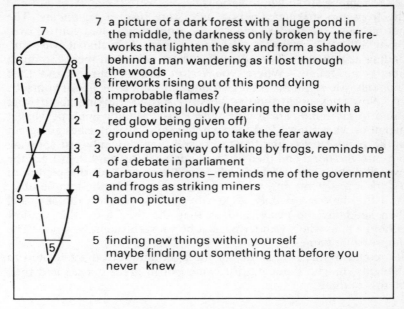

7 a picture of a dark forest with a huge pond in the middle, the darkness only broken by the fireworks that lighten the sky and form a shadow behind a man wandering as if lost through the woods
6 fireworks rising out of this pond dying
8 improbable flames?
1 heart beating loudly (hearing the noise with a red glow being given off)
2 ground opening up to take the fear away
3 overdramatic way of talking by frogs, reminds me of a debate in parliament
4 barbarous herons – reminds me of the government and frogs as striking miners
9 had no picture

5 finding new things within yourself maybe finding out something that before you never knew

Figure 2.20 The movement of Sasha's responses to 'Frogs in the Wood'

disturbing images, the second of which, (7), is 'an overall picture for the whole of the poem'. (TF24) The only additional comment made in her follow-up refers to (8): 'Maybe it's related to thoughts, maybe thoughts just come out in great masses and then there's nothing.' (TF30–32)

Taped follow-up   *Sasha TF1–32*
Sasha 'Frogs in the Wood'

1 I started by reading the first couple of verses but it didn't really make much sense, and then I read it over again and started to work out the second verse. I had this idea where it says, 'Your heart making a deafening noise', it was like a heart beat beating really loudly and it was deafening everything and sort of going through him, and there was this red glow as the heart pumped. Then in verse three, 'And how strange when your fear of being lost has subsided', the ground opening and taking all the fear away and when it suddenly comes up and it's gone. It happened so suddenly,
10 this black and white idea just appeared in my head where it was

really quite scary, like a horror movie. And then, 'Their arguments in the streams,/Condemning the barbarous herons,' it reminded me of the miners' strike where various herons were the government and the frogs the striking miners. There were just all arguments. The herons were the leaders and yet the frogs maybe had control over them. Five, it's probably analysing it more now that it was, um, finding new things within yourself, 'where being lost seems/So much like being found.' Where you're lost inside yourself and then suddenly you're found. You've found out something about yourself. 20 Now back up to the first verse, I started thinking about what came to my mind. For a long time I just couldn't think of what it meant or what I saw. And then when it says, 'Bright ashes going out in the ponds' it was like fireworks, and then suddenly just spraying out into the pond and then suddenly dying away, and then I got the overall picture where for the whole of the poem I got this picture of a dark forest with, um, a sort of an eerie pond in the middle of it. And the darkness is only broken by the fireworks in the sky, and then suddenly die away, and as they die they form this shadow behind a man who's wandering as if he's lost through the wood. The 'improbable flames' 30 could be the irregularity of the light and maybe it's related to thoughts, maybe thoughts just come out in great masses and then there's nothing.

Elizabeth

As we noted earlier, Elizabeth's taped follow-up (TF1–94) guides us through the event.

> after that first line I thought that the rest of the lines would be
> sort of funny so I went through the first verse line by line.
> (TF10–13)

IR3 is revealed as a clear image in response to the last line of the opening stanza. She then reads through more quickly, not pausing over 'difficulties' such as 'improbable flames' and 'invented grief'. By the end of the first reading, it is clear from IR9–12 that she has experienced the movement and emotional life of the text/poem. A lengthy note describes a personal association generated by the text.

She returns to the text, IR13–15, to clarify her interpretation of the opening and closing stanzas.

The follow-up then confirms her experience of the poem she has evoked: 'it leaves me feeling happy' (TF91). After evaluating how her personal experience corresponds to that which lies behind Patten's words, she ends the taped follow-up:

Elizabeth 'Frogs in the Wood' *IR1–15*

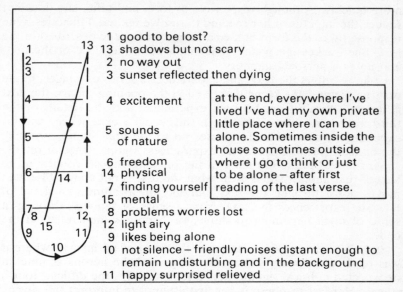

1 good to be lost?
13 shadows but not scary
2 no way out
3 sunset reflected then dying

4 excitement

5 sounds
  of nature

6 freedom
14 physical
7 finding yourself
15 mental
8 problems worries lost
12 light airy
9 likes being alone
10 not silence – friendly noises distant enough to
    remain undisturbing and in the background
11 happy surprised relieved

> at the end, everywhere I've lived I've had my own private little place where I can be alone. Sometimes inside the house sometimes outside where I go to think or just to be alone – after first reading of the last verse.

Figure 2.21   The movement of Elizabeth's responses to 'Frogs in the Wood'

I would like now not to say any more about it but to find the others and find out what they think about it. (TF92–94)

1 What is the significance of the first response?

Elizabeth is the only reader to respond directly to a textual detail, her curiosity aroused by the tone of Patten's unusual assertion in the opening line. Kristina's immediate response is also to the opening stanza, but it is a generalized association, rather than an evaluation of any particular feature. Colin and Sara, however, respond only after reading through the whole text. Colin's response is an attempt to interpret the closing stanzas, whereas Sara, albeit imprecisely, describes what she has experienced of the development within the text. Her response is, at least in part, to the form in which Patten has cast his words: 'the last verse is the strongest, it sums up the poem and gives it its meaning.' The text proves more intractable to Sasha than to the others. After reading the first few stanzas, and returning to the opening, her first response is to the line, 'Your heart making a deafening noise', which she hears and pictures vividly, even frighteningly.

2   What is the significance of the first unbroken series of responses?
Elizabeth continues to close-read the first stanza, but then reads
more quickly. Although responsive to form and tone, she does not
reduce the impetus of her reading to resolve textual difficulties. One
response takes the form of a clear image of a scene described in the
text. She evokes the poem, reflects on her experience of the text,
and notes a personal memory.

Colin re-enters the text, and experiences a series of images; in the
first, he pictures the scene described in the opening stanza; the next
is drawn entirely from his own experience; and the details of the
third image are drawn from both the reader's experience, and his
experience of the text. He presses on to the final stanza, omitting
the difficult fourth stanza, and experiences 'a great sense of relief'.

Sara moves hesitantly back to the opening stanza, confirming to
herself that at least she is clear what the text is not about. She then
moves down through the text, building an awareness in detail of
how she experiences the text: from a sense of sadness, through 'a
sense of force beginning to show', to 'happiness and relief' at the
end.

Sasha's next response also takes the form of an image, 'where it
was really quite scary'. Then, the frogs and the herons assume an
unexpected political significance. She, too, skips the difficult fourth
stanza. Her last response is her first attempt to interpret the closing
stanza – an interpretation which owes at least as much to her own
experience, as to the demands of the text.

*3   What has been achieved by the initial response, and/or series of
responses?*
While the readers have all arrived at the different points on their
journeys, four of them make clear their first destination: a first
apprehension of their felt experience of the whole text. If the
resolution of textual difficulties has not been considered essential to
the achievement of this initial apprehension, then it has been
deliberately postponed.

Sara and Elizabeth have incorporated their initial responses into
their first series of responses. By the final stanza, Elizabeth has
evoked the poems, and she has noted a personal experience
corresponding closely to the experience embodied in the text. Sara
has a firm grasp of the varying effects upon her of the text, while
acknowledging a very vague understanding of 'the plain sense' of
the text. This closes her reading.

The first engagements of Colin and Sasha with the text are much
less coherent. In arriving at a 'sence of relief', Colin has
experienced a series of images, for whose composition he draws
upon both his own experience and the demands of the text. Sasha's

images appear to owe more to reader than to text, but she attempts, on her final response, an interpretation of the significance of the ending of the poem.

Kristina has noted only the feelings of fear and isolation contained in the opening stanza. It is when she re-enters the text that she secures her initial grasp of the whole text.

4   What is the significance of the subsequent re-entry point?

Three of the readers return to the opening stanza, for different purposes, and to different effect.

Elizabeth, whose curiosity had been aroused initially by the opening line, reinterprets her second response, and answers her first question, 'good to be lost?' Kristina notes an explication of the line 'Bright ashes going out in the pond'. In response to the same line, Sasha says:

> For a long time I just couldn't think of what it meant or what I saw. And then . . . it was like fireworks . . . just spraying out into the pond and then suddenly dying away . . . (TF21–24)

Colin literally re-enters the middle section of the text, to resume his 'crashing through the undergrowth'.

5   What is the significance of the subsequent re-reading(s)?

Elizabeth now needs merely to realise the connection between the two closing stanzas to close her reading.

Kristina moves down through the text. The opening and closing stanzas generate memories from childhood and her more recent past, when her feelings, in her opinion, correspond to those described in the text. In response to the middle section, she pictures herself, briefly, within the text, a phenomenon to which she returns on her re-entry to the text for the final time. It is with more particular memories of childhood that she closes her reading.

Colin returns to the fourth stanza, which yields little meaning but gives him 'a sence of relaxation with all of your worries gone' as he closes his reading.

Sasha also closes at the fourth stanza, after seeing 'an overall picture for the whole of the poem' which extends the image which occurred on her re-entry to the text: 'as (the fireworks) die, they form this shadow behind a man who's wandering as if he's lost through the wood'. (TF28–29)

6   What has been achieved by the time the reader closes the process of responding privately?

Elizabeth's responses provide the most complete account of the activity of reading to emerge during the week.

Sara, as we have already noted, closed her reading at a very early stage. The other three readings are also incomplete. At this stage they are all more aware of 'what's inside' them than they are of 'what's inside the text'. Kristina has projected on to the text memories not yet incorporated into her reading as the text demands. Colin has experienced a series of images which oscillate on a continuum between reader and text. Sasha has had a frightening experience, curiously at odds with the speculation that at the heart of the text lies the notion of self-discovery.

This is the mental and emotional baggage they will carry into the discussion. There are a few more items to be added.

7 What is the significance of the follow-up?

To 'what's inside the poem' and 'what's inside us when we're reading the poem' Elizabeth adds her thoughts on 'what's inside the poet when he's writing the poem'. She sets her understanding of her world against that of the implied author – her final destination. It is one she wishes to share:

> This poem leaves me feeling happy. I don't know what the others will have made of it, but I think I would like now not to say anymore about it but to find the others and find out what they think about it, before I can sort of really close it. (TF91–94)

The others have not evoked the poem, but the text generated a world within them. It is to that they turn. Colin recalls in detail the recent experience which had come to mind during the reading, and had intruded into the text. Sara confides, reluctantly, that 'Personally, it makes me think of death', and Kristina reflects on how children and adults react differently to the loss of love.

The inclusion of Kristina's reading of 'Days' as one of two reading events recorded during the week, and the analysis of the responses which occured during the evocation, demonstrate its singular quality: it is a unique glimpse into the complex process of editing and re-editing which a competent reader may undertake when reading poetry. And yet, it resembles the other readings in a number of important respects.

As with Elizabeth, her curiosity is first aroused by the unusual expression of a striking idea in the opening stanza. She then moves quickly through to the end of the text, to complete her initial apprehension. The first stanza seems 'straightforward'; she pictures the closing lines of the second stanza. She is content at this stage not to make connections between the two stanzas.

Her subsequent re-entries alternate between the question she says she understands and the opening lines of the text, when she reads part or all of the text aloud. Her re-readings exemplify the self-ordering, self-correcting process that occurs in the transactional relationship between reader and text.

When the poem emerges, she notes the effect of the event: 'it's quite a powerful poem, it's very simple language, but it's quite a succinct little poem about mortality' (TF95–97)

As does Elizabeth, she closes her reading by reflecting on the two worlds of the reader and the text.

D   Responding to real readers

(i)   'You can't have a poem explained to you, can you?'

Later in the week, I asked the readers whether jotting around the text was making their reading harder:

Sasha 15: No, I find it easier . . . maybe it's because before I was thinking about it in an order and now I just write down anything and piece it together afterwards.
Elizabeth 16: I find it harder because I'm thinking more and it – it's not actually physically harder to do but it's harder, once you've finished you feel like you've accomplished more than I did before.
J.T. 17: Is it more or less helpful?
E. 18: More, more.
J.T. 19: Why?
S. 20: 'Cos before I never had a clue what the poem was about at the end.
J.T. 21: Can you explain that a bit more?
S. 20: In the lessons sometimes we've gone through a poem but I still wouldn't know what it really meant to me by the end of the lesson.
J.T. 23: Even if it had been explained to you during the lesson?
E. 24: You can't have a poem explained to you, can you? You can't really say, 'even if it had been explained to you' because there isn't a wrong or a right answer . . . You can explain what the words and metaphors mean but you can't explain a poem.

The correspondence between the readers' observations and Rosenblatt's model went further, in the direction signposted by Elizabeth in her final utterance. Having chosen the Patten text for our first group session, Holub's 'History Lesson' was chosen for the second session. Once again, the readers had enthusiastically chosen for themselves a complex text. After a group session, which I had found taxing, I asked the readers whether it might not have been better if I had simply explained the text to them – what would the response have been then?

Colin 171: No one would bother.

J.T. 172: Because?

Sasha 173: There's lots of different versions and you're just being given one and you're not being given time to think it out for yourself to come to your own version.

J.T. 174 Do you think you can actually be told, be taught what a poem means?

C. 175 No, each person would think something different about the poem and each poem would be different.

J.T. 176 So you wouldn't want to be taught?

C. 177: No, I wouldn't want to be taught because each poem will be different.

(ii) 'This poem . . . wants me to find out . . . the secret that he holds'

On Friday, the readers were asked to compile, from the week's reading, a group anthology, and to explain the reasons for their choices in the form of, 'I like this poem because . . .'. Their reasons fell into four categories: predictably, because the texts dealt with familiar themes, or were well-written; less predictably, I felt, because the texts addressed disturbing areas of human experience, or because the texts were puzzling. In fact, all of the texts offered for group discussion fell into this last category. Had I listened more carefully to the conversation after reading 'History Lesson', I would not have been so surprised by the inclusion of 'puzzling texts'.

J.T. 156: This was a poem you all agreed on as wanting in your anthology. Why did you all decide on this out of 20/25 poems as it's obviously a poem to begin with you hadn't understood?

Colin 157: The puzzle of it.

J.T. 158: Explain that.

C. 159: You don't understand it, you want to find out what it means, you can see there's something there worth finding out.

J.T. 160: What was the something that was there that hooked you, that made you want to push it further?

C. 161: The boy's question.

J.T. 162: Did anyone else have a different reason for doing it?

Elizabeth 163: No, I think it was the last line.

J.T. 164: The last line, Sara?

Sara 165: I hadn't read this one before.

J.T. 166: Before today. What about you, Sasha? You were the one who . . .

Sasha 167: Because I didn't understand it.

Perhaps it would be more accurate to say three categories, for being 'puzzling' is an element of being 'well-written'. The delight experienced by these readers in the puzzling quality of language is a measure of their awareness of the way words work. Colin's reason for choosing 'Tom Bone' makes the point, memorably:

> I like this poem because it wants me to find out the kind of house he lives in and the secret that he holds.

(iii)   *'At first I thought the poem had something to do with frogs'*

The risks and the rewards of working with the reader-response model are well illustrated by the final, two extracts.

If, as happened with Sasha – and often happens with many young readers – the reader is overwhelmed by the transactional relationship with the text, it is crucial that the reader be encouraged to talk about the reading experience. On the first day, the group discussion, led by Elizabeth and Kristina, focused on Sasha's unusual reading of 'Frogs in the Wood'. I was drawn into what happens so rarely in the classroom, a lively exploration of the 'wrong' answer.

J.T. 74: Did you make any assocation?

Sasha 75: Um, just finding out something about yourself was mine. And it wasn't really a picture.

J.T. 76: What was the association then?

S. 77: I'm not really sure. But I could relate to it 'cos I found out quite a bit about myself recently, and um, not all of it's good I'm afraid to say. I don't know, it just immediately clicked that I had found out something about myself.

J.T. 78: How did you know, how could you tell that when you were looking at these words on the page that it 'clicked' as you said? Did you feel different? Did your mind go away from the poem? Or what happened?

S. 79: It was just being lost and just being confused and quite scared, and I was really scared before I found out what I was really like.

J.T. 80: As a person?

S. 81: Yeah.

J. T. 82: So the whole idea of being lost in a strange wood was less important . . .

Elizabeth 83: That's why you thought it was in the head!

S. 84: Yeah.

J.T. 85: Can you explain that a bit more? What did you say about being in the head?

S. 86: I thought the wood was the mind and the things that go on inside the mind instead of being in an actual forest or a wood.

It came as much of a surprise to Sasha, as it did to the rest of us, to realise the origins of her initial response, with its disturbing, surreal images and sense of self-discovery.

At the end of the week, when Elizabeth chose to write her own poem, and Kristina to begin her own sketches (see pp. 217–18), Sasha chose to write about how she came to her understanding of 'Frogs in the Wood'. I think that there are two important lessons to be drawn from what she writes below. First, she is learning about herself as a reader; with increasing maturity, she will learn to keep in balance the contrary impulses set up by the text. Second, she has not learned to distrust her instinct to make her own meaning.

It is all too easy to make literature appear inaccessible by the teacher adopting an unnecessary and inappropriate role as assessor. With more experience, Sasha will learn to carry on her reading activity, to include the editing process characteristic of mature reading. Talk rather than writing, will enable her to learn to edit, and to continue to attend to herself, at the same time as attending to the text. Her account of 'Frogs in the Wood', shows the potential and the challenge of a model of learning based on the responses of the readers.

Sasha Sturgess   10th August
Frogs in the wood by Brian Patten

At first I thought this poem had something to do with frogs, and that they were the theme behind the poem. The idea of the poem has more to it than just being about frogs and their reactions but is about learning to understand yourself. To me 'Frogs in the wood' as a title is misleading, it should be something about coming to terms with yourself and not having self pity take you over.

The word 'lost' that keeps appearing isn't being lost physically but mentally confused and once you've overcome the fear and invented grief' (meaning self pity). you will be able to find yourself. 'Wood' in the title and second verse I look to mean a dark eerie forest but as my understanding of the poem grew, the picture changed into a confused mind with thoughts, confused about which way to turn.

In the second verse when it says where you are the loudest thing, "your heart making a deafening noise". to me the person is beginning to realise that he's human and that he needs to think about what is actually happening to his mind. The frogs and barbarous herons are the two sides in the mind, the wrong and the right that is always in the mind and the person starting to weigh up the questions and what he should do. 'Bright ashes going out in the ponds' is like escape routes closing and him being forced to choose, and inevitability coming to terms with himself and how the word around him reacts.

Chapter 3

Four Readers' Readings

Ray Bell

A   Children Talking – Teacher Learning

At the heart of the following enquiry is a tentative notion of a methodology which encourages enjoyment of reading poetry by trusting poems to work without too much teacher 'direction' and trusting readers to sort out their own responses. If poetry is presented as a kind of mental obstacle course, readers are easily discouraged and the experience may be truly deadly: but if they are encouraged to read lots of poems for the pleasure they afford, then genuine enthusiasm can result.

Providing time and space to respond to, and reflect on, the imaginative experience generated by a poet's words, can create the climate: trusting the reader *and* trusting the poem can create the opportunity.

This chapter is about listening and learning. Four young readers talk enthusiastically about their responses to poems and I, as the teacher-researcher, try to learn from their discoveries. In exploring the effects of different approaches to monitoring readers' responses, it becomes clear that the sorts of response elicted are dictated by the methods used and that the nature of the 'learning' that takes place also depends upon the strategic decisions that are implemented.

As can be seen in section (B) following, a pilot study was used to clarify the procedures and to establish a working relationship of mutual trust between the four readers and the teacher-researcher. This is followed by section (C) The Main Study which provides the data for the development of a pattern fo the stages of response outlined in section (D).

B   The Pilot Study

(i)   *Monitoring the readers' responses*

The focus of the Pilot Study was deliberately wide: 'to explore the mental activities that occur during and after the reading of poetic texts'. The data collected was primarily immediate and considered responses which were 'stated' in speech or in writing, elicited by methods which were constantly refined as four readers worked with various texts, individually, and as a group.

Four children, one male and three female, aged fourteen, volunteered to be members of the study group from a mixed ability third year class. I had been teaching this class for two terms, three periods each week. Weekly group 'talk-sessions' were arranged as well as organizational meetings and preparatory/follow-up activities.

Since poetic texts provoke shared interpreting, I wanted to use this opportunity of working with a small group to collect both individual and group responses for later analysis, a decision which I felt would throw some light upon what enthusiastic, committed readers do with poems despite the difficulties that would be encountered with matters of group dynamics.

The children's individual and collaborative efforts clearly established that talking about poems is a natural, easy and sometimes exciting business and proved to be highly productive for the teacher-researcher seeking to devise a manageable means of monitoring readers' responses.

The four group 'talk-sessions' were organized in the following way:

Session One	*Free discussion*
	'Blackberry Picking' – Seamus Heaney
Session Two	*A new group member: the teacher-researcher*
	'The Warm and the Cold' – Ted Hughes
Session Three	*Individual tape-recorded responses*
	'George and the Dragonfly' – Roger McGough
Session Four	*Personal constructions*
	Poems chosen by the readers

Each 'talk-session' was tape-recorded, transcribed, then carefully studied.

Session One, without the teacher-researcher, allowed the readers to begin to create their own methods of working by first recognizing the importance of private 'mental space' before public utterance. The transcript of their discussion shows how the group did not leave sufficient time for personal reflection before becoming involved in discussing the poem in a social, interactive situation.

In *Session Two*, I involved myself in the group discussion and by presenting several reading and jotting 'prompts' in the form of a short series of 'open' questions, I was able to investigate the important practical problem of how directive the teacher-researcher should be in eliciting responses. This method increased involvement by providing a supportive framework for all four readers to bring their unique, individual responses to the shared interpreting. Questioning oneself before questioning the text appeared to be a fruitful first step in encouraging responsive listening and talking, and clearly demonstrated that formulating one's own questions is a vital prerequisite in developing the ability to make meaning out of what is read. Careful preparation and structuring by the teacher, if not over directive, proved to be helpful and productive.

To prepare for *Session Three*, the children were given the text in advance and made individual tape recordings of their responses before meeting to share their ideas. This change of method to monitoring individual tape-recorded responses provided another fascinating insight into how readers approach a poem. The nature and quality of the transcribed responses show very clearly the importance of personal styles of reading. From such data, 'reading' a poem appears to involve a form of mental 'flickering' between an involved engagement with the text and a critical evaluation of it. From close study of individuals 'inside' a poetic text, 'making' a poem, the teacher-researcher is able to come closer to the unarticulated element in the reading process, which appears to take place both as the reader reads and when the reader reflects upon that reading.

The readers spent a week with a poem of their own choice to prepare for *Session Four*, when each student would lead the group discussion. Confidence in each other had developed to such an extent that I felt it worthwhile to make time for each reader to show the group what their first steps toward articulating feelings and ideas had entailed, before discussing each selected poem together. The emphasis at this stage was on the quality of the shared interpreting because the readers had reached a point where they all recognized how exploratory talk can bring out existing knowledge to be reshaped by new points of view being presented. This opened up the basic question of how much the reader is deducing from the text itself, and how much he is reading a construction of his own into it. By placing the emphasis on the readers' own choices, their keenness to read was maintained and helped to flourish. I felt that I had come close to their thought-tracks by employing this method because it had encouraged genuine involvement in poetic texts that were already personally possessed.

(ii)   A basis for further research

Throughout these preliminary investigations, a major research problem concerning response to literature – how to describe the content of spoken or written responses of individuals and groups – had become a pressing concern. The designations of certain critical schools do not seem to me to suffice for educational research of this type, and the terms of rhetorical analysis encompass the form of the stated response only. A number of researchers have worked on classificatory systems but I disregarded such methods at this stage in my enquiry because of the arbitrary nature of such schema in employing content analysis techniques. Meta-description of the responses was eschewed in favour of a concentration on the informality of the personal responses that refer to the reader and his associations, his feelings about the work, and his relation to it.

Several important principles did emerge from the Pilot Study. First, the reader's role needs to be recognized as that of a challenging, active participant in reading activities. Second, the willingness to be involved in a text hinges on the amount of pleasure that the reader finds in it. Third, the reader needs to learn to trust his own perceptions and judgments. Fourth, the personality of the reader appears to be of central importance, a factor that perhaps can best be examined by methods of investigation that focus upon what the reader 'means'. Fifth, the style, context and approach of the teacher-researcher is vital in affecting the reader's learning stance and the strategies he employs.

These principles underpin the more detailed investigations of the Main Study which places transcription of individual and group 'talk' at its centre. Careful transcription of tape-recordings and informal, reflective commentary by the teacher-researcher can create important data which can be freely interpreted to gain insights into the process of reading a poem. Such an approach, free from the constraints imposed by content analysis techniques, is able to concern itself with what a reader 'means' rather than with how a response might be labelled, and thus, this research method was repeated in the Main Study. The benefits of such an approach are flexibility, accuracy, and subtlety.

C   The Main Study

(i)   *Methods of monitoring*

The Pilot Study showed that talking about poems is both demanding and rewarding, though few people actually do it, except the captive participants who are required to demonstrate what they know of certain poems 'read' during the specified hours of an English course. However, the same four volunteer readers were willing to continue to work with me in my attempt to explore the response phenomenon and my search for good practice in poetry teaching. It was certainly clear that students do not necessarily become tongue-tied when asked to discuss a poem: animated and articulate conversations about poetic texts *can* be as lively and natural as conversations about fashion, sport or popular culture. The problem for the teacher-researcher is how to help readers to find a fruitful way into conversation.

Reading poetry is especially rich in possibilities for both independent and group work and for the teacher to create strategies which will encourage active participation and enjoyment. David Swanger highlights this notion of the potential for pleasure very well:

> We can experience poetry privately, never attempting to share our excitement with others, and be content. The poem is then like the damsel in the high tower who lets her hair down just for us, a private love. . . . But for those of us who wish to bring the damsel down from the tower and have her dance and converse among our friends, there is the challenging task of learning to build the ladder.[1]

The Main Study which follows therefore, not only attempts to learn about what happens when readers express their responses to poems, but also seeks to discover how best 'to build the ladder'.

The means of monitoring responses used in the Pilot Study and the Main Study – individual writing and tape-recording, and group discussion – allows detailed observation of how readers explore poems and also throws light upon how decisions that the teacher-researcher takes about procedures influence the nature of the responses elicited. Joint exploration with keen readers is the keynote of these investigations. Thus, rather than applying an approach which prompts the teacher, directly or indirectly, to tell the readers what to think and feel about what is read, the emphasis is shifted to attempting to encourage and study constructive interactions between readers and texts. Knowledge about readers and their transactions with poetic texts can then perhaps play a part in enhancing the teacher's effectiveness in the classroom.

David Jackson's stages of response[2] were particularly useful in my attempts to understand more about the creative process involved in reading poems and the need for teachers to successfully structure poetry reading and writing experiences to cater for children's differing expressive needs and personal 'timetables'. Jackson establishes *three* stages of response: the first encounter, coming to terms and making a statement, as a means of describing a reader's reading stance and the strategies he might employ when experiencing a poem. These three stages were used in the Main Study to begin the attempt to describe what was being observed.

The success of the first encounter depends upon preliminary space and time being given to the individual reader to begin to find his own way of gaining entry to the poem and perhaps possessing the reading experience for himself. This avoids a premature rush into final product writing or talking, which is a 'public' stage that may hinder active involvement with the text if it is encouraged before an independent, personal response has had time to develop. In other words, experiencing the text should come before analysis. The evidence of the transcripts which follow supports this notion that it is from such 'first impressions' that reflection, criticism and commentary grow. Notice, for example, how recording excitement or puzzlement through the tentative or assertive contributions to small group talk in Transcripts Two, Six and Eight is capable of generating 'sufficient momentum . . . to carry a reader on to a more detailed, considered stance where commentary, intelligence and feeling can intertwine with and inform each other'.[3]

Jackson's second stage of response – the coming to terms – brings the questions, speculations and impressions of the earlier stage into contact with the opinions and perspectives of other readers. In the transcripts of group discussions detailed later in this chapter, one can see that through shared talk particularly, modification into a more coherent and developed shape is possible by the way the readers balance and reconcile different ideas and feelings through collaborative effort. For example, a closer reading of the text, prompted by the view of another reader, is encouraged and a reconstruction of 'sketchy' first impressions is seen to take place. This complex, awkward 'journey' through small group exchanges may result in a reader arriving (though not necessarily in a sequential order), at Jackson's third stage of response.

The making a statement stage, is seen to grow out of the earlier stages. Perhaps it is worthwhile noting at this point that it is this stage that is so often most highly valued by teachers as 'evidence' of 'learning' – a judgement which seems to me to be to the detriment of the true nature of the experience of 'reading' a poem. This is the synthesizing, more carefully reflective stage which need not necessarily be a final statement, nor be valued as highly as the earlier stages. Such a 'considered' view may be frequently revised by the reader going back to early impressions and modifications – as seen in transcript Three.

In section D of this chapter, this sense of linked stages of response is expanded in the light of the findings of the Main Study research, which does try to allow readers to find their own ways into experiencing poetic texts, though guided and supported by a teacher-researcher who is aware that the decisions that both readers and teachers make about different procedures to adopt, dictate the nature of the responses evoked and the learning that takes place. Such an understanding might help to develop a teacher's sensitivity about when to intervene and when not to intervene in the process of reading a poem.

The procedure that was followed throughout the Main Study is outlined in Table 3.1 – collaborative group discussions, with and without the teacher-researcher, and individual activities, which were planned to both prepare for and follow up the 'talk' sessions of the group. In my view, such methods of monitoring response allow for modifications to be made as the study progresses, by remaining flexible enough to respond to the unpredictable nature of the response phenomenon under investigation, while at the same time, a clear sense of direction can be maintained by both the readers and the teacher-researcher.

At first examination, the following transcriptions of the readers' spoken and written responses to the three poems used in the Main Study may appear as gossipy pieces of chat, but the more carefully one considers their words, the more the process of responding to poems is illuminated. The readers can be observed developing from the first encounter with a poem, through the stage of coming to terms with it (either helped or hindered by the teacher-researcher's involvement!), to the more reflective phase of making a considered statement about it. The readers make their meanings slowly, over time, by various methods, and the teacher-researcher's role, in this context, is to assist them to demonstrate, explain and share their responses, then pay close attention to their individual, unique voices.

Though the process of responding to poems is never brought into completely clear focus, as a slide might be when seen beneath a microscope, perhaps the twilight of the dimly apprehended can be recognized in the following transcripts to be as significant as the clear light of the tidily explained.

Table 3.1   Methods of Monitoring

'*The Tyger*' – William Blake

Transcript One	Individual tape-recorded response, before group discussion
Transcript Two	Group discussion, including teacher-researcher
Transcript Three	Individual written response, after group discussion

'*The Sick Rose*' – William Blake

Transcript Four	Individual written response, before group discussion
Transcript Five	Individual tape-recorded response, before group discussion
Transcript Six	Group discussion, without teacher-researcher

'*The Jaguar*' – Ted Hughes

Transcript Seven	Individual tape-recorded response, before group discussion
Transcript Eight	Group discussion, including teacher-researcher

(ii)   Finding a Tyger

The focus of the first enquiry was to explore the notion of the three stages of responding to a poem, described earlier: the first encounter, as seen in the individual tape-recorded response of Transcript One; the coming to terms response stage as reflected in the group discussion of Transcript Two, which included the teacher-researcher as a group member; and the making a statement stage, as seen in the considered, post-discussion written response of Transcript Three.

The readers were given two copies of William Blake's poem, 'The Tyger', one of which was his illustrated version, one week in advance of the scheduled group discussion. Their preparatory task was to read the poem carefully and 'to talk about it, in writing or on tape, in any way you want'. The same suggestion was made after the group discussion had taken place.

'The Tyger' was chosen for several reasons: it is a poem I enjoy and admire; the readers had responded well to poems used in the Pilot Study that had challenged them to consider their place in the natural world; and, because I believe that restricting children to texts that are supposed to be 'appropriate' to their age or ability level deprives them of too many good things. In other words, my knowledge of the readers and their 'tastes' could now be brought into practical use to test my notion that readers can get more out of genuinely good poems than out of mediocre ones, even if the superior poem is difficult in some ways.

The chief aim was not that the readers would come to admire Blake and his achievement, but that each reader would be able to find a Tyger of his or her own.

In Transcript One, we can watch Michele easing herself into the poem. Because there has been no demand to write a finished product, she can be seen to be reacting freely to the poem's 'feeling centre', clear of any such constraints. Her personal associations help her to begin to take possession of the poem inwardly. The important point in this is that Michele is allowing her thinking processes to be made known to herself; in the act of talking out loud on to recording tape, one can see a sorting and self-testing process going on. This is made more clear in her 'jottings', made immediately before the group discussion:

> I think that the poem reflects on a tyger prowling at night, hunting and foraging for food. The lines about the lamb made me think of it being had for the tyger's tea. I think that the tyger has no mercy for anyone and he is always living, no matter how many times he dies.... No-one wants to stop him and I think Hell made him. Why did God make him and is he the same creator of the meek little lamb and the big fearsome creature? Why is it spelt 'Tyger'? What do 'sinews' mean?

Both methods of presenting her response to the poem show a developing understanding of her own thoughts. She is selecting the significant ideas from an initial bewildering confusion, and then in the acts of talking and writing, she is able to articulate them to herself more clearly.

The importance of providing time and space for such first encounter responses is clearly demonstrated in Michele's highly personal reconstruction of the poem's meaning. In Transcript Two, her active participation in the group discussion then demonstrates how such a struggle to independently possess a poem can be refined in the act of sharing such responses with other people. The way that Michele finds her own Tyger highlights two important features of the response phenomenon: first, that starting to see yourself as a person capable of independently making sense of what you read takes more time than teachers often suspect; and second, a vital foundation on which to build might be said to be for the reader to start from where she is rather than from where the teacher thinks she is.

The group discussion of Transcript Two shows that talking together about a poem is a natural, challenging, and sometimes exciting business. The readers do not, by this stage, need convincing that their discussions are worthwhile and valued. They appear to understand this aspect of sharing thoughts and feelings because of previous experience. As Janine said: 'Listening to others . . . makes you change your ideas. You might have an idea . . . but as you listen, you may feel you could change what you think'.

In the commentary on this Transcript, I focus attention on Michele's modification of her ideas into a more coherent and developed shape, made possible by collaborative effort. The group responded positively to Blake's poem and were able to re-establish the 'work-in-progress' atmosphere of the earlier small group discussion sessions. They listened carefully, used language skilfully, responded positively to the suggestions and problems of others, and were all *actively involved* (though Leigh said very little on this particular occasion). Thus, the sharing of responses appeared to be a natural development from the individual's own response to the text, achieved in her own way according to her own individual timetable.

However, I was disappointed that the shared exploration failed to relate 'The Tyger' to their own experiences. I believe that this was due to the presence of the teacher-researcher. An 'open' and hypothetical style of discussion *is* possible in such circumstances, but free association of the text with personal experiences, in this instance, was prevented rather than encouraged by the teacher's inclusion in the discussion. (In contrast, in a later group discussion [Transcript Six], without the teacher present, a much more imaginative approach is used whereby each reader's own feelings and personal experiences are brought alongside the whole experience of the poem to give many new, rewarding insights.) Perhaps the idea of talking to an animal could have opened up this area of personal experience –

'Have you ever talked with a pet?'
'Have you ever seen an animal's eyes in the dark?'

The readers seemed to have needed help in getting past the difficulties of Blake's language and syntax, to get closer to the heart of the mysterious, magical creation of a Superpowered Being. Perhaps an 'experiential' task as suggested above, could have prepared a way into the poem by questioning the readers' own experiences. With hindsight, the group discussion could have been invigorated by the teacher-researcher's intervention: not in this instance by becoming involved in the 'shared talk', but by initiating a preparatory task such as:

> Write a poem in which you are talking to a beautiful and mysterious creature. You can ask it anything you wish. You have the power to do so because you can speak its secret language.

Such an idea might well have drawn the readers to the main question Blake asks: 'How did the Tyger get the way it is?'

Natalie's post-discussion, written response to 'The Tyger' (Transcript Three), very clearly demonstrates the importance of creating a personal context for understanding. In making a considered statement about the poem, she successfully balances the claims of the print (rhythm, tone, imagery, sound, and diction, etc.) against the claims of her personal associations. A keen, discriminating intelligence can be seen working alongside personal feeling – an approach which enabled her to transcend the too tentative and 'safe' approach which handicapped the group discussion.

'The Tyger' William Blake

Transcript One	Individual tape-recorded response Michele
Transcript Two	Group discussion, including the teacher-researcher: Janine, Natalie, Leigh and Michele
Transcript Three	Individual written response Natalie

The Tyger

Tyger! Tyger! burning bright
In the forests of the night,
What immortal hand or eye
Could frame thy fearful symmetry?

In what distant deeps or skies
Burnt the fire of thine eyes?
On what wings dare he aspire?
What the hand dare seize the fire?

What the shoulder, and what art,
Could twist the sinews of thy heart?
And when thy heart began to beat,
What dread hand? And what dread feet?

What the hammer? What the chain?
In what furnace was thy brain?
What the anvil? What dread grasp
Dare its deadly terrors clasp?

When the stars threw down their spears,
And water'd heaven with their tears,
Did He smile His work to see?
Did He who made the Lamb make thee?

Tyger! Tyger! burning bright
In the forests of the night,
What immortal hand or eye,
Dare frame thy fearful symmetry?

William Blake

The Tyger

Tyger Tyger, burning bright,
In the forests of the night;
What immortal hand or eye,
Could frame thy fearful symmetry?

In what distant deeps or skies
Burnt the fire of thine eyes!
On what wings dare he aspire?
What the hand, dare seize the fire?

And what shoulder, & what art,
Could twist the sinews of thy heart?
And when thy heart began to beat,
What dread hand? & what dread feet?

What the hammer? what the chain,
In what furnace was thy brain?
What the anvil? what dread grasp,
Dare its deadly terrors clasp!

When the stars threw down their spears
And water'd heaven with their tears:
Did he smile his work to see?
Did he who made the Lamb make thee

Tyger Tyger burning bright,
In the forests of the night:
What immortal hand or eye,
Dare frame thy fearful symmetry?

100

Transcript 1

Michele: 'The Tyger'

Commentary

In this personal commentary, the reader is fully immersed in the 'puzzle' of the poem she is making. The concept of a poem as an experience shaped by the reader under the guidance of the text appears valid when such a personal re-enactment is witnessed (Rosenblatt, 1978).

Involvement is triggered by her initial fascination for the imagery and the reason for writing such a poem.

Individual Tape-recorded Response

This is the first poem – 'Tyger' – William Blake.

The poem made me feel independent . . . and hostile. Independent because the Tyger was by himself, and was hunting for himself and no one really mattered – and hostile because he didn't want . . . didn't want to be with anyone, except himself. And . . . he had a 'couldn't-care-less' sort of attitude, which hung over me . . . I don't know why.

I thought the poem was quite good and had a lot of good rhymes . . . and it went together sort of thing . . . and I think they're quite good words to describe it.

The fifth stanza appeals to me 'cos it says, 'When the stars threw down their spears, And water'd heaven with their tears' . . . it reminded me of a falling star or a shooting star, and then exploding into a thousand pieces . . . like which was heaven crying . . . and it was sort of like a rocket on Guy Fawkes' day, exploding in the sky. I liked that bit . . . that's what I liked.

The first two lines catch my eye – 'Tyger! Tyger!' . . . I think it must be because they're two

101

capitals and two exclamation marks . . . but I haven't got a reason . . . it makes it stand out.

'Did He who made the Lamb make thee?' interests me; 'fearful symmetry'; 'When the stars threw down their spears' . . . ; 'What an anvil'; and that's about it. That's all that interests me.

What I can see is a tiger going through the jungle looking for a prey, and I can see a little lamb, all by itself in a little sheep pen, and the tiger running towards it, chasing it. And I can also see the rockets exploding . . . it comes straight into my mind.

I read it once quickly, then twice thoroughly, and then I started to work on it and . . . I was looking at the words thoroughly, trying to make what they were.

The pattern of this personal discussion shows a clear 'shuttling' or 'leapfrogging' movement between specific ideas and personal anecdotes which illustrate, modify, or advance the ideas.

Here Michele is making a story out of the mental images evoked.

The power, mystery and magic about 'The Tyger' are emphasized.

Transcript 2

'The Tyger'

Group Discussion

Janine 1: I looked at it first . . . then again the next day . . . and I didn't make any sense of it. I looked at it twice, then I put it down and didn't look at it until last night.

Teacher 1: Which one did you look at? You had two versions, the illustrated and a 'straight' one . . .

Commentary

If a teacher encourages a student to start from where she is, rather from where the teacher thinks she is, then this often means drawing blanks at first readings. Janine's frank recognition of difficulty takes courage to own up to, and can be used as an actual problem from which to start, rather than the blind alley of a dutifully 'fake', stock response.

Here the teacher could have explained how Blake illustrated his own text. This is an important role for the teacher to play in providing such background information.

Natalie sees the limitation of an illustrated version in its mediating function very perceptively. She also seeks an explanation that only the teacher can provide; here for example, changes in pronunciation could have been highlighted by the teacher.

J.2: The straight one . . .

Natalie 1: That one . . . the illustrated one . . . makes it look harder I think . . . 'cos it makes you look at all the funny language, like the way he spelt 'Tyger'.

Michele 1: That one's more interesting . . .

N.2: . . . Yeh it's more interesting, but it's harder to understand like that.

J.3: It gives you other ideas . . .

N.3: Yeh . . it makes you think it's actually about a tiger, but you might think something different. 'Cos I don't think it is . . .

N.4: . . . That gives you an idea already, so you can't think of anything else . . . if you can just see a tiger, that's all you're gonna see in the poem unless you read it . . . that's why that's better, 'cos it's got no illustration. So you can use your own imagination . . . It makes you think that that is what is what you've got to think it is . . . Oh yeh, and how . . . if you look at the last two lines, if you're reading that aloud, how would you say that, 'cos 'eye' and 'symmetry' wouldn't really be right? . . . so you'd have to say 'symmet – try'.

J.4: Yeh, that's what I was thinking.

N.5: . . . I think it starts off saying about a tiger,

then . . . I don't understand the rest, I mean, it's sort of . . . more than it, in it? . . . I think it's got a meaning in it.

M.2: No . . . I think it's about the tiger and what he does and what he looks like and every-thing . . . the way . . . the natures of them. I like . . . the fifth paragraph . . .

N.6: Yeh . . . that's like the Bible . . . 'He who made the Lamb made thee' . . . that's why I think it's got a meaning, 'cos it's like the Bible . . . capital 'H' it's got.

J.5: 'And when thy heart began to beat' . . . it's sort of . . . somebody else . . . like some-body coming into the world . . . maybe it's the tiger just being born.

T.2: Somebody's made it. It starts life.

N.7: Yeh.

T.3: You mentioned the Lamb . . . there's an-other poem by Blake called 'The Lamb' . . . we might get a chance to look at that later.

N.8: Why's it all in questions? Did you notice that? It makes you think . . .

M.3: Your own ideas about what it's about.

T.4: But what's the question it's asking? I think you have to sort out that question . . .

N.9: I dunno!

J.6: Shall I read it?

Michele not only attempts to concentrate attention on the principal interest she has found in the poem; she directs the readers to her favourite stanza.

A crucial focusing question. However, the teacher 'blocks' a development of this understanding that the poem is a series of questions by rushing too quickly towards *the* question.

When in doubt re-read the text carefully. This is a practice, established previously, which is initiated by a reader who understands the process involved. Natalie answers her own question. Voicing her 'problem' aloud helps.

Michele has been listening carefully. Here, she seizes the opportunity to try out her theory about hell. The anecdotal additions are a deliberate attempt to catch the other readers' attention.

N.10: *(Janine reads the poem aloud).* Oh!

J.7: Oh, what?

N.11: Where it says . . . 'Tyger! Tyger! burning bright' . . . I don't understand that . . . 'cos how would a tiger? . . . it's the colours I suppose.

J.8: I thought it made it appear . . . in the jungle. Colours burning through the trees . . .

N.12: It makes it sound really bad!

J.9: He stands out from all the other animals . . . You know in the fourth verse where it says, 'What dread grasp/Dare its deadly terrors clasp?' . . . when I first read that, I thought he was killing somebody.

M.4: I think that's the bit about the devil. I think he's possessed by the devil . . .

N.13: . . . making it . . . yeh . . . sound really bad.

M.5: . . . and he's down with the devil . . . sort of, with the anvil and that . . . and putting on a ball and chain on sort of thing.

N.14: Where it says . . . where the tiger is created . . . where it sounds like the Bible. I think that's supposed to mean created by God, but that sounds like it was created by something bad! . . . to terrorize all the animals.

T.5: So Blake is asking if God created the tiger, which is so ferocious – did the same being who made the Lamb, make it?

N.15: Look at the 'He', capital . . . that's why I said it was like the Bible . . . they always do that.

M.6: It doesn't on the illustration one . . . it's made it clearer.

N.16: The Lamb's gentle and that . . .

T.6: They also call Jesus the Lamb of God because he was sent to earth and was slain for us . . . he was quiet and gentle.

N.17: Yeh . . .

T.7: I liked Michele's ideas on the hammer, chain, and furnace, and the anvil . . .

N.18: I don't get that!

M.7: I think that's hell . . . he's gone to hell or something. You know, he's been made . . . *conjured* up from the devil . . . he's got a sort of . . . like a duty to do what he does.

T.8: He can't help it.

M.8: Like the Lamb . . . the Lamb is made by God . . . he's got a duty to be like God.

T.9: You mean, the way God made him?

M.9: Yeh.

T.10: So why did God make the tiger as well as the lamb?

In attempting to become part of such a group, teachers also need *time* to adjust!

Note the insistence on precision.

Michele seeks to draw attention back to her present concern: the evil, hostile independence of the creature that so fascinates her. Her early involvement in the sharing of ideas about the poem has centred on her personal concerns which were noted in her jottings and her tape-recorded response. She listens to the other readers but, at the moment, her own concerns dominate her thinking. Such a small group experience provides an important, and perhaps unique,

	reality test for her own ideas as well as developing a set of interpersonal skills not typically developed in the whole class discussions.
N.19: He could be saying . . . if he made the lamb and the tiger, then he can't be as good as he makes out he is, or as good as everyone says he is. He could be questioning how good God really is or who he is? Why should you have to understand the Lamb . . .?	
T.11: Why make both?	
J.10: In the second verse though, it says . . . it questions you, where it belongs to . . . 'cos you can see he's evil 'cos it says 'In what distant deeps or skies/Burnt the fire of thine eyes?' . . . so he's evil because of fire, and you've got to imagine where he is . . . in the world or whatever . . . 'cos he might be down in hell there mightn't he? – 'cos it doesn't say where he is . . .	
T.12: Like saying, what brought this tiger into being and why? (Silence) How many of you read it when you were younger? (Two had)	
Leigh.1: In the colours of this . . . the tiger, say it's come from the devil and that, all the colours are like flames . . . whereas lambs . . . gentle white . . .	Leigh's first contribution. The text had been chosen to possibly encourage comparison of earlier readings with responses at present. However, Leigh's new involvement was more important than such an intention being pursued at this stage.
J.11: I've just got a good idea. You know that 'symmetry'? . . . Is it because . . you know you know	

how he's got stripes, if you put him over half between him, then he'd be exactly the same both sides.

M.10: Or it could mean that one side's got . . .

L.2: . . . no good one side, no evil the other side – he's all evil.

M.11: Yeh . . .

N.20: Oh Yeh, and who's to say that? Who's William Blake to say that then?

M.12: He's questioning religion . . . .

T.13: What's good and what's bad?

J.12: . . .'Cos a tiger is a cat in't it?

M.13: Cats used to be gods in Egypt . . . and lambs used to be slaughtered . . . .

T.14: Like Christ was sacrificed?

M.14: Yeh . . . like that sheep was dragged out the other day, the other week.

T.15: Cats were later thought to be connected with evil, like a witch's cat . . . their eyes . . . some people are frightened of the eyes. So if the poem's asking is it the same person that made the tiger as well as the lamb, then I'm suddenly thinking, what does the tiger represent . . . stand for . . . Evil?

N.21: Who's to say what is good and evil?

J.13: We're going off the poem now . . . that's a bit stupid.

Janine's 'good idea' illustrates an important feature of the response phenomenon. The phrase 'fearful symmetry' has gone underground into the group subconscious since N.4 and J.4. Here, it suddenly surfaces again.

Michele provides the background information, both historical and current. The associations she makes at this point prove to be very valuable later in the discussion and are undoubtedly more useful in advancing understanding than the efforts of the teacher.

Michele deliberately steers the conversation away. She is having difficulty coming to terms with this aspect of the poem, so she points to another area that fascinated her at the first encounter stage of response.

Michele again uses ideas from her personal first encounter. Her way of gaining entry to the poem remains the vital motivating force.

T.16: No we're not you know . . . we're . . .
N.22: . . . getting deeper!
M.15: To go straight off that . . . I like the bit about . . . 'When the stars threw down their spears, And water'd heaven with their tears'.
T.11: Tell us why.
M.16: I don't know . . . I think it's like . . . like a sort of shooting star, exploding like a rocket.
N.23: Like when the world was created.
T.18: I get a really good image of that . . . I really see that in my head . . . like light coming to the world, or the Big Bang . . . that theory of, you know, how the world began.
M.17: . . . like a rocket on Guy Fawkes' day.
T.19: . . . and then 'water'd heaven . . .' life depends on light and water and you suddenly get . . . .
N.24: I think that's a really good line.
T.20: What?
N.25: 'And water'd heaven with their tears'.
M.18: Yeh . . . .
N.26: I think the whole of that part is really good.
J.14: But who 'water'd heaven with their tears'? Who's them?
T.21: The poem asks those questions . . . .

M.19: But He might have said . . . 'I've done a bad job', and cried (laughs).

J.15: *Yes!* Michele . . .

N.27: That was my first impression . . .

M.20: Yeh . . . when you talk in a group . . . you can't really do it on your own.

N.28: It's better when you talk to other people.

J.16: When you're sitting in your bedroom, with everything else on your mind, you can't really . . . just looking at it . . .

T.22: But can you all try . . . first on your own, in the week before we talk . . . in advance . . . ? Do something yourself first, before you talk with me or the group . . .

J.17: I don't mind doing it, sort of separate, if you're gonna *join in the talking* . . . *but if you're gonna just ask questions*, then I don't want to do it.

N.29: Why create two opposites in the first place? For comparison . . . I suppose then you know what good *is* . . . but then if you always have good, then you don't need bad.

T.23: Why have good *and* evil? Natalie suggests . . . in order to have an opposite of good.

N.30: Yeh . . . we've all got the option to be bad.

T.24: You've got free will.

Janine's protest succinctly highlights the dilemma of the teacher being involved as a group member. It is interesting to note how Natalie's thoughts are still with the text; she wants to pursue the sharing of ideas despite the obvious failings of the teacher's technique.

N.31: Yeh, then you'll hopefully do the right thing . . . 'cos you just go against . . . So the tiger's a symbol then . . . like a symbol of what you can think of as evil.

T.25: In the sense that evil is created with a purpose of good – somewhere.

N.32: I think it's amazing! He's got a lot of meaning into it . . . .

J.18: This morning, you said you hated it! (laughter)

N.33: I know, because I didn't understand it . . .

J.19: If one person says . . . like Michele said about the devil . . . that's brought us along to one thing, but we didn't think of that, so . . .

T.26: The sharing helps then?

N.34: The first and last verses . . is the easiest to understand. It didn't really discuss the more important bits of it.

M.21: Really basic . . . not gone into it in detail . . . just the basic idea . . .

T.27: Why did someone make it that way . . . 'framed' it?

N.35: Why does it say 'hand or eye'? . . . how can an eye . . . ah : . . just frame it in your mind . . . in your eye . . . I see, to get an idea.

Natalie tries out this idea as a direct result of recent classroom discussion of the nature of symbolism.

Note the discussion that follows from the idea proposed by the teacher at T.31. The suggestion 'Think of an apple' provides an entry into a full exploration of symbol, which is not directed toward 'The Tyger', but creates a fortuitous way-in to 'The Sick Rose', the second poem considered (see N.39).

| | | These two questions were both asked in Michele's jottings. She has waited with patience until a suitable moment for them to be considered has been reached. The 'moment' stems from Natalie's concern with the language employed. |

L.3: He's watching over all that He's made.
M.22: What's 'sinews'?
T.28: Why did he spell 'tyger' like that?
M.23: Can anybody suggest a reason?
       I don't understand that bit (points to verse 2).
T.29: Does it bother you when you don't understand all of it?
M.24: Yeh.
J.20: I don't understand *any* of it, so it doesn't really matter!
L.4: I think the bit you don't know the meaning of is the main meaning.
T.30: The key? Janine's saying that it hasn't 'come together' for her.
M.25: I think it does.
T.31: It does seem to mean a lot more than just describing a tiger which is where we *all* start . . .
       It makes you see the tiger in a different way, maybe for the first time.
       Think of an apple.
       What can an apple suggest, besides something to eat?
N.36: Adam and Eve . . . Garden of Eden.
M.26: Isaac Newton and . . .
T.32: Gravity?

Here, I attempted to emphasize the idea of symbol, referring back to N.31 and forward to the planned session on 'The Sick Rose'.

J.21: That's stupid!

M.27: Maggots.

N.37: Yeh, the maggots get into the apple and do horrible things to it . . . destroy it.

T.33: A poet might say, because an apple's round . . . he might say that the world is *like* an apple. Now then, if he said that . . . you could say that people exploit the world . . . go down in the ocean and rip out the oil, down in the earth to rip the coal out. . . .

N.38: . . . like how the apple goes mouldy where the worm's been.

M.28: Or when it rots, you've got the pips and it renews itself.

T.34: OK. If the apple falls and rots . . . it 'bubbles'. Have you ever heard that word used to describe an apple rotting in the grass? There's a poem, by Laurie Lee, describing apples in autumn – the apples, if left in the grass, change.

N.39: Like the cycle of life.

T.35: The idea of the world like an apple. If you'd just been watching something like the *Threads* programme on television.

N.40: Oh . . . that was really good!

T.36: . . . On nuclear war, and you thought of all the warheads all over the world, that are

Janine's exasperation, which began at J.17, is voiced again. This is most probably a direct response to the fact that the group are moving steadily away from the text. Janine wants to solve the puzzle of the poem, and on this occasion, the sharing of ideas has not had the desired outcome for her. Indeed, the group have not 'solved' the mystery of 'The Tyger'; they have explored its mystery.

Natalie provoked the discussion in the first place (see N.31). She also provides a fortuitous way-in to 'The Sick Rose', the poem considered in Transcripts Five and Six.

sunk into the ground . . . you could think
that what we're doing to the earth is a bit
like . . . infesting it . . . putting things into it
that could destroy it . . . like a worm cor-
rupting an apple, until the whole thing is
destroyed.

N.41: But all those pieces . . . little pieces, might
make new planets.

T.37: Look at all the possibilities . . . Just say
'apple' to someone – all the ideas a poet
could use.

M.29: The Big Apple!
N.42: New York
T.38: They're called associations . . .

Transcript 3　　　　　Natalie: 'The Tyger'

Individual Written Response

I didn't understand this poem at all to start with
but when we all talked about it all together I started
to realize how many other meanings there were. It's
not just about a tyger, I think it's really powerful
(especially stanza 5) although the poet seems to be a
bit of a religious maniac.

This poem makes me start to think. It gets you to

Commentary

This post-discussion 'considered' written response
shows how Natalie's enthusiasm for the poem has
been sustained and developed.

read it in greater depth. I liked it more because of this. It's not just another boring poem.

I like 5 best, it sounds like it was written about 2,000 years ago. 'What immortal hand or eye Could frame thy fearful symmetry', and 'In what distant deeps or skies Burnt the fire of thine eyes' and 'When the stars threw down their spears And water'd heaven with their tears'. I think all those are really good. The last one is brilliant, I don't quite get it but it's really powerful and it gets you thinking (well it did me). I like the way the first and last bits (?) are the same. When I read this through again I didn't really see a lot then I switched the light off and closed my eyes. I saw first a tiger which changed into a ball of fire for some reason unknown. Then I saw a furnace and was surrounded by darkness. It changed colour to white and exploded into little stars which fell down. This reminded me of the Bible so I started thinking about all that 'In the beginning . . .', stuff so I imagined that, grey clay-like lump of something or other but it was round anyway. These little sparks fell on to it and it became a jungle full of creatures. The fire turned into a tiger and walked off, very satisfied. After that someone came in and switched the light on so I lost concentration but that's about it anyway. All I can say is, this poem is amazing.

PS: I prefer the ordinary sheet to the picture one.

Her own personal re-construction of the poem's central images could have vitalized the group discussion. Natalie gets on the inside of the poem by using her personal, imaginative insights as an interpretative tool. She balances the claims of the print (the poem as a poem establishing its meaning through rhythm, tone, imagery, sound, diction . . .) against the claims of her personal associations. Natalie successfully creates her own personal context for an understanding of 'The Tyger'.

(iii) Discovering a Rose

The focus of the second enquiry was primarily to examine the workings of a small discussion group without the teacher-researcher present. The four readers were given a copy of William Blake's 'The Sick Rose' one week in advance of the scheduled discussion session. Two examples of preparatory individual work are included below (Transcripts Four and Five), to demonstrate the contrasting emotional ambience felt for the poem by the two readers who then go on to engage with the text in group discussion. In this instance, it is interesting to note what the two readers have brought *to* the poem, and what they have *made of it*, after sharing their responses.

The selection of a second poem by William Blake is important in this context. I wanted the readers to attempt to build upon the ideas discussed earlier with 'The Tyger', with particular reference to metaphorical language and symbolism. Both the individual reponses and the group discussion that followed show how individual readers deploy a contrasting degree of sensitivity and empathy in responding to a text. It also shows how the recent experience of Blake both informed and hindered their engaging in a ready commerce between the experience of their reading and other relevant experience.

Transcript Six demonstrates the value of 'free' discussion in a small group. It is valuable for a number of reasons. The group were asked to: 'Discuss the poem in any way you wish', then left to collaborate in order to explore their responses to the 'open' topic. The transcript shows how their social interaction allows, and sometimes compels, the participants to modify their points of view as they go along, adapting and editing as they 'test' their thoughts by setting their own responses against those of others in the group. The readers are both tentative and assertive in this coming to terms phase, as they try to find their own way to whatever discoveries they make.

For example, compare the more literal approach of Janine with the more imaginative stance characterized by Natalie and Leigh. Their speculative approach to the text was less obvious in the earlier group discussion which included the teacher-researcher: perhaps in that instance, the tape-recorder, like the teacher, had an inhibiting effect (see Transcript Two). In the 'free' discussion of Transcript Six, the group were, in a sense, compelled to talk, regardless of what they said, and had become used to talking while tape-recording. In such circumstances, the readers might have been expected to attempt to define the 'meaning' of the poem, in order to be seen to be 'doing something, getting somewhere': but in fact, they appear to understand their need for time and space to clarify their own thoughts and feelings and therefore, they do not become obsessed with getting at 'the facts'. What the discussion of 'The Sick Rose' primarily demonstrates is the value of encouraging readers, through shared talk, to consider their own ideas away from what can often be the inhibiting influence of teacher opinion and pronouncements.

Such a conversation can be criticized because it lacks the direction and bite of a discussion in which the teacher shapes the talk and enlarges upon significant points made by the pupils. However, it is my view that the 'aimlessness' of such a discussion is potentially one of its greatest advantages and may bring it nearer to 'natural' or 'real' conversation. Everyday conversations are in reality much less tidily structured than the talk that is often envisaged *should* take place in school discussion groups. Divergent thinking, unpredictable changes of subject and new information, for example, can be seen in the discussion to effect changes in the direction of the talk. Far from limiting and devaluing the conversation, these digressions and unexpected turns of direction enrich the collaborative search for understanding. The experience of talking in this way allows the expression of individual ideas and opinions – an outlet which is essential to personal and social development. Even more significantly, the experience of sharing responses can be seen to be developing and refining the readers' sense of *how to talk about poems*.

An emphasis on such an active, re-creative response needs to be based upon the encouragement of what John Stuart Mill calls:

> . . . that conscious and intelligent incompleteness which carries with it the principle of growth . . . the organization that represents a measure of real understanding, and seeks of its very nature to extend and complete itself.[4]

Clearly, the readers involved in this group discussion did not 'solve' every difficulty in 'The Sick Rose', but I believe that this does not matter. The concentration and richness of the discussion are what really matter: readers entering into the poem as fully as they are able. However, in commenting on such unsupervised discussion, it is necessary to voice a gnawing doubt that can initially beset research that aims to pay close attention to the very varied ways in which readers attempt to verbalize their responses. Harold Rosen points out the dilemma succinctly:

> Surely we can show some responses to be irrelevant and we should not be content to applaud any strong reaction?[5]

Leigh's storytelling in the group discussion answers this question. By paying close attention to such responses transcribed from a tape-recorded discussion, it is clear that readers must often find their own ways of saying things, pre-analytical ways that are couched in personal characteristic modes of thought. Again, Rosen is helpful:

> It may well be that certain responses are irrelevant, may arise
> from inattention and the loud inner voice which drowns the poet,
> but we had better be very sure that the responses are irrelevant,
> that the reader is not attending, that the inner voice is not joining
> the conversation.[6]

Leigh's contribution to the group discussion is crucial. He
fictionalizes a story about a poltergeist which allows the group to
move into a mode of abstracting which provides a voice for some of
their inner material that could not be expressed directly and
explicitly. His invented story stimulates a fruitful approach by which
the readers are able to move towards each others' meanings. An
utterance count of this discussion clearly fails to show how
important Leigh's metaphorical fictionalizing was to the collaborative effort; yet even the bare figures indicate a much increased
contribution (see Transcript Two):

Natalie – 34
Janine – 22
Michele – 19
Leigh – 14

Close attention to the evidence of the transcript in showing what
actually happens when readers are reading can bring this aspect of
reading poetry into focus.

'The Sick Rose' William Blake

Transcript Four   Individual written response: Janine

Transcript Five   Individual tape-recorded response: Michele

Transcript Six   Group discussion, without the
                       teacher-researcher

                    The Sick Rose

O Rose, thou art sick,
The invisible worm
That flies in the night
In the howling storm

Has found out thy bed
Of crimson joy,
And his dark secret love
Does thy life destroy.

                 William Blake

Transcript 4

Janine: 'The Sick Rose'

Individual Written Response

First impression . . . none. I looked at it at least ten times before this. At first I didn't understand it, but now I think that the invisible worm is some sort of bug, like the black fly, which flies through the night and settles on the rose. And then attacks it and kills it. 'Does thy life destroy.' If it did mean this, every line would fit in except for 'And his dark secret love', I don't understand that, it could be the rose. When it says 'Has found out thy bed', it means the worm has found a place to settle.

I don't think this poem has a meaning. It's just about a bug killing a rose. Unless it's an evil thing killing a rose. Unless it's an evil thing killing a beautiful thing, as roses are always thought of as being beautiful.

When you think of a sick rose, it makes you think that the worm is trying to help the rose, and by trying to help, kills it.

Commentary

Janine experienced considerable difficulty coming to terms with 'The Tyger' and became exasperated with talk of symbolism. These *pre-discussion* jottings show a reaction to that first session. She seeks a literal interpretation: 'It's just about a bug killing a rose'. However, she then destroys that notion very successfully by seeing the possibilities in the destruction of good by evil. Janine is taking longer than the other readers to understand the potential inherent in metaphorical language.

119

Transcript 5

Michele: 'The Sick Rose'

Individual Tape-recorded Response

The poem is called 'The Sick Rose', by William Blake. I don't think much of the poem 'cos I didn't understand it that much and it's too short I think. But, it's probably got a lot of meaning.

I think, looking at it, it makes me feel sort of sad, 'cos it . . . I think the rose is killing somebody or something . . . killing somebody's love etc., you know? I don't think much of it! (very emphatically). It didn't really give anything to me . . . sort of . . . express anything really. Nothing really jumped out at me either.

I think the bit about . . . 'has found out thy bed' . . . appears to be something . . . cos it says there's a bed of roses and . . . somebody gets taken away or something, somebody's love is shattered, by a rose. . . and bled, their heart bleeds sort of thing.

Nothing really catches my eye . . . apart from 'Oh Rose' . . . it sounds a bit of a sob-story really, 'cos it's all sad and everything and nothing really interests me. 'Has found out thy bed' . . . and 'his dark secret love' and 'the invisible worm' do.

Commentary

Michele is prepared to state her emotional response; the poem is 'sad', but leaves her cold, despite the fact that she is able to interpret the destruction by the invisible worm in terms of 'killing somebody's love' – an interpretation that Janine (in Transcript 4) deliberately refuses to pursue further than recognizing that the rose may represent beauty.

What I can see, like I've already said, is a man sort of bleeding . . . being cut by a rose . . . his heart bleeding . . . he's given the rose to a girl and she hasn't accepted it . . . she said 'No, I don't want *your* love', or something like that (something silly!) and he died from that . . . and his love is destroyed 'cos of this rose that she didn't accept. I don't know why . . . .

This reader is confident enough to admit the symbolism into her personal re-enactment of the poem's meaning, despite the judgement that it is a 'silly' emotion. Yet, to cope with the symbolism, she works it into a simple story.

Transcript 6

'The Sick Rose'

Group Discussion	*Commentary*
(Natalie reads the poem aloud)	
Michele 1: I think it means . . . right? . . . it's very sad and I think somebody's lover has died. I think he had a rose in his hand and . . .	Michele attempts to get the conversation started by testing her personal theory, detailed on her tape.
Janine 1: Did anybody find out what 'crimson' meant?	Janine, characteristically, is concerned first with vocabulary difficulties.
Natalie 1: It's a red . . . a red colour isn't it?	
Leigh 1: It's a colour of joy.	Leigh enters earlier in this discussion and succeeds in making a vital contribution to the sharing of responses.
N.2: What's the 'invisible worm'?	
M.2: That's the thing that's destroying the rose but . . . has it got a deep meaning or something?	
J.2: I just thought that it was . . sort of . . . a worm is like a black fly or something . . . something.	Like Michele, Janine also 'uses' her initial jottings.

121

N.3: Yeah. I tried to find a meaning but I couldn't . . . I suppose it's just about a worm.

J.3: 'Cos those little bugs . . . you can't really see them like can you? . . . that's why he says 'invisible'. And 'flies through the night' . . . it settles on the bed . . . 'cos like bees are attracted to . . .

N.4: But why's the rose 'sick'?

M.3: 'Cos it's being eaten by the bugs.

J.4: So they settle on the rose . . . they kill the rose by sitting on it . . . and sucking the thing out of it.

N.5: But . . . the 'R' is a capital . . . like a girl's name.

L.2: In the verse, it's a bit like a poltergeist . . . like 'the invisible worm in the night . . . in the howling storm' and . . . 'has *found* thy bed', so it could be coming back to (inde-cipherable) . . . memories.

M.4: Yeah.

N.6: Eh?

M.5: Yeah . . . 'invisible' . . . .

N.7: That's really good . . .

J.5: But it's nothing to do with the rose though!

L.3: 'And its dark secret love' . . . so she

A 'story' is initiated, despite the reference to a girl's name. Excited telling follows which breaks the flow, leaving early ideas 'un-finished' as a rush of possibilities arise. This element of response was missing from the first discussion which included the teacher.

The 'natural' storyteller continues . . .

M.6: probably killed him or something . . .
N.8: She killed him and the last thing he . . .
M.7: That's a good idea isn't it?
 The last thing that she gave him was a rose, or he gave her . . .
N.9: No . . . that could just be . . . her name . . . or it could be just a way of describing her, 'cos maybe she was like . . .
J.6: Listen . . . if it's *sick* . . . then the poltergeist has come come back to . . .
M.8: I know. The poltergeist has come back to . . . to try and make the rose better.
N.10: No . . . he wants her to die with him or something.
L.4: Or if rose is the name . . . Rose could be the poltergeist.
N.11: No!
J.7: No . . . it's not, 'cos otherwise 'thou art sick' . . . 'cos it's . . .
N.12: I don't understand why it says *sick* . . . (reads lines) – and 'the howling storm' – what's the howling storm?
J.8: Yeh . . . but . . . it wouldn't have a 'crimson joy' would it?
N.13: . . . the anger . . . the anger that he's feeling. . .
L.5: The poltergeist causes the . . .
N.14: Anger . . . .

This question is never answered though the readers move on to show their understanding of the idea of symbolism – i.e. things 'standing for' other things. This understanding becomes explicit at N.25.

123

L.6: Yeah.
J.9: But it wouldn't have the 'crimson joy' would it? . . . 'cos that's deep red. That's nothing to do with it is it?
N.15: Red joy . . .
L.7: No . . . he's found a 'bed of crimson joy' which, if it's Rose, the name, he's . . .
N.16: See, that's how . . .
L.8: . . . She's happy . . .
N.17: If she'd have murdered him that would be red . . . blood . . . you know . . . 'crimson joy', . . . so she'd be . . .
M.9: Yeah, she'd be happy then.
(General agreement)
And she destroyed his love . . .
N.18: He's destroying *her* . . . .
J.10: A rose is always thought of being the most beautiful flower isn't it?
M.10: Yeah, but it can be . . . the pricks . . . .
N.19: Yeah, 'cos it's the flower of love isn't it?
J.11: Yeah, it could be a really beautiful girl that's destroyed his love . . . ages ago . . . and he went out and killed himself or something, and he's come to . . . something like that.
N.20: Yeah, cos it's . . . .
M.11: He's the worm!
J.12: . . . 'cos it's 'his dark secret love', so it must

Natalie reuses the idea of Leigh suggested in L.1.

Janine's use of her initial jottings gets her closest to breaking free from her fear of *not* understanding.

124

have been . . . he's come back to get her . . .
(pause)

N.21: I don't *get* it anyway! So . . .

M.12: I think it's a silly poem anyway, 'cos it's too short . . . it doesn't explain it . . .

J.13: I don't think it's got any deep meaning, like the other one.

N.22: 'Cos of William Blake, you *think* it's got a deep meaning though, 'cos of the last one.

J.14: I couldn't . . . I didn't know what it was until that bug thing but as it . . . .

N.23: It's all in Old English, that 'thou' and 'thy' and all that.

L.9: No but . . . the worm . . . it's always wriggling places . . . trying to get in places to find out things . . . so where it says 'the invisible worm', it can't be seen. It's always creeping in places, trying to find out things about . . . the rose.

N.24: That's why it could be a ghost or whatever you said.

M.13: It could be a . . . .

N.25: But why worm? . . . Oh yeah. The rose and the worm are just symbolizing it aren't they? Could be . . . 'cos a worm destroys the rose . . . it could just be symbolic.

Past experience is important here in bringing Natalie to the idea of symbolism which eventually allows her to synthesize a full response to the poem.

From this silence in the first discussion, Leigh emerges as a stimulating contributor – he offers a hypothetical and 'open' approach to the seeking out of meaning.

Natalie and Leigh are 'feeding off' each other's ideas very profitably, despite the fact that two other readers are offering suggestions too. Natalie again shows a clear understanding of symbolism.

J.15: I think it could be somebody . . .

L.10: Where it says 'has found out thy bed' . . . it's found out the secret of the rose.

J.16: Yeah but . . . I don't think it is a person though, I think it's something to do with nature.

M.14: Well it could be both . . .

L.11: The first verse could be explaining what it goes through during the winter . . . the weather.

N.26: (excitedly) A flowerbed . . . 'cos you know worms *undermine* the rose, 'cos it would go in the earth . . .

In finding this apt term. Natalie makes the poem her own.

M.15: That's right . . .

N.27: . . . and undermine . . . .

J.17: Kill the roots or something!

N.28: Yeah! I've just realised (very excited).

L.12: It destroys its life . . . .
So we've got two meanings for the poem.

Leigh summarizes. It is interesting to note how he assumes such a leading role here, in contrast to the first discussion where he said so little (see Transcript 2).

J.18: It could either be the bug on top of the . . .

M.16: 'Has found out thy bed' is the worm going into the bed, destroying the roots of the rose . . . 'of crimson joy, And his dark secret love' . . . Does thy life destroy' . . . so the love, of being in the air, free and everything . . .

J.19: It could be one of those blackfly creatures

126

M.17: that land on the thing and suck up all the . . . what's inside the . . .

L.13: Puss . . . sap . . . But if the poem refers to a woman's . . . a girl's name, I don't think it would be called 'The Sick Rose', it would be called 'Rose, The Sick'.

N.29: It might not have done . . . that was the opinion of the poet to call it 'The Sick Rose'.

M.18: But I can't work out the title . . . it seems stupid . . .

N.30: Because as the worm gets deeper and deeper . . . it gets sicker and sicker, because it's having its life ripped out.

M.19: . . . I know, the worm might be trying to help the rose . . . to live . . . but it can't 'cos . . .

J.20: I thought that the worm or bug or whatever . . . tries to help the rose by settling on it and by trying to give it fluid . . . or whatever it does . . . and it's sucking into it or something. And by doing it, it kills the rose. But I think it must represemble [sic] something of evil and beauty . . . 'cos a rose is beauty and the . . .

N.31: 'cos he's always doing that in his poems . . .

127

J.21: and the worm is trying to kill it and it's evil, so beauty and evil . . . any views of that?

N.32: Yeah, like Beauty and the Beast.

J.22: I've just thought of something . . . it's really horrible. There's something in there that's trying to get through (laughs) . . .
Maybe it's something like that!
So a rose is always beautiful and a worm is something evil.

L.14: Yeah, the rose could be good and the . . .

N.33: . . . worm is evil, referring to the Tyger . . .

N.34: A worm is good but it's horrible compared to a rose . . .

(*Teacher joins the group*)

Having refused to recognize the power of symbolism in her initial jottings, the discussion has led Janine to see the sexual connotations of the destructive force. The learning potential of such a process is thus highlighted.

(iv) Meeting a Jaguar

The focus of the third enquiry was to investigate further the role of the teacher in small group discussion work with particular reference to pupils' and teachers' questions. Thus far, I have presented learning as something which the learner does, and which the teacher cannot do for him. I have argued that in finding words to express ideas and feelings to others, the reader will be reshaping them for himself. It cannot be assumed, however, that this reshaping will go on whenever a group of readers is put together; task planning is necessary. The quality of the discussion, and therefore the quality of the learning, is not determined solely by the ability of the readers. The nature of the task, their familiarity with the poetic text, their confidence in themselves, their sense of what is expected of them, all affect the quality of the discussion, and these factors are all open to influence by the teacher. At this stage of the enquiry, I was particularly concerned with what the teacher can do to contribute to successful discussion of a poem by taking part in it. To ask how and whether a teacher should intervene, and to what end, then necessarily follows.

The findings of my comparative investigation of the group's discussion of poems, with and without the teacher, detailed earlier in this chapter, suggest that readers left on their own talk more fruitfully than when under the guidance of a teacher. The research of Williams (1971), supports this notion:

> They talk more, and with more vitality and involvement; they are freer to explore their own feelings; they don't linger impressively, conclusively, but they cover the same ground and are far less restricted in their range of enquiry. [7]

This is not surprising because I acknowledge from the evidence of my own attempt to join the group after their unsupervised discussion of 'The Sick Rose' that, like many teachers, I am inclined to direct and therefore, restrict overmuch.

The nub of this problem is how to encourage children to talk as well *with* the teacher present as they appear to do *without* his presence.

It is understandable that teachers feel a need to be present at some stage in group discussions in order to ensure that some form of learning is going on and that time is not being wasted. Perhaps if group conversations were regularly recorded on tape (which immediately raises the problems of classroom layout, architecture, and availability of tape-recorders), or if reporting back on a discussion was encouraged, then a real concern with a reader's need to share ideas and feeling about literature could be stimulated. It would also signal genuine interest in children's oral development. Such practices could also serve to quiet the teacher's concern that he may be abdicating his duty in taking some responsibility for what his pupils learn in such discussion work. However, as Douglas Barnes (1976) points out, such 'reporting back' alters the kind of talk and the pace of group discussions, though he also suggests that this is not necessarily harmful to active learning.[8]

Such methods of monitoring response to literature would enable the teacher to listen to and learn from the tape-recorded transcriptions or written reports of 'open' discussions and could encourage a shift of focus from the over-emphasis on 'finished' writing. Individual and group tape-recordings could point teachers toward a more balanced provision of opportunities for children to show their personal reading styles as well as their 'learning'.

Students' and teachers' questions need particularly close investigation. The relatively small number of questions asked by pupils themselves in the traditional classroom raises the problem of what determines the rate of question asking. It is clearly impossible to monitor such activity by recording whole class lessons, and as Barnes (1971) emphasizes:

> . . . a teacher may unintentionally brush away pupils' contributions which are perfectly valid but which in the flow of the lesson he fails to recognize. Some teachers, however, are able to draw pupils more actively into the formulating of knowledge, so that what is accepted as valid . . . is the result of negotiation between pupil and teacher.[9]

Such negotiation, whatever methods are employed, aims to raise the value of contributions to discussion in the pupils' own eyes and seeks to encourage the learner to struggle to sort out something for himself or for someone who really wants to know. Hence, my intention to investigate the role of the teacher in small discussion group work begins with the notion of fostering negotiation between teacher and pupils.

In setting up the reading and discussion group activities concerned with 'The Jaguar', a copy of the poem was given to the readers one week in advance of the discussion session. The poet's name was deleted because 'The Warm and the Cold', another poem by Ted Hughes, had been used in the Pilot Study – a fact which was recognized by one particularly alert reader who could see the stylistic similarity in the two texts (see Transcript Eight). The pupils were simply asked to read the poem carefully before the next session.

At the beginning of the session, I read the poem to the group, then asked for questions to be written down with the intention of using the readers' questions as the springboard into a group discussion. As in Alcock's study (1976), I suspected that perhaps finding the right questions might be, at first, more useful than finding answers to less important questions.[10] Earlier sessions had pointed out the importance of continual reference to personal experience as a reader's major method of questioning, considering and understanding a poem. Personal 'stories' appeared to be the basic fabric of such conversations, the *means* by which readers enter into other people's experiences, try them on for size, and advance into generalizations. The role of the pupils' own questions appeared to be vital to this reshaping of experience.

The readers produced the following questions, given here as a group effort to avoid duplication:

Boa-constrictor's coil – why a fossil?
What does 'fatigued with indolence' mean?
'mesmerized?
Why is it called 'The Jaguar'?
'drills of his eyes'?
'visionary his cell'?
Why is it 'breathing straw'?
Why does the fourth line start on the next verse again?

Transcript Eight shows how some of these pupil-initiated questions were used by the group. This method most certainly helped to avoid the teacher being cast in the role of indirectly asking the children: 'Can you guess what I'm thinking? Can you guess the answer I want someone to give me?'

The pupils' questions focus intently on the poem itself. At this stage, there is no movement outside, beyond the poem into individual experience. However, by maintaining the strategy of basing the conversation upon the pupils' questions, my own questions reinforce or expand them, as my statements recapitulate their own discoveries. The students do not find explanations from the teacher, nor do I offer totally new questions when their own questions go unanswered. Instead, a pupil's question is used to enable the sense of discovery to revive (T.12, T.14). The problem for the teacher is to avoid rigid direction. The pupils, in fact, respond to the flexible structure which creates a sense of discovery. The right 'tone' is critical and is carried not only in the words but in intontation, gesture, expression, and even in the context of the discussion – by the way in which expectations are set up from what had been previously said and done.

An utterance count of the discussion demonstrates that every individual played a full part in sharing ideas and feelings about the poem:

Natalie – 43
Michele – 32
Janine – 31
Teacher – 28
Leigh – 26

The teacher did not do most of the talking, but played a crucial role in discussing the poem in a speculative tone of voice, reinforcing the pupils' hypotheses in a tentative, thoughtful, reflective manner. Such a stance allows each reader to co-operate at the same time as operating as an individual and encourages tentative enquiry. Notice, for example, how the use of words like: 'think', 'seems', 'probably', 'perhaps' indicate the creative element in the enquiry process.

The findings summarized below were investigated further in other sessions which concentrated on the group, including the teacher, meeting an unseen poem together without preparatory readings. As far as this group was concerned, the enquiries suggested that where a poem is easily assimilated and concerns a familiar topic, pupils' questions are varied in purpose and form. Often, they will be directed to related matters of special interest to the individuals. Some students appear to prefer such confirmatory discussions. However, when assimilation is blocked, pupils' questions tend to concentrate mainly within the text itself and on its interpretation. It is here that the teachers' supplementary questions and his structuring of pupils' questions is of critical importance. Alcock (1976), neatly sums up my own findings in the following statement:

> Students may be able to discuss without the teacher at times, but the teacher ultimately has a vital role, not only in formulating the most helpful supplementary questions and in using students' questions in a structure which will aid a discussion that might otherwise grind to a halt. His summaries of answers are most valuable in clarifying discussion and in giving a new 'take-off point' when discussion becomes repetitive and nonprogressive.[11]

If pupils' questions fall flat, a teacher needs to be ready to encourage, stimulate and guide by asking questions that open up possibilities. In this respect, if students learn how to enquire both by enquiring themselves and by observing others do so, then the teacher's questions can serve as a guide to the enquiry process itself.

'*The Jaguar*' *Ted Hughes*
Transcript Seven   Individual tape-recorded response
                    Michele
Transcript Eight   Group discussion, including the
                    teacher-researcher

The Jaguar

The apes yawn and adore their fleas in the sun.
The parrots shriek as if they were on fire, or strut
Like cheap tarts to attract the stroller with the nut.
Fatigued with indolence, tiger and lion

Lie still as the sun. The boa-constrictor's coil
Is a fossil. Cage after cage seems empty, or
Stinks of sleepers from the breathing straw.
It might be painted on a nursery wall.

But who runs like the rest past these arrives
At a cage where the crowd stands, stares, mesmerized,
As a child at a dream, at a jaguar hurrying enraged
Through prison darkness after the drills of his eyes

On a short fierce fuse. Not in boredom –
The eye satisfied to be blind in fire,
By the bang of blood in the brain deaf the ear –
He spins from the bars, but there's no cage to him

More than to the visionary his cell:
His stride is wildernesses of freedom:
The world rolls under the long thrust of his heel.
Over the cage floor the horizons come.

Ted Hughes

Transcript 7

Michele: 'The Jaguar'

Individual Tape-recorded Responses	*Commentary*

Individual Tape-recorded Responses

. . . It's Sunday. I look at it and I don't really understand it, but I've just written in my book . . . and I'm slowly beginning to unravel the poem.

Reads: 'The apes yawn and adore their fleas in the sun'. I think that describes the apes slowly waking up . . . and they're inspecting each other for fleas, 'cos they do, don't they? Inspect each other's fur, to get the fleas out . . . in the sun.

Reads: 'The parrots shriek as if they were on fire, or strut Like cheap tarts to attract the stroller with a nut'. I think that means when they shriek in the morning – yarhh – like that . . . they're on fire, sort of like they're screaming in a burning house or something. And they strut like a tart in London . . . to try to attract the boys, . . . but they're not attracting boys . . . they're trying to attract people . . . yeh, people outside of their cages who are feeding them with nuts which you can buy. (Excitedly), Ah, yeh! *Reads*: 'fatigued with indolence' . . . don't get that bit!

Reads: 'tiger and lion lie still as the sun'. That means they're all quiet and being sort of . . . just waking up . . . . still, before they wake up.

Commentary

First reading. Note how a second attempt is made two days later. (Her personal journal.) Michele later makes use of her jottings in the group discussion. Michele employs a line-by-line, close analysis method in preparing for the group work.

Michele makes full use of the space she finds by using this method of analysis. She makes the poem her own by freely admitting difficulty alongside a growing excitement at finding meaning for herself.

Another reader, in the group discussion, has problems interpreting this image. Michele however, achieves a very clear picture that allows her to understand the purpose behind the chosen words.

Articulating her difficulties produces questions that can be opened up to discussion with the other readers. At the same time, Michele will clearly have much to offer in sharing her own ideas and feelings.

What might appear to be a rather restricting, linear method of close examination of the text is seen here to work very successfully for Michele. Her readings

Reads: 'The boa-constrictor's coil is a fossil'. Well, when you've got a fossil . . . it's all sort of ravelled up and indented, so the boa-constrictor's indented in, like a coil . . . it means he's sort of like a fossil 'cos he doesn't move . . . soundless . . . but he's still alive sort of thing.

Reads: 'cage after cage seems empty or stinks of sleepers' Well I think the cages *seem* empty because there's no life, at the moment, they're all asleep.

Reads: 'stinks of sleepers from the breathing straw' – I don't understand that bit, or *reads*: 'might be painted on a nursery wall' – I don't understand that either.

Reads: 'But who runs like the rest past these arrives At a cage where the crowd stands, stares, mesmerized'. I think that means . . . they're going to sort of see a new arrival. They all stand there gazing at it . . . mesmerized . . . hypnotized by it. Like an owl sort of looking at you . . . staring at you . . . hypnotizing you.

Reads: 'As a child at a dream' . . . I think the child at a dream means that it's sort of like a dream to a child . . . a dream come true, 'cos he hasn't been to the zoo before, because I think they're in a zoo.

Reads: 'at a jaguar hurrying enraged Through prison darkness after the drills of his eyes' . . . means that he's very sad, and annoyed that he's been taken into and comments are after all, only a first stage in coming to terms with the text – an initial exploration which will be used as a foundation for further consideration.

captivity. He's being held, as it were, like a prisoner. And the drills . . . the sort of the daily drill like going through feeding time . . . seeing the visitors . . . dinner time . . . sort of all like that. Daily drills. *Reads*: 'short fuse' . . . I think he's just got to the end of his tether now . . .

Reads: 'Not in boredom – the eye satisfied to be blind in fire', . . . I think that he's not all that bored, he's satisfied to a certain content . . . to a certain amount . . . but, he's not *very* content, he's sort of blind. He's going, blind with enragement and and boredom.

I think when it says, *Reads*: 'By the bang of blood in the brain deaf the ear' – it means he's trying to get out, and he's trying so hard that he's jumping up against the cage . . . and he's banging his ear, and making it bleed . . . banging his brains out sort of thing. 'Cos it says . . .

Reads: 'He spins from the bars, but there's no cage to him' . . . that's sort of like . . . he spins . . . he jumps up and he gets down, dazed and he spins around . . . but he can't really see any . . . he can't really see any cage because he's been blinded by the boredom.

Reads: 'More than to the visionary his cell . . . I don't understand the last verse, *at all*!

Right, it's now Tuesday and I've come back to it . . . and I still think the same about the first four . . . paragraphs, but looking at the fifth paragraph, I understand it a bit more. *Reads*: 'More than to the visionary his cell . . . His stride is wildernesses of freedom' . . . I think that's meaning that his visionary cell and wilderness freedom . . . mean that he's not really going to go, but he's *imagining* it . . . he thinks that he's going to go . . . he's just got a little sort of . . . in the back of his mind . . . that he could possibly get out, but he know it's not true. He'll never get out! *Reads*: 'The world rolls under the long thrust of his heel' . . . I think that means that cats are supposed to be kings of the jungle . . . aren't they? So he thinks that everybody's under his heel and he's the one . . . he's the king . . . and, *Reads*: 'Over the cage floor the horizons come' . . . I think that means it's beyond the horizons of him, you know? . . . but they're still coming to him, they're still there . . . in his mind. But he knows they're just not going to happen! I don't really think the poem's about a jaguar . . . I think it's about the animals waking up . . . in a zoo . . . but the jaguar's only got about the last two verses about him . . . all the three verses are about the animals in the zoo and everything like that.

Contrast this statement with the earlier bewilderment: 'I don't understand the last verse at all!'

Time has produced a more rich and full understanding of captivity in a zoo.

Here Michele is close to understanding how the poet has used the jaguar. In sharing her carefully considered response with the other readers in the group discussion that follows, one can see how important her two 'readings' have been to her making a full engagement with the puzzle of the poem. Such a process of discovery will be used to enmesh individual understanding with group collaboration.

Transcript 8

'The Jaguar'

	Group Discussion	*Commentary*
Teacher 1:	Right. Let's use *your* questions then.	The posing of the question – hearing it
Natalie 1:	Why does it say 'The boa-constrictor's coil is	aloud, begins to provide an answer.
	a fossil'? (pause)	
	Well is it because it's so still?	
Michele 1:	It's still like a fossil – fossils are sort of cap-	Michele is interested in the form of the
	tured for ages . . . preserved.	poem. I judged it inappropriate to talk of
M.2:	Why does he end the sentence suddenly and	enjambment at such an early stage in the
	go on to the next paragraph? . . . 'cos when	discussion, thus avoiding the 'teaching' role.
	I was reading it, I wasn't reading it right.	
Janine 1:	What's mesmerized mean?	
	(silence)	
T.2:	If you mesmerize somebody, you do it	In contrast, it seemed necessary to provide
	generally with your eyes . . . fix somebody	the required information in this instance,
	in a stare, like . . .	following silence.
N.2:	. . . you're hypnotized . . . That's what	
	snakes do!	
Leigh 1:	The crowd just stare . . .	
J.2:	I thought of 'The Elephant Man' when I	
	read that. It was the first thing I wrote down	
	when I read it . . . I watched the film where	

everybody just stares at him . . . it reminded me of that, staring.

T.3: They were fascinated . . . in the freak-show circus, with his ugliness. Just like William Blake being fascinated by the beauty of a rose. That's a good connection . . . it makes. a lot of sense.

N.3: Why's it called 'The Jaguar'?

M.3: . . . it hasn't anything to do with a jaguar.

N.4: I mean . . . it only comes in the third . . .

M.4: I thought it was going to be all about jaguars . . . like 'The Tyger' . . . but it's not all to do with him.

N.5: It's different . . .

T.4: It uses the jaguar as one animal among many . . . but it picks up the jaguar especially. Leigh – you mentioned that?

L.2: It's the first time he's been behind bars like . . . it's explaining his first morning.

T.5: Where's this set?

All: In a zoo!

M.5: When you read it first, I thought it was about the jungle.

N.6: No, but, you can tell . . . when it says . . . after 'the stroller with the nut'.

M.6: 'Cage after cage seems empty'. You can tell there.

This is an attempt to encourage such personal associations as Janine's above. It is also an honest attempt to connect the idea with the previous experience of the group.

A direct attempt to involve Leigh. Janine plays this role later in the discussion (see J.14).

N.7: The jaguar can't *accept* being caged up.

T.6: Well let's look at the other animals first then.

N.8: The apes accept being caged!
Reads: 'The parrots shriek . . . or strut like cheap tarts'

M.7: I like that line . . .

J.3: Yeh, it's really good. You can see it . . .

M.8: . . . sort of like prostitutes in London

J.4: *posing*, sort of . . .
(Natalie demonstrates the strutting to the amusement of all).

T.7: 'Fatigued with indolence, tiger and lion lie still as the sun'.

N.9: Well, if they were in the jungle, they'd be running about. That's why I thought it must be a zoo there. (pause)

J.5: Sphinxs

N.10: You know where they're going (demonstrates the cat-like posture, again amusing all)

M.9: You know . . . the sun never moves . . . .

N.11: It does . . . it moves 'round the . . .

L.3: But you don't see it move . . . it's fixed in one spot.

J.6: Not as good as the cheap tarts!

The finding of a single word stirs a rush of activity.

The teacher uses Natalie's method (see N.8) of reading aloud to redirect attention to the text. In this discussion, the teacher is not forcing a method upon the readers; he is following their lead.

Leigh adopts a logical, information-giving role.

T.8: Was 'cheap tarts' good because you actually *saw* the parrots wobbling? . . . (laughter and agreement)
Why parrots and cheap tarts?

N.12: The bright colours . . .

L.4: They're greedy as well.

J.7: . . loud . . . .

L.5: A tart's a person who puts loads of make-up on to attract the boys . . .

T.9: Well we started to look at the first verse . . . in detail . . . to see how the jaguar fitted in. Because you said the title makes you think it's about the jaguar, but it's about other things. Well we've just looked at how the start is all about other animals and it comes to the jaguar . . .

N.13: Yeh . . . it's a comparison between them and the jaguar.

J.8: Where does the jaguar come in and is it really a comparison?

M.10: Third verse . . . 'at a cage'.

N.14: Like a journey through the zoo . . . then you get the jaguar imagining himself free . . . so he's using a limited space to be the whole world. He's imagining . . . *in his mind*, he's gone back to . . . .

J.9: It says 'prison darkness' doesn't it?

Such a summary appears to be needed at this point. Sometimes the onus falls on the teacher in a small group discussion to provide the stimulus and encouragement for all the pupils to be actively involved.

Natalie plays a leading role throughout this discussion. Her perceptive comments are vital to the flow of the discussion.

141

L.6: So he's prowling . . . the others are just doing little, he's free.

M.11: He's *aware* . . . the others can't be bothered
any more.

N.15: 'Cage after cage seems empty' . . . there's
no life.

M.12: That's why I thought it was early morning . . . they're all in bed.

N.16: 'breathing straw'?

M.13: It camouflages them . . .

J.10: In their little holes . . .

L.7: You might smell them but you can't see
them.

M.14: Why's it '*breathing* straw'?

N.17: 'Cos they're breathing, asleep, I suppose . .
under the straw. The straw looks as though
it's moving . . .

T.10: So the idea of breathing is transferred from
the animal, underneath, to the straw.

J.11: I thought about 'Jungle Book' then, 'cos
I've got this little friend . . . and they've got
all . . . in their bedroom . . . all these pictures of snakes, beasts and that sort of
thing . . .

N.18: It might be a painting . . . so still . . .

M.15: I didn't understand that bit . . .

N.19: . . . everything's so still . . .

Note how this phase of the readers' talk
leads to Michele picturing the poem 'like a
picture 'round the wall' (M.16). This notion
of the 'story' of the poem existing like a
series of 'mental stills' characterizes
Michele's personal reading strategy. It can
be contrasted with Natalie's sense of the
poem's 'whole' meaning (N.20).

Natalie makes full use of Janine's idea. She
goes on to repeat the essential idea as if to
emphasize it to herself.

142

M.16: I didn't understand it before, but now we've gone through it, I do. Like a big picture 'round the wall . . .

N.20: So that line sums up . . . on its own . . . everything described up to then might just as well have been a picture. So instead of taking an animal and putting it in a cage, from freedom, to let people stare at it . . . they might just as well have seen a picture . . . (pause)

N.21: Locking the animals up takes *more* than their freedom away 'cos I mean, they die, in a way. They're all free and running about, but if you lock them up, you're sort of locking away their freedom and their life that they had before . . . and that was their natural life and so they don't know how to live.

J.12: They give up their will.

T.11: So the opening describes the zoo – how all the life has gone out of the animals. *Reads:* 'But who runs like the rest past these animals arrives At a cage . . .', so if you pass these animals, what is it that makes the crowd stand, stare; be mesmerized? 'as a child at a dream'.

J.13: That's really good, that line . . . when you're dreaming, you can imagine it . . . you

Natalie is now ready to expand the idea, by close reference to the text.
Natalie's sense of the 'whole' meaning of the poem is clarified by Michele's suggestion that the reader needs to 'picture' the 'story' of the poem . . . 'like a big picture 'round the wall'.

Natalie has come a long way. Her vigorous talk and relevant comments, analysis and evaluation, have not emerged with Wordsworthian spontaneity – *the questions asked by the other readers, and herself, have determined, more than any other factor, the quality of her answers.*

143

can see it, really real. A child might never have seen one in real life, and if they come along . . . they can see it, like a child for the . . . first time.

L.8: So now the jaguar comes in. Right in the middle of the poem.

M.17: I think that's quite good there, 'cos the jaguar's the subject and it brings you right back into it . . . like an . . . *impact.*

T.12: Well put. So the poet has saved up the jaguar? To come after the dull, lifeless animals. That's why Natalie used the word *contrast* earlier. It's been deliberately saved until the best moment, like Michele suggests. What do you think of it Leigh? (pause)

M.18: Now we get him, *annoyed* . . . cos he's in prison.

J.15: I think that's difficult to understand . . . and the next line.

T.13: *Reads:* 'stares . . . at a jaguar hurrying enraged Through prison darkness after the drills of his eyes on a short fierce fuse'.

N.22: Is that meaning, he's trying to get free? . . . like drilling through the bars.

L.9: He's in a darkness . . . he's trying to get through . . . but it says in the next verse, 'The eye satisfied to be blind in fire.'

Note the sensitivity of Janine to the dynamics of the group. Leigh doesn't respond to this prompt – not until his own ideas are clarified by the others (see L.10).

144

N.23: If the fire is his anger, then he would be satisfied ... no ... I don't know ... if the fire was his anger then he'd be satisfied with ... I can't say it. He's satisfied with being *angry*.

L.10: ... his anger ... like a fire, he's trying to get through ...

J.16: He's like a ball of fire ... he'll get through the bars in the end.

M.19: Yeh ... he's determined to get through.

N.24: So he's still got his anger – in his eyes – he's still got fire in his belly. He'd like to get out and rip a few people apart ... for doing this to him. Isn't that it? He's happy in that ... it's his anger that keeps him going.
(Discussion of prisons followed).

T.14: Isn't that similar to what the jaguar has?

N.25: He has his anger ... his fire. All he sees is his anger ... he's 'blind in fire'.

M.20: He's not accepted it ... yeh ... all the other animals have. That's why I thought he was new ... it sounds like he's just come there and he can't accept that he's in captivity. The others have been there a long time and they have.

N.26: Unless there's something *special* about a jaguar – like they never settle.

Natalie's interpretation once again 'fires' the enthusiasm of the whole group. Her tentative suggestions show the importance of asking hypothetical questions in a context of 'open' discussion.

This involved a consideration of how hatred of a warder may keep a prisoner going while locked up. The idea of 'feeding' off hatred was carefully explored.

Returns to her original question. 'Why is it called 'The Jaguar'? Different words are

145

M.21: They don't . . . they're the fastest, full of energy . . . the fittest.

L.11: If he's only just got there, the other animals been there a long time . . .

N.27: And he's angered by their . . .

L.12: He doesn't want that to happen to him.

N.28: 'Cos their lack of . . . they don't care . . . that makes him angry even more.

M.22: I think he's shut his ears off to the world . . . he doesn't hear anybody, except only the padding of his own feet. He's trying to get out . . . 'the bang of blood in the brain' . . . he tries to get out the cage, he jumps up at the bars, he bangs his head . . . (general laughter) . . . then he turns round, like in the cartoons . . .

N.29: I've just thought of something . . . because if you shot him, that would be 'bang of blood in the brain' so that would be like killing him – like taking him away from freedom – so that's just like what's happened to him.

L.13: Like he's wrapped up in himself – deaf – in his own anger . . . not aware of what's around him – like the darkness earlier.

J.17: This is really bugging me. I like this poem

---

used, but the same question is asked again.

I wanted to inject ideas here about how the poet is obviously impressed by a 'special' quality in the jaguar. I deliberately held back to see if the readers would begin to relate their own experiences of zoo visits, without direct prompting.

Michele's idea, rejected in a sense by the group's laughter, is taken up by Natalie and ultimately helps her to clarify her thinking.

but I don't understand half of it! No . . . but if . . . can you like a poem when you don't understand it?

T.15: I think you can.

A deliberately short response. Janine raises an interesting and important question about responding to poems, but at this point in the discussion, I decided not to interrupt the flow of the group's concentration on this particular text in favour of exploring such a general issue.

J.18: I like it a lot . . . I think it's the best poem we've done, but . . . the third and fourth verse . . .

T.16: Well we might not understand *every* detail, but have you got a good sense of the jaguar's rage? Maybe that's enough if you've got so far . . .

J.19: I don't think he's expressed it very well.

T.17: The word order is the difficult bit – change the order a bit . . . So 'He spins from the bars', . . . turns around . . .

M.23: Oh – I imagined a cartoon where he jumps and spins around.

A simple, but very helpful prompt.

L.14: He goes up and down – he spins 'round as soon as he reaches the bars.

M.24: Yeh, but why does he do that?

N.30: He hopes the bars won't be there.

L.15: 'But there's no cage to him'. We've just said he's still free in his own head . . . he hasn't accepted it . . .

N.31: Yeh.

L.16: . . . so 'there's no cage to him'.

M.25: Like a bird going into a window, thinking

that there's nothing there . . . a moth or something. He won't understand what's there. A bird has to accept its cage, otherwise it'll keep flying into the bars . . . this jaguar goes up and down *daring* the bars to contain him.

N.32: He's just in his own little world.

T.18: The acres of his jungle have shrunk down and he's saying, this is still mine . . .

N.33: Yeh, he's just expanded it all . . . in his head.

M.26: So he doesn't see the bars . . . so he says 'Oh well, I'll go over there today' . . . and it's not . . .
(pause)

M.27: . . . like he decides where he'll go, as far as *he* wants to go.

J.20: I've just seen a bit and I really don't know what it is. Is 'His stride is wildernesses of freedom' . . . is it every time he walks he wishes he was free? . . . and so he . . . I can't describe it.

T.19: What you're saying Janine, is pretty well what we're talking about now. What that line does is it . . *encapsulates* . . do you you remember that word, about the

Specific knowledge of readers can greatly aid a teacher in producing appropriate responses to pupils' questions. Here, specific help is given to Janine, based on shared experience of a previously considered poem. (See Pilot Study) Janine's confidence is low at this stage – perhaps such a response will help maintain her interest and encourage her to persevere.

spit? . . . it wraps up what we're talking about.

L.17: What about 'More than to the visionary his cell'?

J.21: People are looking into it . . . and imagine different things than he does when he looks out . . .

N.34: His cell appears to the outsiders as a cell . . . but to him it's . . .

J.22: It's *not* a cell, it's his own world. His own world in there. You just look at vision and you know what that is . . .

T.20: So suppose you're in class and there's a really rotten lesson going on . . . you're bored. And . . . so what you do is you . . . say to yourself, 'You've got me in this classroom until the bell goes, you're boring me . . . but you haven't got me really because in my mind . . . I'm having all kinds of good ideas. In there is mine! You can't get in there!'

L.18: So a visionary has like . . . free thoughts . . . like a prisoner can be locked up . . . but you can't lock up his mind. If he can keep freedom in his head, he's not really

Leigh takes up the idea and uses it with great insight. The reference to comparative experience solves the difficulty for one reader.

locked in . . . Is that what the jaguar's doing? Is he still free? . . . 'there's no cage to him' . . . Natalie said the same thing at the beginning . . .

J.23: Now you've read the first line . . . it makes more sense. If he's free in his own mind and so he thinks he's somewhere else . . . so the stride he walks, he thinks he's somewhere else, in the jungle . . .

L.19: . . . for every stride he takes, the more freedom he wants . . .

J.24: I like this verse best because I . . . especially, 'The world rolls under the long thrust of his heel' . . . that's really good that . . .

M.28: I think it means the world is his stride when they move their paws, sort of like rolling . . .

N.35: Yeh, but he's accepted being in a zoo by doing that!

L.20: Why?

J.25: He covers the whole world with his thoughts . . . that's quite good in it? – I hadn't seen that! It's the whole world in his mind. I didn't understand it when I read it but I've written down that that's my best bit . . . but now . . . it's *really* good in it?

Janine's confidence has returned. The mutual support of the group has helped her through her bewilderment.

150

Now she feels confident enough to make judgments. Earlier, she predominantly sought solutions to interpretative difficulties.

T.21: And the last line? . . . 'Over the cage floor the horizons come', . . .

J.26: Brilliant! . . . I think that whole last verse is brilliant . . . You can see, just outside the cage . . . everything coming true . . .

N.36: How about when the sun rises, out of the darkness, 'cos it was all dark before . . . now he can *see*, in his head . . .

L.21: I've just had a weird idea. He might have been locked up and that . . . and he's thinking back . . . while asleep, about the past. He's just woken up . . . back to reality like. (pause)

L.22: Like the second half is in the jungle for the *jaguar* . . . against the opening description of the zoo.

M.29: I reckon he's thinking about wider horizons . . . like I'll get out one day, but he knows he never will.

J.27: His future . . .

M.30: . . . he's thinking beyond the horizon . . . because you can never catch the horizon can you? You can never catch up with it, so he'll never really be able to get out.

J.28: Looking at a horizon . . . you can see your future . . . where you're going to go, from then on . . .

151

N.37: His world is rolling under his paws.
J.29: I really like that . . . it's really good.
N.38: I do too. I think it's really powerful.
M.31: I like it too. I didn't when I first read it.
J.30: I knew it wouldn't be boring . . . even
       though I didn't understand it, I knew it
       wasn't a boring poem . . . like William
       Blake's . . . I couldn't get into that.
N.39: I could!
T.22: That's personal taste isn't it?
N.40: But I didn't like it from the start, because
       the first time I read it, we had a really bor-
       ing teacher so . . .
L.23: It's between alright and good.
T.23: I've enjoyed talking through it with you.
J.31: It's much better talking with a group than
       talking . . . than talking separately . . .
T.24: It's interesting that Natalie sort of had a
       sense of the whole poem, early on, and you
       were still worrying about certain bits Janine.
       Maybe there's something to learn from that?
       (General discussion followed about visiting
       zoos and safari parks)
L.24: It reminds me of a zoo . . . a snow leopard
       going up and down.
T.25: Did you wonder why it did that?

A preparatory conversation about visiting
caged animals might have enhanced the
group's discussion. It has taken a long time

L.25: Not at the time.

T.26: If we went to a zoo together now, it would be interesting to see if people do hurry past . . . to watch such an animal. The poet suggests that for him, and the people visiting the zoo, the most fascinating animal is the one that hasn't accepted its restrictions. Maybe that's true of people?

N.41: It could be about how some people accept . . . they just accept being . . . led, and some are leaders.

T.27: Like getting institutionalized. People in a school, ring a bell every so often, and they never think about what they're doing . . . they just react to one bell after the next.

L.26: At the end of a lesson, the bell goes . . . you want to quickly rush out, but really you don't want to go to the next lesson.

M.32: Yeh, I know, that's what I've wondered . . . like escaping one 'cell' to go to another one . . . and sometimes you leave a lesson that's not bad, to go to one that you know is going to be awful – without thinking.

N.42: I've never thought of that . . . even if you're enjoying the lesson . . . yeh! . . . but you might want to get to your freedom . . . like dinner time . . . the quicker you're free.

for a reader to tell of his personal experience.

Only Natalie appears to take up the idea of applying the idea to people.

153

T.28: Like free in your thoughts?
But some people seem to be able to keep
more of their freedom than others . . .

N.43: That Jaguar stands apart . . . from all the
other animals.

Throughout this session, the individuals
involved have shown an uninhibited,
creative stance which remains flexible and
open to the intake of ideas. The atmosphere
of collaborative activity also points to the
teacher's role being critical. A constant care
for the individual and his self-esteem
appears to be crucial. This may mean disturbing any complacency with a challenge. It
may also mean, where pupils' questions fail,
that the teacher's questions must encourage,
guide and stimulate. Such questions should
open the way to discovery; they should not
test or instruct directly, although one can see
in this transcript how pupils learn to enquire
both by enquiring themselves and by observing others do so. Both pupils' and teacher's
questions can be a stimulating guide to the
enquiry process.

D The Stages of Response

The main concern of this series of enquiries was both to explore responses to poetic texts and to investigate and strive for successful practices in teaching methodology. My role as teacher-researcher was certainly enjoyable and rewarding because of the interest and quality of the four readers' efforts. By attempting to honour the individuality of their responses and observe what committed readers 'do' with poems, some pointers towards a rationale for helping children respond positively to poetry have hopefully been suggested as well as stimulating opportunities for further enquiries.

Studies of this kind may well be able to begin to construct a picture of what it means to be 'inside' a poem. Such 'response research' may also illuminate how the transactional relationship between author and reader creatively brings about the personal satisfactions that child and adult alike seek from poetic texts. Knowledge about readers and their transactions with poems can only enhance a teacher's effectiveness in his attempts to encourage constructive conversations about what is read.

Outlined below is a summary of four stages in the response process that appeared to me in the light of my investigations, a tentative formulation that clearly requires refinement from further research. Such a description is no more than a useful starting-point and three important considerations need to be swiftly added. First, any model that delineates general stages in the highly complex response process is apt to appear too neat and linear. In attempting to describe the movement from passivity to involvement for example, the shuttling back and forth actions of the reader are lost from view. Second, this description is both the product of response as well as process itself, in the same way that the decisions that teachers make about procedures to adopt in 'teaching' poetry dictate the nature of the responses elicted. Third, many sub-stages must exist within such a staged framework, a feature recognized in the conceptual model offered by Keith Hurst in Chapter Four.

Four stages in the response process

Stage One Identification of the Individual with the Poem
The reader engages with the text in a highly idiosyncratic manner, attempting to decide whether or not he feels he can identify or sympathize with any part of the poem.

Stage Two Projection of Self into the Poem
Following an initial engagement with the puzzle of the poem, the reader begins to view the text in terms of his own experiences and

associations. By perceiving the poem in terms of his own personal interests and ideas, he attempts to involve himself more fully in the experience offered by the poet.

Stage Three   Clarifying an Emotional Response
Here the reader moves his attention from the words and images of the poem to the feelings and attitudes that are evoked within him. In interpreting metaphor, for example, the reader utilizes his own emotional responses to seek to tell himself what the poem 'means'.

Stage Four   Intellectual or Conscious Insight
This is the result of the previous stages, the flow toward insight which involves both primary and secondary emotion and the shuttling back and forth actions of the reader. At best, the reader gains 'satisfaction' from his interpretation and, to evaluate his own re-creation of the poem, may seek to test what he now holds at the forefront of his attention by comparison with the 'readings' of others.

Chapter 4

Group Discussions of Poetry

Keith Hurst

Introduction

In my early days of teaching, all my attempts at poetry lessons followed roughly the same pattern. I would read the poem, sometimes only once, and begin to fire questions at the twenty-odd bewildered faces looking up to me. 'What does the poet mean when he says . . .?' After all, the poem had been chosen because it was pretty straightforward; no archaic language, no difficult ideas; here were the poet's comments on everyday encounters and experiences which I was sure we could understand perfectly well. We were pressing our noses against the windows of life and all we had to do was talk about what we could see. At least, I was able to tell them what *I* could see since, after twenty faltering minutes, we had only got down to line nine and, at this rate, there wouldn't be time for me to explain how I wanted them to write their own poems on a similar idea. 'And if you find poetry too difficult, write in prose instead.'

It wasn't long before I realized that I would either have to improve my teaching of poetry or leave it alone altogether, and I chose the latter course for some time. My first tentative steps towards a guilt-ridden comeback gave me some encouragement, reinforced by advice from colleagues and writers and, although I confess to having had the occasional regressive tendency, the butcher's cleaver was no longer called into use. Nevertheless, a sense of unease and doubt continued: what I wanted to happen with poems in the classroom did not seem to square with what the students made of them and, although I could easily refer to research into what happens when young people read narrative prose, there was a noticeable scarcity of similar studies on the reading of poetry. Indeed, many writers refuse to recognise a difference.

Obviously, I had to carry out my own research so that my quest for successful poetry-teaching could be focused. I wanted to find out what teachers tended to do with poems, what students did with them, and whether the twain could ever hope to meet.

A clue to the way I should proceed was provided by Barrie Wade's article in the *Journal of Education for Teaching*[1]. A central finding of the modest experiment he carried out and reported was that a teacher will lead a small group of students discussing a poem and concentrate on explicating the text, whereas, if the teacher is removed, explication practically disappears and a wider range of tentative explorations begins to occur. I therefore asked the teachers, who had kindly agreed to help me, to teach a poem (chosen from a short list we negotiated) in the way they wanted to in their classes, whilst small groups of students were removed to discuss the same poem, in any way they wished, around a tape recorder.

The data I collected were varied (written comments on the poems by teachers and class-members, lesson notes or tapes), but the most enlightening were provided by taped group discussions. It was these, above all, that told me something about what students did with poems and enabled me to adapt my teaching strategies accordingly. Indeed, I am sure that a small group of students talking around a tape-recorder is a worthwhile teaching strategy in itself.

One of my intentions was to make comparisons: between the teachers' own written responses to the poems and their students'; between the performances of students in the presence of their teacher and those left with their peers or in isolation; between the teachers' intentions in preparing lessons and their assessments of how the lessons actually went. Occasionally, I will make reference to the written and taped material which I collected from the teachers with this in mind but my principal focus will be on the transcripts of group discussions.

A Group discussion: 'The Stag' by Ted Hughes

(i) *Following the pupils' responses*

In presenting some extracts from the transcripts here, I realize that I am putting you at a disadvantage. You do not have the tapes to listen to and, as was my situation initially, you probably do not know what you are looking for. There is always a problem in presenting transcript material. Should I interrupt the extracts to present my interpretations along the way, or should I provide parallel columns of transcript and commentary? Because the first transcript is lengthy, I feel it is necessary to interject periodically, not least to provide some thinking space. When doing so, I believe it is important to adopt a clear strategy of 'reading' or interpretation from a number that are possible. Initially, therefore, I will compare the students' apparent reading of the poem under discussion (Ted Hughes' 'The Stag') with my own understanding of it, together with some impressionistic observations on their approach. Please adopt a strategy of your own and ignore my interjections if you wish. At the end of the transcript I will suggest further strategies which could be employed and you are, of course, free to read these before you begin (p. 174).

Please note, however, the method of punctuation I have employed in the transcript:

/	represents a brief pause in speech,
–	indicates when an utterance has been cut short or interrupted,
...	indicates the continuation of an utterance through an interruption.

This group consists of four girls; Karen, Laura, Susan and Jane. They are all members of a high ability set in the third year (age range around thirteen) of a co-educational comprehensive school. Their teacher has just read to them Ted Hughes' 'The Stag', has asked them to 'discuss the poem in any way you wish', and left them to it.

The Stag

While the rain fell on the November woodland shoulder of Exmoor
While the traffic jam along the road honked and shouted
Because the farmers were parking wherever they could
And scrambling to the bank-top to stare through the tree-fringe
Which was leafless,
The stag ran through his private forest.

While the rain drummed on the roofs of the parked cars
And the kids inside cried and daubed their chocolate and fought
And mothers and aunts and grandmothers
Were a tangle of undoing sandwiches and screwed-round
    gossiping heads
Steaming up the windows,
The stag loped through his favourite valley.

While the blue horsemen down in the boggy meadow
Sodden nearly black, on sodden horses,
Spaced as at a military parade,
Moved a few paces to the right and a few to the left and
    felt rather foolish
Looking at the brown impassable river,
The stag came over the last hill of Exmoor.

While everybody high-kneed it to the bank-top all along the road
Where steady men in oilskins were stationed at binoculars,
And the horsemen by the river galloped anxiously this way and that
And the cry of hounds came tumbling invisibly with their
   echoes down through the draggle of trees,
Swinging across the wall of dark woodland,
The stag dropped into a strange country.

And turned at the river
Hearing the hound-pack smash the undergrowth, hearing the
   bell-note
Of the voice that carried all the others,
Then while his limbs all cried different directions to his lungs,
   which only wanted to rest,
The blue horsemen on the bank opposite
Pulled aside the camouflage of their terrible planet.

And the stag doubled back weeping and looking for home up
   a valley and down a valley
White the strange trees struck at him and the brambles
   lashed him,
And the strange earth came galloping after him carrying the
   loll-tongued hounds to fling all over him,
And his heart became just a club beating his ribs and his
   own hooves shouted with hounds' voices,
And the crowd on the road got back into their cars
Wet-through and disappointed.

                                          Ted Hughes

Karen 1: say something/it only/does the stag actually die then in
the end do you think
Laura 2: no/I don't think so because –
Susan 3: it says they're 'wet through and disappointed' so they
might –
Jane 4: or is it just saying that they didn't see it die/we don't
really know do we/'cos the stag disappears off into the trees and
all the spectators –
K.5: it doesn't actually say that he dies though does it/I mean it
says/'his heart became just a club beating his ribs and his own
hooves shouted with hounds' voices'
(inaudible)
(laughter)
J.6: as I was saying –
(laughter)
J.7: I reckon it's just that you don't know whether he dies

because he disappears off into the bushes/all the people/you go
from his point of view to the people/the spectators/the farmers
and that they mention first of al . . .
K.8:   they kind of –
J.9:   . . . they can't see so they're wet through and disappointed/
if you see what I mean
K.10:   Ted Hughes is leaving it up to your own discretion
whether he dies or not/isn't he
L.11:   yeh
J.12:   exactly
S.13:   he jumps from one thing to another doesn't he
J.14:   well do you reckon he dies
S.15:   leaves it up to your own imagination
K.16:   erm/I don't think he does actually . . .
S.17:   no
K.18:   . . .'cos it says when his heart –
J.19:   I reckon he does
K.20:   they'd say a more final thing wouldn't they/really
J.21:   I reckon he really means it because you see/they were
saying/the hounds/it's obviously/the hounds were obviously with
him because/it says 'his own hooves shouted with the hounds
voices' so they were obviously really really close –
S.22:   yeh/but I don't think they got him in the end/and then it
says the crowd got into their cars though so what happened
J.23:   I know but they wouldn't be able to see would they/they'd
all –
S.24:   no they got back into their cars so they would have got out
wouldn't they
L.25:   they would've tried to/'cos
S.26:   yeh
L.27:   yesterday we were discussing it and . . .
J.28:   that's not fair/you cheated
L.29:   . . . they followed it/in cars/they followed it –
S.30:   no/no/we weren't doing this/it was an article . . .
J.31:   oh
S.32:   . . . *The Sunday Times*
L.33:   they followed it/they follow stag-hunting in cars as well/so
they 'got back into their cars/wet through and disappointed' . . .
K.34:   that's true
L.35:   . . . then they didn't try to follow in the cars so it just
leaves it up to you

The girls seem to have apprehended the whole poem quite quickly
and hit against the problem posed by the final word: 'disappointed'.
This can either lead beyond the text to a consideration of 'what

really happened' or back into the text as a consideration of the crowd's psychological state. I can only reflect and speculate on the crowd's expectations and that invites me to inspect my own.

The comments from L.27 and L.33 are made more understandable if you are aware that the girls' teacher presented them with a magazine article on stag hunting in the lesson prior to this. Jane was absent.

J.36: would you feel sorry for the stag/do you feel sorry for the stag or the people or the hounds or what

K.37: the stag of course/it's a bit unfair isn't it/having a whole load of horses and dogs and people chasing you/so you haven't got a chance have you really . . .

J.38: no

K.39: . . . the actual survival thing

L.40: and/the stag's quite a big animal/you can't exactly hide can you

J.41: no

K.42: does this mean he's run along the road in the first verse/or very near the road/'cos it says 'the traffic jam along the road honked and shouted'.

S.43: 'because the farmers were parking' (inaudible)/oh

J.44: yeh because it's/obviously a day out/innit/for everybody 'cos the kids inside/you know –

?45: mm

J.46: the sandwiches and things

?.47: yeh

J.48: it's obviously a big day out and the first two/verses they're just when they all get there/isn't it . . .

?49: yeh

J.50: . . . and the third one as well/because you hear about the/the horses standing there waiting for the start –

?51: yeh

?52: 'in the boggy meadow'/yeh

J.53: I don't know much about hunting personally/but –

(laughter)

Concern with the ending has led to some consideration of the way sympathies have been directed (36) but this is not developed just yet. The girls are, I imagine, following their individual lines of thought, scanning the text and attempting to find points of entry into it by rereading and considering single phrases. At this stage, the concern is with trying to 'image' the scene depicted in the text.

K.54: what does it mean by 'the stag ran through his private forest'

J.55: well you know/they each have their own sort of . . .

L.56: territory

J.57: . . . territory/I suppose that his/you know/he's all comfy and at home

S.58: there is/some places that are done off for deer and that/couldn't they

?59: (inaudible) yeh

J.60: and then you see it goes/it says/you get 'the stag ran through private forest'/the 'stag loped through his favourite valley'/'the stag came over the last hill of Exmoor' . . .

J.62: . . . but the next verse/'dropped into a strange country'/-you've got the strange country and that's where the hunt starts/isn't it

?63: yeh

?64: yeh

S.65: they all end/the first, second and third verse/they all end with something about the stag

J.66: yeh

S.67: 'the stag ran through his private forest'/'the stag loped through his favourite valley'/'the stag came over the last hill of Exmoor'

?68: yeh

J.69: also 'the stag dropped into'/yeh

L.70: sort of build up the atmosphere by . . .

J.71: it is/isn't it/yeh

L.72: the people and that/and then –

L.73: yeh/erm –

(laughter)

J.74: yeh

K.75: you know when it says/you got the last line of the first three verses/it's going on about his favourite valley/private forest . . .

J.76: yeh

K.77: . . . and last hill of Exmoor/are they chasing him there/ they aren't are they . . .

J.78: yeh

K.79: . . . it's just when he gets into a strange country

S.80: no

J.81: no/because if you read the third verse/it says/er/the blue horsemen 'moved a few paces to the right and a few to the left

and felt rather foolish'/so they're obviously just waiting there
aren't they –
L.82: 'cos it's –
?.83: mm
J.84: 'cos that's like when you're foxhunting isn't it/you wait till
you sight a fox/you don't –
?.85: yeh
(inaudible)
L.86: yeh but they're marked aren't they/they have to chase a
certain stag
K.87: this is from yesterday as well
J.88: oh/they're obviously waiting/they obviously know there's a
stag around them don't they/they're waiting till they see it . . .
?.89: mm
J.90: . . . before they make a move/do anything
K.91: so why is the stag running everywhere/though/I mean if
they
J.92: well wouldn't you
K.93: . . . aren't chasing him
J.94: it's like/erm/you know . . .
?.95: walking everywhere
J.96: . . . just walking/like we're walking/he's just having a walk
through his territory isn't he/it's natural (laughter)
S.99: he's just at his leisure
K.100: then why did he actually go over into a strange country
then
?.101: well he was –
S.102: the stag came over the last hill of Exmoor and then they
all/then he sees these people –
J.103: you know probably/he's just/(inaudible) to go right to the
boundary/thinks he'll go for a little run/you know/well what's
wrong with it/you might not know/somewhere but you go for a
walk over there/don't you/he comes over and then he/he's jumped
upon by this bunch of idiots/you know (laughter)
K.104: OK
S.105: yeh/er –
(pause 6 secs)

The imaging continues, taking into account the girls' perception of
the patterning of the text – its repetitions and contrasts. This, in
turn, leads to consideration of the stag's situation, a change of focus
that Jane prompts with her venture into anthropomorphism.

J.106: just sort of look through the verses/right/start with the first one/erm/yeh/er/good idea –

(pause 7 secs)

J.107: right/it gives you a description of the day/doesn't it/you've got the idea of a wet November don't you/particularly cold and miserable

S.108: yeh

L.109: mm

J.110: but/and you think nobody'd be out on those days/but/you see that the hunt draws so many people –

L.111: mm

S.112: yeh

S.113: so it's obviously a very popular thing

K.114: but notice it's all male who are actually at the hunt/and around the hunt/because it says 'the kids inside cried'/and –

J.115: 'and mothers and aunts and grandmothers' are in the cars . . .

?116: yeh

J.117: . . . whereas the husbands –

S.118: so it's more the male –

K.119: yeh

J.120: so they stayed in the car and all the men got out with their binoculars/'cos it says –

K.121: yeh

S.122: yeh

J.123: well/'where steady men in oilskins were stationed at binoculars'

L.124: mm

J.125: yeh

K.126: 'cos they were undoing sandwiches/and 'screwed-round gossiping heads'/and things like that.

J.127: yeh/and . . .

S.128: 'steaming up the windows'

J.129: . . . parking/then he could have scrambled into the bank

S.130: 'steaming up the windows'

K.131: so they could be really quite bored . . .

?132: yeh

K.133: . . . just sitting there in the car

J.134: but it's obviously a sort of day out for the family isn't it

S.135: yeh

K.136: yeh

J.137: 'cos I mean you/you know/presumably you don't want to drive on a wet November day into a bank/but they're actually going to stay there because they've got their sandwiches/and/so its obviously a great sort of social event/isn't it

S.138:   yeh
K.139:   yeh
L.140:   notice the colour
S.141:   yeh/that's what I was –
J.142:   I suppose it's the cold isn't it/blue . . .
S.143:   no
J.144:   . . . cold
S.145:   no probably it could be his hunting jacket
J.146:   yeh
K.147:   red is for foxhunting isn't it
J.148:   yeh that's true/red is foxhunting/it might be a different
colour for staghunting
K.149:   yeh/different clubs have different colour collars as
well/so –
J.150:   yeh that's true/it's obviously/it pictures as though it may
be sort of sodden/it's pretty miserable/it's 'sodden nearly black'
and 'sodden horses'
?151:   yeh

Jane suggests a change in strategy; a more ordered approach to
working through the text (106). However, what may become
potentially restrictive leads to the following of a thread which runs
through the whole text: the predicament of the humans and their
'miserable' but unsympathetic state. Then Laura picks out another
phrase which presents problems (152).

L.152:   what does it mean by 'pulled aside the camouflage of
their terrible planet'
J.153:   whereabouts
J.154:   that's –
K.155:   after 'the blue horsemen on the opposite bank' (sic)
L.156:   after/down there
J.157:   do you think it's/as they/rush/rush after them and they're
tearing through the bushes and that
K.158:   'terrible planet'
S.159:   perhaps it's/it is their world isn't it/perhaps it's their world
J.160:   yeh perhaps its/'cos that's from the stag's point of view
again isn't it/it's a terrible planet now for the stag
K.161:   or maybe the author thinks it's a terrible planet/I mean
that we're driven actually to hunt . . .
L.162:   animals
K.163:   . . . like they're –
J.164:   but it says that '*his* limbs all cried different directions to
his lungs, which only wanted to rest'/so it's from his point of view
if you go from there isn't it
K.165:   yeh but there's a comma there though/isn't it

J.166: yeh but it's still the same sentence/it's still his thoughts

L.167: 'the blue horsemen on the opposite bank' (sic)

J.168: 'cos he can see the blue horsemen on the opposite bank . . .

K.169: yeh

J.170: . . . and he's seen them pull aside the camouflage/and he sees their terrible planet

S.171: yeh and it says –

J.172: yeh but it says *their* terrible planet/wouldn't it say *his* terrible planet

S.173: no/their terrible planet

J.174: what/they've made it terrible you mean

K.175: yeh

S.176: revealing them and the horses and the hounds and . . .

J.177: yeh

S.178: . . . something out of everyday life in their life comes into his

J.179: yeh

S.180: then it says 'the stag doubled back weeping and looking for home up a valley'

J.181: that's obviously living in a strange country and wanting to get back to what he knows

S.182: yeh

J.183: 'cos obviously if he doesn't know he's going to crash about all over the place

S.188: yeh it backs up your point on the next line/'the strange earth came'

J.189: yeh/that's true

L.190: and it says/somewhere/about tearing/lashing –

J.191: and you see/in the last verse it says about/erm/and it says 'the strange earth came galloping after him carrying the loll-tongued hounds to fling all over him'

K.192: it seems as if the earth/as though he's still standing still but the earth is still coming after him

J.193: perhaps he's not going as fast as the hounds so it seems/however fast he runs . . .

K.194: mm

J.195: . . . he thinks they're going faster than him/and the hounds/he's panicking as the hounds get nearer and nearer . . .

L.196: perhaps

J.197: . . . and he feels that they're going to fling all over him/perhaps it's *his* point of view

K.198: mm

L.199: perhaps he's going fast/(inaudible)/not moving fast enough for him

S.200: yeh

J.201: would you say the poem's written form the stag's point of view/or –

S.202: more from the stag's/to get you to sympathise

There is an intense realization of the stag's predicament, here, which is dependent on a close reading of the poet's rhetorical cues and controls. The power of words like 'terrible' and 'weeping', together with the use of the stag as a focaliser, is directing sympathy and, at 201, Jane steps back to consider this. It is an interesting example of reflexivity arising out of a very close engagement with those textual cues.

J.203: yeh but it's not –

K.204: I think it's quite factual really I mean he hasn't/he hasn't sort of leaned over either way . . .

S.205: no/that's true

K.206: . . . well he definitely hasn't leaned over towards the horsemen/that's pretty obvious isn't it

?207: no

J.208: yes/and you don't get much/you don't get descriptions of their feelings/so much do you

K.209: no

J.210: more of the way they've spaced and (inaudible)

K.211: towards the end you do . . .

S.212: yeh

K.213: . . . but

J.214: yeh the stag but before then it's all very much a description of the country and . . .

L.215: the people

J.216: . . . the people/as opposed to a description of their thoughts or feelings or whatever

K.217: yeh

S.218: yeh

J.219: 'cos it's not/er/the feelings of the people on the hunt is it/or on the stag at all

L.220: no

S.221: well no one really knows what a stag feels like when it is being chased

K.222: apart from the stag

S.223: yeh apart from the stag you know/but he can't really express his feelings

K.224: no

J.225: but this is very much the human/what he thinks the stag will feel like . . .

S.226: yeh/it's a human point of view isn't it

J.227: . . . it's as though/even though he's putting the stag's/trying to put the stag's point of view forward/you've got/you've got . . .

K.228: it must be –

J.229: . . . you've got to be an –

L.230: I suppose that's/yeh/I suppose that's how you'd just have to put it as if you're/you'd have to imagine you're the stag and what you'd feel like/don't you/really

J.231: yeh

L.232: but it'd be a bit hard –

K.233: it's very unfair though isn't it/I mean a load/a pack of hounds/then a load of horses and human beings directing them/so –

J.234: it's very unfair odds isn't it/but –

(inaudible)

J.235: I don't think you agree with hunting do you

The next 111 exchanges are concerned with a discussion of blood sports and pest control. This is, of course, not to be condemned as irrelevant but I have omitted it because there is no discussion of the text until:

J.346: do you think there is any meaning in his comparison to a military parade in verse three/do you think there's any extra meaning in that or is he just –

K.347: well/er/in the next line it says 'moved a few paces to the left'

J.348: what I mean is –

S.349: so it's well organised

J.350: yeh

?351: yeh/and they've got someone saying now move to the right/now move to the –

K.352: like marching/they sort of/you know/instructing

J.353: mm/do you think he means to say that it's a bit false

S.354: yes

J.355: 'cos you/you think of a hunt/really/it must be really enjoyable you know/I can imagine that/no I mean not after what I said/you go tearing away across the country on a horse

K.356: mm/it is

J.357: it must be very exhilarating and yet/here/he's got/I mean/'spaces as at a military parade' and 'moved a few paces to the left'/it sounds really boring doesn't it

L.358: I know/it's because they're waiting

K.359: you've got to be patient/haven't you/to wait for the actual/animal

?360: (inaudible)

J.361:   you'd think/that line/it sounds really awful/you think/it gives you a really bad impression of hunting/you think oh/you know/blue horsemen in the soggy meadow/sodden/and all these boring –

L.362:   it depends what you're trying to do . . .

J.363:   wet

L.364:   . . . he's trying to say –

?365:   (inaudible)

L.366:   give us a bad impression of it

?367:   he's trying to convey his feelings through the way he –

L.368:   maybe he actually has been on a hunt and that's how it actually was

?369:   yes

J.370:   you can tell by the poem that/obviously/not only does he/think hunting is cruel but he thinks hunting is pretty boring as well . . .

L.371:   yes

J.372:   . . . you know/just not worth the effort/it's a waste of time

?373:   he probably thinks/well/its

S.374:   maybe he just went along for the/he didn't go along as a hunter/sort of thing

K.375:   no/but in the fourth verse

S.376:   spectator (inaudible)

K.377:   'and the horsemen by the river galloped anxiously this way and that'/that shows they do get a bit of movement/actually there

J.378:   yeh but even then you think er/I mean that first/you see –

K.379:   he puts 'anxiously' in though doesn't he

J.380:   'while everybody high-kneed it to the bank top all along the road'/I mean you begin to get a bit of excitement/don't you/er/but then you get the boring bit again/'while steady men in oilskins' and then 'galloped anxiously'

K.381:   mm

J.382:   so even/you think he could have put more feeling into that/don't you/I mean you'd have thought he'd made it (inaudible)

K.383:   if he'd wanted to he could have put the words in

J.384:   it could have been made that/you know –

(pause 6 secs)

J.385:   he could have really made that . . .

K.386:   mm

J.387:   . . . dashed and/but/you know/he just makes it normal/- and boring and –

K.388:   to put you off hunting

S.389:   yes
J.390:   to put you off/really/the whole poem is to –
S.391:   I don't know whether the whole of it is –
J.392:   no/well –
?393:   some of it (inaudible)
S.394:   at the beginning/when they say/'the rain' –
L.395:   'daubed their chocolate and fought'
S.396:   yeh it sounds as though they're all sitting in the car
K.397:   yeh sort of making it sound dreary/you know/boring/-
and –
?398:   mm
L.399:   yes/I suppose so
?400:   let's have a look
K.401:   and he mentions the rain again in the second verse/'while
the rain drummed on the roofs of the parked cars'
?402:   yeh
S.403:   and the steaming up the windows
?404:   yeh
S.405:   so it's really stuffy inside but you can't go out
K.406:   and all the kids inside cried and –
S.407:   yeh
K.408:   yeh it all sounds a bit monotonous sort of thing
L.409:   'and screwed-round, gossiping heads'/I mean/that's the
kind of thing you'd all love to (inaudible) wouldn't it
J.410:   mm
(pause 8 secs)

Further detailed consideration of the way the humans are presented
leads now, to direct and more confident assessments of the poet's
apparent intentions, tested against the text.

L.411:   so you think he makes it imp-/conveys it as/as if he
doesn't like it and trying to put it in (inaudible) direction
?412:   yeh
J.413:   do you think he puts across well though/do you think
after reading this poem/er/puts you –
L.414:   it makes you feel a bit more sorry for the stag
J.415:   do you think it does do that or do you think it would have
an effect on you/or not/or do you think you're just reading a
poem/oh well/so it's a poem
K.416:   I think most people feel sorry for the hunted animal to
begin with anyway/and this wouldn't really help it much I don't
think
L.417:   if a hunter was reading this I don't think he'd sort of
have any feelings to sort of say/right
J.418:   it's just somebody's opinion and my opinions differ –

171

S.419:   yeh
J.420:   do you think it's strong enough to put –
S.421:   no
J.422:   no I don't but on the other hand –
K.423:   it's strong enough to put us off but not –
J.424:   but not (inaudible)
?425:   that's 'cos we've gone –
J.426:   but on the other hand do you think that was his
objective/the poet/do you think it was to . . .
K.427:   to direct future generations
J.428:   . . . to direct/to direct an opinion/ do you reckon it was/or
do you reckon it was just/oh/something he wrote
K.429:   yeh but that –

The first side of the tape runs out here and, after some delay, the
girls are not able to pick up this thread. The next 114 exchanges are
concerned with some discussion comparing 'The Stag' with Hughes'
'View of a Pig' and commenting on the stag-hunting tradition on
Exmoor. Then, they return to the poem via a need to explain 'bell-
note'.

L.544:   and they're all barking
J.545:   and their echoes just through the draggle of trees/yeh/it's
just very faintly/it's obviously the first –
S.546:   he can hear them/he can't see them but he can hear them
J.547:   yeh/this is just before he drops into the strange
country/isn't it/so it's obviously his first warning/which obviously
he doesn't sort of take much notice of if he's dropping down into
a strange country –
L.548:   and then he turns at the river/and he turns at the river
and obviously he's sighted because the hounds smash through the
undergrowth
L.550:   yeh
S.551:   mm
J.552:   you get a picture of hounds sort of going mad/don't you
L.553:   'hearing the hound-pack smash the undergrowth'
J.544:   and you get this bell-note
K.555:   you know that bell-note/well the hounds sort of bark or
whatever is always called music/that's what you can call it
J.556:   yeh it's true isn't it/I reckon it's the leading hound/one
hound is out in front

Some repeated references to the strangeness which the situation
presents to the stag follow, as do comments on the physical and
mental state of the stag.

The final stage in the discussion (604 to 630) returns neatly to the
point made at its beginning, indicating that the detailed discussion

has confirmed and enriched the girls' initial reactions.

J.604: and if you hear footsteps you think they're a lot closer to you than they are and things like that/I reckon he's just so frightened that everything's got muddled up/and that the hounds are so close it's really panicking and I suppose it's a bit sort of frightened

L.605: yeh

S.606: for him

J.607: for him/because you begin to realize what he feels like/or what you imagine he would feel like

K.608: he ends it in a sort of very cold way/sort of when the crowd got back –

J.609: you suddenly get this/suddenly/sorry/carry on/sorry/I'm interrupting aren't I

S.610: yes you are/very rude

K.611: when the crowd get back in/on the road and back into their cars wet through and disappointed/one moment you're all with the hounds and . . .

J.612: yeh/really excited

K.613: . . . getting really excited/yeh he builds up the atmosphere and then he just ends/and the next moment –

S.614: you're dropped aren't you/kind of thing

J.615: yeh but that is just/its a real build-up/isn't it

S.616: yeh/you get a build up and then you go –

J.617: the hounds are so close and then you suddenly get –

K.618: just left

J.619: it goes all –

S.620: it just drops and kind of – .

J.621: 'and the crowd on the road got back into their cars wet-through and disappointed'

K.622: you feel as though you ought to have a bit more on there or something don't you

J.623: yeh

L.624: it comes to such a climax and then it just drops it

J.625: mm

L.626: it just drops it

J.627: do you think that helps the poem or do you think that spoils the poem

K.628: maybe he intended to do that/you know/to give you/ (inaudible)/impact

J.629: but do you reckon it does spoil the poem/or does it make it better or –

L.630: no/I think (inaudible)/it goes back to the first point/ doesn't it/about leaving it to your own discretion

(ii)   Theorising the pattern of talk

There are, as I suggested earlier, a number of ways in which to read this transcript, and I would like to indicate a few possibilities.

First, it could be viewed as exemplifying the pattern of small-group talk. That there is such a pattern is made clear in *Communication and Learning in Small Groups*[2] by Barnes and Todd, a book which helped me considerably in pointing out the shape of conversations like this.

Barnes and Todd make the distinction between social (interactive) and cognitive aspects of speech, and create their categories to deal with either aspect. Since the social aspects are not my prime concern, I shall deal only with the cognitive – and that at the second level proposed by Barnes and Todd (the first level was a system of categorising single utterances which they themselves did not find useful). The cognitive strategies involved in group discussion were listed and subdivided by Barnes and Todd as follows:

1	Constructing the question	– 'Closed' tasks
		– 'Open' tasks
2	Raising new questions	
3	Setting up hypotheses	– Beyond the given
		– Explicit hypotheses
4	Using evidence	– Anecdote
		– Hypothetical cases
		– Using everyday knowledge
		– Challenging generalities
5	Expressing feelings and recreating experience	– Expressing ethical judgements
		– Shared recreation of literary experience[2]

In applying this descriptive framework to my own data, it is necessary to make two adjustments. Since the task set each group of students is an 'open' one, it is impossible to distinguish between strategies 1 and 2; it is clear that both are happening at the same time. Second, since the printed text is the most immediate piece of evidence in the discussion, I would add 'textual reference' to the list under strategy 4. Moreover, it must be stressed that, in any cycle of utterance, strategy 5 is taking place simultaneously with any or all of 1, 2, 3 and 4.

As can be seen from the transcript, the pattern of discussion follows, as Barnes and Todd indicate, a series of cyclical changes. Each cycle begins with a question (not always phrased as a question) which suggests one or more hypothetical answers, or which requires explanation or opinion. Each hypothesis is, then, questioned, challenged, tested or confirmed by a process of referring to evidence of various kinds, or by creating the poem in order to clarify, demonstrate or negate the hypothesis. Alternative hypotheses may be suggested or the original one is reworded or restated.

The cycle is completed by what I would term a 'provisional resolution' in which at least one of the group seems to accept a favoured hypothesis and any further dissent or testing is subdued, at least for the time being. A new question is asked as a direct consequence and development of the accepted hypothesis, or as a result of a group member encountering another problem in the text, or to force attention back on the text after a digression.

Such a cycle can be illustrated by rereading the first 12 utterances of the extract. Karen begins with a question (1), Laura responds with a hypothesis (2), there is a process of testing and seeking evidence which leads to a provisional resolution (10, 11, 12).

This descriptive approach to the transcript allows several complementary perspectives to be taken. First, one may focus on trying to assess the quality of the talk. It may be possible to distinguish between the worth of each girl's contribution, according to the way she initiates, hypothesises, tests out or provides evidence. Second, one could attempt to judge the effectiveness of each girl's communication or her interpersonal skills; the onset of GSCE oral assessment encourages teachers to think in this way.

Another strategy, again focusing on assessment, involves making judgements about the success with which the girls demonstrate their understanding of, and response to, the poem. There is certainly some evidence of deep personal engagement with the poem on the part of at least one group member. However, it is probably sensible to defer judgement, seeing the discussion as one stage, or element, in the gradual and tentative process of forming response.

A fourth strategy involves asking oneself: 'What learning is taking place here?' Or, put another way: 'Are the girls gaining any benefit from reading the poem and, if so, what?' Certainly, they have an interesting discussion about bloodsports and are led into formulating their views in the company of others. But this could have been initiated without the help of the poem and it is debatable whether pre-existing attitudes in the girls are modified at all by the experience of reading and discussing. The exchange between Jane and Karen (36 to 39) indicates the presence of these pre-existing attitudes and any modification of them might be primarily due to the exchange of views with others on this kind of talk. This was certainly recognised by a number of teachers who taught the poem as part of the research programme. Several of them dispensed with 'The Stag' after one reading and concentrated on eliciting and developing their students' opinions on blood sports. One, who felt very strongly that hunting animals was barbaric, very quickly asked her students to write on other subjects about which they had passionate views (nuclear weapons featured here) and the poem became, perhaps, an irrelevance.

If the poem is useful in this respect it may be in inviting the students to focus on what they think is Hughes' attitude to staghunting and then responding to it. (The exchanges between 361 and 429 illustrate how this can take place.) Or it may be in inviting an imaginative engagement in the plight of the stag, as intensely realised in the exchanges between 544 and 630. The encouragement of empathy is an oft-stated and apparently respectable aim shared by many teachers, but it does beg the question about whether we believe in the redemptive values of literature or would rather concentrate on helping students to realise the potentialities of language and form in shaping response.

In fact, the strategy I principally employed when reading and listening to this, and all the other data, was shaped by my intention to discover and describe a general pattern in the way students read poems. I characterize it as follows.

The students engage in cycles of exchange (discussion), in the way described above, initiated by questions. These questions can be sparked off by thoughts hovering around the edges of the text ('I don't think you agree with hunting do you', 235) but they often arise from some line or word in the text. Although many groups tended to work through a text line by line, it was clear that such questions could come from a 'problem' set by any part of the text at any time. This seems to be a result of the formal nature of poetry, as opposed to narrative prose.

Each question seems to be centred on one of three ways in which the text is perceived by the students. I refer to these ways as 'frames' through which the text is viewed, as students are creating their own meaning from it. One frame is the text as *story*. This involves a simple construction of the events which the text seems to be relating ('does this mean he's run along the road in the first verse', 42) and a positioning of the protagonists in a kind of mental theatre (see the exchange from 17 to 81). It depends on the students being able to relate the 'events' of the text to recognisable human experience, as in the discussion about jackets (140 to 151). Much time is spent on retelling the story of the text, sometimes from a focalised position (as the stag, 544 to 614).

A second frame requires that the text be viewed as the product of a *poet* as the voice of its creator, and the result of his/her choices and opinions. Much discussion centres on what Ted Hughes is intending (10 to 24 and 201 to 206).

Third, there is the frame of text as *form*, as selected words and

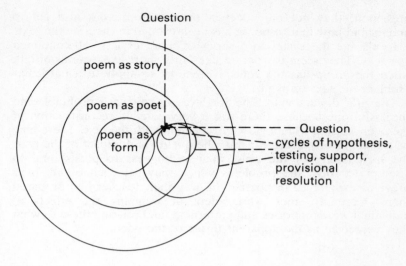

Figure 4.1

shape, the way in which the poet has presented the story. It is well not to have too narrow a conception of this frame. It may involve the perception of conscious patterning (as in the discussion of repetition, from 60 to 73), or of focalising (201), or of intention conveyed by association and connotation (the military images discussed from 346 to 361).

Once a cycle has been initiated in one of the three frames, it can move into any combination of the other two; an idea represented by figure 4.1.

I would also like to illustrate the process by referring to one such cycle, from 152 to 179. Laura begins by focusing on the phrase 'pulled aside the camouflage of their terrible planet', in a question which is initially treated as part of the recreation of *story* (by Jane, at 157). When Karen repeats 'terrible planet' (158), Susan responds in the frame of *form*, implying that the phrase is a metaphor ('it is their world, isn't it', 159). This is developed by Jane (160) and Karen presses the point further by referring to the viewpoint of the *poet* ('maybe the author thinks it's a terrible planet', 161). Consideration moves back to *form* (discussion of the comma, and the stag as focaliser) and thence to an understanding of what happens in the *story* and its significance for the stag before the provisional resolution at 175 to 179.

A phrase such as 'the camouflage of their terrible planet' draws attention to itself and, when students rise to the challenge thus presented, they not only deepen their response but also get to understand how that response has been evoked in them by the text.

I envisage the cycles as a series of more or less self-contained episodes. They seem to operate like fairly short-lived spirals of talk when the group has the collective energy to apply to a particular problem the text turns up.

The girls' discussion of 'The Stag' was a particularly profitable and successful one because there was a very detailed reconstruction of the poem arising from a close engagement with the text. There may be a number of reasons for this: the quality and impact of the text; the high ability of the girls; their willingness to persist and to attempt to solve the problems which they set each other; their previous experience of poetry; the way their teacher had prepared them. Certainly, they were adept at weighing the effects of individual words, phrases and patterning, and relating these to what they perceived as the apparent thrust of the poem.

B   The Three Frames

(i)   Story: the 'simple construction' of the text

The majority of discussions and written responses got little further than simple constructions of the text as story. This bald statement appears rather dismissive of the efforts of many students but that is not the impression that I wish to give. Paradoxically, simple construction is really quite a complex business.

The term 'construction', also, suggests an association with what Richards called the 'construing' of a text, or making out 'the plain sense'[3]. Richards' term *is* an over-simplification; one which fails to take account of the fact that one cannot, as it were, translate the meaning of words, devoid of context, tone and feeling. My view of 'construction' recognizes that it takes place alongside and in conjunction with a number of other important reading processes and that it does not necessarily have to take place *before* the other processes can be brought into operation. I use the term to describe the act of putting the language of the text into the language of the reader within the frame of 'poem as story', or a recognisable account of experience.

I will develop this and other ideas I have outlined, with the help of a number of brief extracts from other data I collected in my research.

Producing the mental theatre
Here, a group of four boys are also discussing 'The Stag' and constructing an imaginable scene from the text.

Gary 43: 'While the blue horsemen down in the boggy meadow. Sodden nearly black on sodden horses, Spaced as at a military parade'/that means they're waiting to see the stag
David 44: well it's a hunt isn't it/these are the huntsmen and they're
Steven 45: the horse/the horses that are going out
D.46: yeh/the stag's taking them through all the woodland and that and they're absolutely filthy and spattered with mud and that and the horses are . . .
G.47: soaking wet
D.48: . . . sodden and/yeh/they're all wet and dirty and that
Martin 49: and they've just come to a river
D.50: and 'spaced as at a military parade'/they're all waiting for it/for the hounds to chase it out of the wood aren't they
M.51: 'moved a few paces to the right, and a few to the left and felt rather foolish'
D.52: they're trying to chase it but the stag's –
S.53: but who's moving/is that the stag moving
M.54: look at the next line it says 'looking at the brown impassable river'/its the horses refusing/its going from side to side
D.55: yeh
S.56: oh 'cos they can't see it/oh yeh they're waiting for it to come out
D.57: 'The stag came over the last hill of Exmoor'
M.58: in other words that was the last hill before the moor/the flat moor-'cos it says it comes up to the/the flat/you know/just flat/cos it says there's no more valleys and that
D.59: 'while everybody high-kneed it to the bank-top all along the road'/they're all getting out of their cars and wanting to see · this
? 60: yeh
G.61: all running up to get there
?.62: yeh
D.63: there's something different and they all want to see it

The exchanges, here, deal with the text on a literal level. There seems to be no attempt to engage with the complexities of association implied in 'spaced as at a military parade', nor to explore the exact nature of what it is to have 'high-kneed it' – except to substitute 'running' as an intended synonym. But there is an attempt to work out who is doing what and where; to position the protagonists in a kind of mental theatre. Simultan-

179

eously, there is a need to explain why these protagonists are acting as they do. Why, for example, the horsemen are 'sodden nearly black' and why 'everybody' seems so eager to reach the bank-top.

For most of their discussion the boys concerned themselves with this business of trying to decide what was happening in the text, one, two or three lines at a time, rarely attempting to unravel the complexities suggested by metaphor or simile (explaining 'camouflage', for example as the undergrowth which disguises the stag, but ignoring 'their terrible planet' which may have caused them to revise this conclusion and perhaps got them to focus on the way the poet is manipulating our view of events).

Such a line by line construction of the text was, not surprisingly, a method favoured by many discussion groups. Very often, however, figurative language was considered, albeit, on occasions, only to present it in literal terms, as with this group who are considering Seamus Heaney's 'Follower' (see p. 237 for text of poem):

Shaun 47. erm/how is/how is the sod 'polished'
Karl 48. its all been turned over/its new underneath
Shaun 49. yeh/of course/yeh
Lee 50. hasn't been dried by the sun yet

These two brief extracts, from discussions on 'The Stag' and 'Follower', are intended to show what I mean by 'simple construction'. It is a concern with the surface of the text as a recognisable depiction of reality: a description, a chain of events or a train of thought. It is something akin to the initial apprehension of a text, although it involves further colouring in of detail. The search for motive or explanation is part of the process of linking the depiction of experience presented by the text with the reader's experience of life.

The process of simple construction would seem to be a common one in the experience of making meaning from the text, and certainly an essential one. In the responses of individual students who were isolated to write about the poem unaided, it is frequently evident that such a process has taken place although it is presented in something like summary form. It is a feature of such responses even in cases when the text bears little relationship to sequential narrative, such as 'Anthem for Doomed Youth' by Wilfred Owen (see p. 238 for text):

'1   A battle is on, and all there is are dead people all around them, all they can hear is the rapid rattle from the guns, which seem to block out all our chances of living. No more fun for them, no prayers, will be said, they will just be forgotten, no one will remember what they have done, the sound of the bombs is all they

will hear, and in time just the sound of trumpets calling them back.
2   What encouragement can they have, to help them battle on? No
one else can give them help, only they can do it, and they know they
will be killed.
All they will remember are the pale looks on the faces of their
wives, that will be the only thing they would like to remember.
Their flowers the only love of friendly memories, and each day a
closing of all of my mind leaving it blank.'

Obviously, a great deal of very hard thinking about the text had
taken place before this response had been articulated. But it is a
characteristic of what I have termed 'simple construction' that there
is no overt consideration of the text as a crafted artefact,
representing the mental processes of the poet.

Most participants in the research respond by means of simple
construction but quite often (this is true, at any rate, of many
discussion groups) call a halt to proceedings after working through
the text just once, line by line. Where there is a desire to persist
there is a willingness to work through the text a number of times,
colouring in more and more details. The line by line movement is
not strictly observed: provisional resolutions are revised as new
'evidence' comes to light or new problems are set, but the overall
pattern of exchanges produces a spiralling effect with each new turn
leading further into a close engagement with the text. Essentially,
this process is a form of storying or, at very least, a viewing of the
text through the frame of story. It involves arranging the
protagonists in the mental theatre, trying to understand their
actions, emotional reactions and motives and speculating on the
details of the action where the poet has left room for that
speculation.

Collaborative storying

The discussion of another group of three boys (of 'The Stag')
demonstrates the process most clearly, for the *story* of the text is in
the foreground of what they say. It is true that they show some
awareness of text as form, particularly in their recognition of
repetition and the irregularity of rhythm which becomes evident as
they read it aloud ('It's a bad one to read I can tell you that'). It is
also true that they focus on text as poet, but this results from their
attempts to answer the question posed by one of their number:
'What's actually happening in the poem?'

The following extract from their discussion illustrates the way re-
reading and storying can modify and deepen response to part of the
text. The group here demonstrates what Rosenblatt calls the 'lived
through experience' of the poem. They do so collaboratively,

picking up the thread of the narrative from one to the other in a series of short, often unfinished exchanges. Cumulatively, their individual fragments build into the group's shared realisation of the stag's plight.

Colin 185: (reads stanza six)
Ben 186: hurray/it's obviously got away by the looks of it
C.187: only just
B.188: but no blood for them/the crowd/er/he's very/he's just about had it now
Alan. 189: sad/he doubles back/sad/looking for his –
B.190: yeh/weeping/for home
C.191: he's obviously lost
B.192: he's lost now and he doesn't know where to go
A.193: and he's turning up and down the valley looking for –
B.194: yeh/and he's getting lashed by –
C.195: it seems he's left the hunter behind
B.196: and he's getting lashed by the brambles
A.197: so he's obviously going through some woodland
B.198: and he's panicking
A.199: yeh
B.200: he's galloping this way and that looking for home/or somewhere he recognises
C.20: and the crowd have lost the stag and the hunt's been lost and so they're –
B.202: they all go home
A.203: and 'the strange earth came galloping after him, carrying the loll-tongued hounds to fling all over him'
B.204: hounds that is/isn't it
A.205: oh yeh
B.206: so the hounds are still coming after him there
A.207: so 'strange earth'/he doesn't know where he is at the moment does he
B.208: no/'And his heart became just a club beating his ribs and his own hooves shouted with hounds' voices'/Mm
A.209: come to think of it/it looks to me as if he's been caught
B.210: yeh

It is this kind of storying and subsequent close engagement with the stag's situation and state of mind which enables them to take up the question of the poet's viewpoint:

C.272: he describes how the stag's feeling quite effectively
B.273: yes/but –
A.274: but its not an advertisement for killing/is it/because I mean/they would have it a nice sunny day/wouldn't they/not a wet day

One would, of course, expect 'The Stag' to be approached as a story. It can be regarded as a narrative which observes the unities of place, time and action. But even with the texts where this is not so overtly the case, students find a need to construct some form of story from the text. 'Follower', (p. 237), for example, deals with a much greater span of time and is a description of changing experience and attitude, not a single action. Nevertheless, the group quoted below attempt to shape some kind of story from the text: not, in this case, the story which the text *tells*, but the story which lies behind the writing of the text. Again, though in a different way from the discussion of 'The Stag', this gives rise to an awareness of the poet as present in the text:

> *Colin 39:*   could it be anything to do with the actual/what the/
> bloke who's wroten it/written it/what he's actually experienced
> *Steven 40:*   Seemus Hanney (sic)
> *C.41:*   is it one of his experiences/though/or what
> *Keith 42:*   well its written from/as if he was . . .
> *S.43:*   yeh
> *K.44:*   . . . sort of the one that's . . .
> *M.45:*   yeh
> *K.46:*   . . . following
> *C.47:*   yeh I know/yeh/but is it sort of/do you think its likely to
> be true/he seems/he seems to know quite a lot about/erm –
> *K.48:*   perhaps his father was a . . .
> *C.49:*   yeh/well/perhaps it was/you know –
> *K.50:*   . . . a plough puller or whatever
> *C.51:*   ploughman

This leads into speculation about the poet; his age when he first followed his father, his age when he wrote the poem, how much time he spent on the farm, whether he went to school, and exactly where the action of the poem is located.

One teacher, writing his own response to 'Epitaph in Lydford Churchyard' (as asked to do, as part of the research, before teaching the poem to his class) constructed a story to provide a context for the writing of the poem. Claiming that the epitaph 'facilitates association and identification', he went on:

> What the poet has done to my mind, is taken a simple idea from a
> 'pleasant' stroll through a very old churchyard. The epitaph
> catches his eye and fires his imagination . . . the poet allows the
> reader to bring experiences and awareness to the poem. One is
> invited to picture the poet's walk in the churchyard. I connect it
> with a similar walk I enjoyed in a Dorset churchyard . . .

This is a curiously idiosyncratic reaction, which may arise from the poem's rune-like quality, but a group of girls discussing 'Epitaph' (they were not even from the same school as the teacher quoted above) reacted to it in a similar way. The text of the poem is to be found on p. 236.

> *Deena 60:*   I dunno though/because if it's words/words inscribed on a tomb this is like he's reading what's written on it/is it
> *Rachel 61:*   well it doesn't actually say whether he actually knew the person or whether its just what he's read/what he's –
> *Fiona 62:*   on the tomb
> *D.63:*   the first two lines must be what's written on the tombstone
> *R.64:*   yes so what/about him/telling them about him and that
> *D.65:*   so the first two lines is on the tombstone
> *R.66:*   the last one
> *F.67:*   it must be a sort of history/it's rather a lot to have written on a tombstone/isn't it

Speculation about the context involves or becomes speculation about the poet.

In other cases, information about the context and the poet is already known. The girls of one group who discussed 'Anthem for Doomed Youth' had some knowledge of the First World War, of war poetry and of Wilfred Owen. In the course of their exchanges, they mention that this knowledge was instrumental in getting them started on the poem, that the making of meaning would have been more difficult without it. Similarly, the students who took part in the discussion, whose transcript we read first, obviously brought to their work on 'The Stag' a context partly drawn from the article on stag-hunting which the teacher had asked them to read in an earlier lesson.

Simple construction moves along a continuum which becomes the frame of seeing the text as story; and seeing the text as story is *one* way into the frame of text as poet. But this conclusion involves the recognition that 'text as story' can mean either the events or the recreation of the story depicted in the text or the context in which the text was produced. Such a distinction is, indeed, similar to the one made by Genette, between 'recit' and 'histoire'[4].

(ii)   Poet: responses to the implied author

The concept of the text as poet can involve no fewer than three things.

First, the poet can appear, quite overtly, as a character in his/her poem. This is clearly the case in 'Follower' and the Michael Rosen poem 'I share my bedroom with my brother', which was also used in the research (text on p. 236).

Second, the poet can be seen as a participant in the circumstances which gave rise to the poem. This does not only involve knowledge of historical or autobiographical detail (as in Owen's 'Anthem') but can also comprise speculation where no facts are immediately verifiable (as in 'Epitaph').

Third, the poet may be sensed within the text as expressing feelings and manipulating tone. This is a notion similar to what Richards called the author's 'intention', although it is a misleading term – 'intention' is not absolute or clearly verifiable. Like everything else involved in the reading of a text, it is the creation of the reader according to certain constraints.

It is possible to regard all three views of the text as poet in the light of the concept of 'implied author'. This is the term used by Wayne C. Booth to describe the impression of the author gained by the reader when reading the text.[5] Booth demonstrates that an author makes use of rhetorical devices which guide a reader's response. At the same time, the author reveals a 'self' to the reader with which the reader forms some kind of relationship. Poetry has often been regarded as a 'pure' form of literary art in which little or nothing of the author is displayed – a view which Booth feels is impossible and even undesirable:

> Even if there are permanent, universal responses embodied in the work, then, they are unlikely to move us strongly and they may be unclear – without the author's rhetoric.

He refutes any claims that a text can be the pure expression of a natural object because 'it is not enough to say that it need not say anything because it simply is.'

The poems used by teachers and students in this research display a variety of rhetorical devices used by each poet to direct the response of the reader. For an accomplished and experienced reader it should be no surprise to find them there. Such a reader perceives the so-called 'implied author' who is discernible even when the poet attempts to efface his personality from the poem.

For younger, less experienced readers who are unfamiliar with the notion, one would expect to find little conscious apprehension of the poem as poet, except in cases where an explicit 'I' is the subject or narrator of the text. As we shall see, the students in the discussion groups often found it difficult to break the code of 'controls' designed to direct response when a more subtle or distanced method was used. Nevertheless, there was often a subconscious awareness that the implied author was there, requiring certain reactions to his/her poem.

Empathising with the real poet

Michael Rosen, whose poem 'I share a bedroom with my brother' is
the subject of one discussion group's work which is discussed below,
evidently sees a poem as a direct encounter between reader and
writer:

> Poets are comedians, teachers, smarty pants, show-offs, nags,
> hecklers, gassers, frauds, actors, conjurors, mimics, orators,
> conversationalists, teasers, thinkers . . . I see each poem I write
> > each poem I read
> > each poem I hear
> as part of a conversation, a chat. When you meet someone and he
> or she says something to you, they expect you to react – do
> something. It's the same with a poem – answer back, laugh, cry,
> tell a story, run away or call him or her a liar.[6]

Regardless of the merits or demerits of this view, one may expect to
find that a reader of one of Rosen's texts would have a direct and
immediate awareness of the poet and that some kind of reaction to
the poet would be provoked.

In 'I share my bedroom . . .', the relationship between reader and
text as poet is characterized by a strong element of recognition and
association. The students of the group quoted below (all girls) have
no difficulty in recognizing the area of experience depicted in the
text. Not only is the business of sharing a bedroom familiar to them;
they see strong connections between what the poet-narrator claims
to have done and felt, and themselves.

In the discussion of this group, we see something rather more
than a comparing and exchanging of experiences and reaction. The
use of the first person seems to encourage, at one time, close
association between reader and poet and, at other times, a
distancing from and judgement of the poet.

Rebecca 1: yeh
(laughter)
Liz 2: yeh/it's a girl and boy in this bedroom and they're/-
brothers and you normally think/sort of/ooer with your brother
but when you/think back at it you know its a really great laugh
Julie 3: you'd miss him if he . . .
R.4: yeh
L.5: you haven't got anyone in there
J.6: it's just the way he describes it/though/about the left eye
peeping out and . . .
R.7: yeh
J.8: you can see it all
R.9: yeh

Karen 10:   yeh
L.11:   it's sort of . . . it's good cos he thinks he's stopped
breathing then he pulls his . . .
(laughter)
R.12:   yeh
L.13:   you can just imagine it/cheeky little brother/can't you/
doing that
R.14:   yeh
?15:   (inaudible)
K.16:   he's probably younger than him anyway/the brother
J.17:   and the way he describes about the picture/it was a railway
thing
?18:   yeh
K.19:   mm
L.20:   the brother's probably/erm/younger . . .
?21:   younger
R.22:   yeh
L.23:   . . . than the other one because/when he jumps on him
K.24:   yeh/you can imagine this cheeky little boy/can't you
L.25:   yeh
K.26:   aaah
(laughter)
J.27:   oh –
(pause 5 secs)
L.28:   it's good where/the bit where it says/erm/'the paint on the
skirting board wrinkles when I push it with my thumb'/cos I mean
I do that/(laughs) . . .
?.29:   (inaudible)
L.30:   . . . pulling the paintwork apart/and yet in the mornings
you sit there and you see a bit of your wallpaper and . . .
J.31:   you get
?32:   (inaudible)
L.33:   . . . you start pulling it
R.34:   yeh
K.35:   yeh/do that
(laughter)
J.36:   and when he makes pillow dens/cos I know I'm always
having pillow fights with my sister/cos . . .
R.37:   yeh/you share a room don't you
J.38:   . . . me and my sister share a room
K.39:   so you know what it's like really
?40:   I like the bit when
R.41:   yeh
j.42:   I'd feel ever so lonely if I was an only child because
R.43:   yeh

?44: (inaudible)

(laughter)

L.45: even though you fight you'd miss them/so I expect she'd miss him in here

?46: yeh

?47: I like . . .

K.48: she said she didn't like it at the beginning but then when . . .

?49: yeh

K.50: . . . she thought about it she liked it

L.51: I like the bit when it says/erm/when he makes pillow dens (pause 4 secs)

R.52: yeh/where

?53: but where they

K.54: 'His left eye's shows'/cos you can just imagine him under the clothes

(laughter)

K.55: and you can see the left eye peeping out of the bedclothes

J.56: yeh/I know what it's like cos me and my sister we're always fighting

(pause 5 secs)

R.57: I like the bit when it says about the elastoplast spools that scatter on my feet the night before

J.58: yeh

L.59: and the ways he says/er . . .

R.60: she

L.61: . . . she says/where she goes down into the blankets and she pretends she's diving down somewhere . . .

R.62: yeh

L.63: . . . and she's got ever such a good imagination

R.64: yeh

(pause)

R.65: I think it's quite good

J.66: I think it's good

K.67: yeh

?68: I think it's good

K.69: I think it's a poem in itself that doesn't have to rhyme

K.70: no

L.71: it's interesting

?72: yeh

R.73: it's well described

K.74: it's realistic

R.75: yeh

K.76: it tells you a story/I mean poems when they rhyme/some of the words are so stupid.

?77:   yeh/and you don't . . .
J.78:   although some of the poems you can't really imagine
L.79:   cos you have to think of something that actually rhymes
J.80:   yeh you can't imagine it/but you can this/can't you
?81:   mm
?82:   like –
J.83:   I think it's very realistic
L.84:   I do/I think it's ever so good
R.85:   yeh
J.86:   cos it's just what me and my sister do

One feels that the 'seeing' and 'imagining' referred to (8 and 13) are the result of reader and poet having had very similar experiences at some point in their lives. This is also clear from 28, 30 and 33. The following exchange illustrates quite clearly the relationship between reader, poet and common experience.

L.126: I really think the author/Michael Rosen/has wrote this really well
R.127: yeh
L.128: I think he's wrote it very good
J.129: he's described –
K.130: yeh/what life is really like/he's described –
R.131: in the bedroom
J.132: it's best for teenagers cos all the poems/really/are either for adults or for children/really babyish/and none of them are for us
L.133: yeh/but this is for teenagers/really/isn't it
?134:   yeh
?135:   our age/sort of thing
?136:   yeh
K.137: I keep on/thinking about that bit where he hides himself in the pillow/cos when I used to stay up/right/and I used to watch a horror movie/I used to get really scared and so I'd go to bed and I'd sort of lay there and I'd sort of cover myself all up/cover myself all up and/erm/have just a little peephole/through the thing/so I could see if any monsters were coming to get me

It is significant to see how this creation of the poem through common experience can enter a more intense level in which the reader comes to own or possess the poem as poet as well as the poem as event. This is particularly evident in the assumption that the poet is female (at 2, 45, 48, 50, 60, 61, 63) even though Rosen's name was acknowledged on the copy of the poem they were using and even though they use it themselves (126).

189

There is, later, even a point at which a member of the group claims to possess the actual emotions of the poet.

R.157: the bit where/I think/where she's breathing/you know/she goes 'Now breathe now breathe' and there's quick silence/when she pulls it away I bet she feels really cross cos he's laughing/I bet she feels . . .

L.158: yeh

R.159: aagh/I hate him

J.160: yes/sort of/aargh/you stupid boy

L.161: and it seems to this that she's sort of sitting somewhere or that/when she's a bit older and that/or maybe sort of thinking back to what she was doing –

J.162: what/you think/that's what this sounds like

L.163: yeh

R.164: yeh

L.165: and she's thinking back to what she did around her younger days like/and beforehand she was saying to her mates and that/she hates sharing with her brother/then she says/goes back/and thinks about it and then she says well no it's right really because she probably feel lost without him

We see, yet again, here, a case of the students creating a story/context for the poem they are creating. Liz is talking about her own reactions interlinked with those that she imagines are the poet's.

It would seem, then, that Rosen's (perhaps limited) aims in writing a text, with a relatively unsophisticated way of presenting himself, are realized here. The relationship between reader and text as poet is a clear and fairly intense one but it relies, in the main, on the common ground of experience which writer and reader share.

Searching for the implied poet

Seamus Heaney's 'Follower' also uses anecdote and reflection on personal experience as its material, presented in the first person. There is a strong contrast, however, with Rosen's text in two ways. First, the experience recorded attempts to grasp a truth which, whilst it may not be more profound than Rosen's, can only be perceived when the cycle of relationship between father and son has evolved to maturity. Secondly, it is therefore presented, not in Rosen's childlike colloquialisms, but as a measured exposition of a paradox – with little or no explicit reference to emotional reaction.

The implied author is not only recounting an experience, the significance of which only became clear fairly late in life, but doing so in a way which distances himself emotionally from the experience. The reader is guided to a revelation of a truth which has some general application and a sense of irony and sadness; but the implied author does not present his reactions for us to share.

Most of the discussion groups which encountered 'Follower' did not approach it with enthusiasm. Several pupils found it very difficult to create the poem by reference to personal experience.

In the following exchanges between students discussing 'Follower', we see the group remaining rather distant from their construction of the poem. Occasionally, they light upon a word or phrase which carries some emotional weight ('yapping', for instance) and they certainly seem to grasp a considerable change of attitude on the part of the poet (197 to 206), but these are emotions and attitudes which the students cannot easily find in themselves. Perhaps the potential force of the poem is, consequently, diluted.

Alan 1: I liked it in general 'cos it gets the effect of all the sort of hard work that's when he's ploughing and that
John 2: yes it does and it gets the feeling of time progressing doesn't it/from . . .
A.3: yeh
J.4: . . . the beginning to the end/especially the last/what/three verses
A.5: yeh/'cos I think it's that his dad gets old/he gets old and senile or whatever . . .
J.6: yeh
A.7: . . . and now he does the ploughing
J.8: yeh/the kid does the ploughing
Nathan 9: I don't like it/it's self-explanatory and I don't really like those sort of poems
Dean 10: I like the last verse
N.11: mm/yeh
A.12: although when it says yapping it makes him sound like a Jack Russell
J.13: yes it does/doesn't it
(laughter)
J.14: I suppose that's all he was/just yapping . . .
D.15: I don't think so
J.16: . . . round his ankles all the time

A.48: it makes him seem rather pathetic/doesn't it/'It is my father who keeps stumbling'
J.49: yes
A.50: I mean if my dad was stumbling along/I'd feel right embarrassed
D.51: yeh in the middle it gives the impression of his father being a real expert

191

A.52: mm
N.53: and then his son wanting to be an expert and sort of doing/I think
A.54: yeh
D.55: now what do you think about the fifth verse (reads it)
A.56: mm/it doesn't seem to do much
J.57: it doesn't get anywhere
N.58: no
A.59: I mean it just sort of states that he wanted to be like his/father but it takes a whole verse to do it
J.60: yeh/he could have put on the end of one of the verses or the beginning of another
N.61: he's already said that/so it shouldn't really be in there
J.62: yeh
N.63: he could have . . .
D.64: well it could be/you know/a bit more condensed
N.65: he could have said something else about/erm
J.66: yes
N.67: . . . horses or something again/I don't know
J.68: mm
A.69: he puts it across quite well but it seems a long-winded way/'I wanted . . . arm'
N.70: yes/it seems extended/if you're going to put that in you ought to extend the rest of the poem because the rest of the poem's very condensed . . .

N.100: he's always trying to follow in his father's footsteps
D.101: I find it hard to imagine that . . .

J.188: yes/it's a mixture of poems/isn't it/it ought to be either one very short one/very condensed/or one very long one
D.189: one/one moment/you know/he's only a little boy and the next moment he's . . .
J.190: yeh/well/he's making a comparison between the two
D.191: . . . you know/a man
A.192: yeh
D.193: yes/he's grown up and he's looking back on it/really/that's what he's doing
N.194: see it's great/it says 'I was a nuisance'/I mean it's not something present/if it was present he'd say I am a nuisance
A.195: well it's put today isn't it
J.196: mm
(pause 5 secs)
N.197: I think he was/erm/I think he was really proud of his father/'cos he was an expert/ploughing . . .
J.198: mm

N.199:   . . . and he said right/my father's good and . . .
J.200:   he seems sorry that his father's not the expert any more
N.201:   yeh/and he's got to look after him
J.202:   it seems like that now he is the/the one who does the ploughing/it's not half as glorious as he thought it was
D.203:   yeh/but when he was younger/he seemed to/you know/ that/I don't know/that/I know/it seemed that he really wanted to take over his father's plough.
J.204:   mm/and then it's not what it's cracked up to be
D.205:   mm
J.206:   'cos it's just an ordinary job/or whatever

The confusion over time-lapse, the difficulty which the group members have in identifying the poet's attitude, and the problem of meeting it from their own experience all result from the vagueness of their picture of the poet. Consequently, the students cannot find a satisfactory entry into the poem, although this is not to say that the struggles of the group are valueless as part of the desire for understanding. It is just than an imprecise view of the poem-as-poet might lead to a less intense experience when the text is read and studied.

It may be true, then, that children (or less experienced readers of poetry) need a point of entry into the text which draws on an association between the poet and themselves, if the poem is to be created vividly. In 'I share my bedroom', that point of entry is provided both by the common group experience and the explicit reactions of Michael Rosen. In discussions of 'The Stag', however, those conditions certainly did not apply. Nevertheless, the hunting of animals, as an issue, is one in the forefront of many students' minds. More important, the implied author of 'The Stag', directing our responses via some extremely subtle controls, leads us to identify closely with the plight of the stag in a state of high emotional intensity – even though his own sympathies are not explicitly presented. One can get a clear idea of this by rereading the transcript of the first tape we studied, especially from 201 to the end. Ted Hughes' code of rhetorical controls has, to some extent, been 'cracked' by this group. The poem has itself become an experience which the students relive and, although there is sometimes a conflict between this and their own past experiences and assumptions, they are led into an experience of excitement and subsequent anticlimax as the focus switches to the humans.

Most groups had little difficulty with Hughes' point of view and the students would probably agree with one teacher's remark (in her written response to 'The Stag') that, 'I am pleased that the poet refrained from the temptation to lecture me, yet I still feel sure that I know his feelings on the subject'.

Complete engagement with the text and the satisfactory creation of the poem could well depend, then, on the reader's perception of the poet. Each poet creates a picture of him/herself according to the sum of his/her own choices of rhetoric and these choices of rhetoric are, in turn, an integral part of what I have termed to be the poem as form. Apprehension of the form of a poem, even though not explicitly expressed by a student, may therefore be crucial to his/her successful reading. However, form can work upon our consciousness in a number of ways, some of them potentially insidious, and this explicit expression of what the form is doing to us is, as post-structuralist analysts have demonstrated, a vital element in developing a critical response.

(iii) Feeling and form

It is true that students are continuously engaged with the form of a text as they attempt to create it. The making of meaning from the text includes the need to decide on the force of figurative language and diction. These features are variously associated with the processes of building up the action in the mental theatre (for example; the exact position of the boy in 'Follower' when he stumbles in his father's 'hob-nailed wake') or of coming to some decision about the attitude of the poet (assessing the strength of 'terrible planet' as a pointer to the poet's indictment of human values). It is, however, rarer to find evidence (in discussion groups or as isolated writers) of students' conscious *assessment* of the effects of imagery and diction, particularly when it comes to the strands, or recurring families, of imagery which occur in some of the texts. Even when noticed, however, these aspects of the text are given little attention and little attempt is made to articulate the effects which they produce in the reader.

It is also true that as one reads, one is inevitably experiencing the effects of rhythm, movement, rhyme and line-arrangement. Again, however, only scant attention is paid to the effects these have. It is as though the students notice that something is present but, unless it presents a problem during the construction and fuller creation of the text, they do not ask why. In the case of 'The Stag', a number of formal features are treated in this way. A group of boys took turns in reading stanzas of the text out aloud. When one had read 'The Stag' he remarked 'It's a bad one to read I can tell you that'. He may well have been able to sense the breathlessness and panic of the stag at that point but there is no indication that he perceived how Hughes has created it and invites the reader to experience it by the long, run-on lines and the collections of descriptive clauses through which we follow the stag through the landscape.

On a number of occasions, other groups point out the changing pattern of stanzas and lines in 'The Stag', the recurrence of references to the stag at the end of each stanza or the proliferation of 'ands' in the final stanza, but the reasons, in Coleridge's words, why the text 'is so, and not otherwise' remain unexplored.

There may be a combination of possible explanations for this. For one thing, it could be that the groups or writers did not have enough time to get on to this aspect of the text. This is unlikely since most finished, voluntarily, before the end of their allotted time, as the reports of teachers and the timings of, and last comments on, the tapes show. Quite possibly, however, such considerations just did not occur to them, and that might be due to lack of practice, lack of literary experience or conceptual short-comings in their stage of development.

It might also be said that they were not asked to evaluate or judge each text, and that they regarded such consideration of form as an aspect of evaluation. Even so, there are many things which the students were not asked to do and, further, a great deal of evaluation (about individual words, phrases, standards of 'realism' or amounts of detail) does go on.

A lot may depend on the nature of each poem. 'Epitaph' is constructed, principally, from one chain of imagery, and, although no students went into a detailed critical appraisal, most who noticed it signalled some kind of approval.

Whilst recognising that a *poet*'s structuring of narrative is an essential element in the form of a poem, it seems that the students' concern to construct a story from the text and, on occasions, to gain some perception of the poet, overrides conscious considerations of many other aspects of form unless they impose themselves strongly on the reader. The clearest example of this is that of 'Anthem for Doomed Youth'. It is, of course, a sonnet and the teacher who chose to teach it thought this essential to a full understanding. Certain aspects of the diction are particularly obtrusive and two strong threads of imagery (death in battle and the funeral ritual of the church) are closely interlinked. This group of girls made no mention of the sonnet form (even though their teacher confirms these students had been introduced to sonnets some time before). Nevertheless, much of their conversation is concerned with the associations of ideas in the imagery.

The fact that there is a pattern of imagery was noticed quite early in their exchanges.

Clare 64:   and it says/what do you think those candles/it says

what candles would –
Alison 65: I don't know about that
Kirstie 66: well you know you have candles at funerals don't you
C.67: yeh/or you know like the light of God/it's all connected
with death isn't it
K.68: mm
C.69: they're not held in their hands it's in their eyes
A.70: something to do with the/I think it's something to do with
their mind
K.71: it's called 'Anthem for Doomed Youth' so it's something
to do with death
A.72: yeh
C.73: yeh it's a theme/like choirs/its got choirs and candles
K.74: because it's an anthem it's –
C.75: but look/'flowers the tenderness of patient minds'
K.76: it's quite nice because it's all done in this kind of
metaphor isn't it

Once the pattern of extended imagery is established, the group are
able to make some statement about the reason why it has been
employed:

C.107: no it's just/like Kirstie said/a metaphor
K.108: yeh/cos everything's substituted for things like –
A.109: yeh/aren't really there/yeh
C.110: like you've sort of you have/there's two things to this
poem/war and the church
K.111: I think (inaudible) based around war/and the church is
used to bring it across
C.112: yeh
A.113: the message
C.114: yeh
K.115: then you can reflect back so it'll become clearer
C.116: yeh like you can connect the death with the church and
how horrible they are and everything
K.117: and also the flowers

Further, the group continue their creation of the poem within the
context of this pattern and purpose. But, if the use of metaphor, as
they see it, is to *contrast* the horrors of war with the sanctification of
church ritual, Owen's use of the word 'mockeries' presents a
problem, employing, as it does, some inconsistency of emotional
association.

K.150: what does it mean 'no mockeries for them'
A.151: well/you know/mockery/you know when you mock
something/isn't it/I don't know/let's have a look

K.152: I know what to mock means
C.153: does it mean in this sense/no sympathy . . . or –
A.154: yeh
C.155: . . . no sympathy or caring for them or no fuss made of them
K.156: mm
C.157: that/you know/when you mock/it's all in the context really isn't it/when you mock
K.158: mock's when you make fun of them really isn't it
C.159: yeh
A.160: I don't know
C.161: perhaps it's got a double meaning
K.162: ambiguous

Their hypothesis, here, is unconvincing, and is not further developed but represents an attempt to make elements of the text fit into the form they have created for it.

Interestingly, though, the need for students to explain their responses and perceptions to their colleagues produces attempts at interpreting what those responses amount to.

A.224: that bit here 'only the stuttering rifles' rapid rattle'/I mean rifles don't stutter do they/well
K.225: I think that's the bells aren't they/that's it/that/declaring it because you have bells at funerals sometimes
A.226: I don't think/everyone's talking about funerals/I don't think that it's being his funeral/honestly
C.227: I think I don't think/I think it is about/death/but not about funerals/it's just the church is used –
A.228: as a colour
K.229: yeh I know/but you can connect it with the funerals
A.230: as a substitute
C.231: yeh
K.232: so the bells are the rifles rattling around so that the rifles are sort of like declaring/the death/you know
C.233: or it could be/I think/I think of it as being the sort of/dying/dying prayer
K.234: yes 'cos you get shot with a rifle
A235: ooer . . .

K.242: they didn't have bells/they just died like cattle
C.243: oh I see
C.244: oh its heral/it's almost like heralding their death/that's the only sound they die to
K.245: yeh/and you see they don't have any bells when they die/they just die and all they have above them when they are dying is the/are the guns and the rifles

C.246:	mm
K.247:	which can –
C.248:	yeh/they're the only sort of –
K.249:	which they can say their last prayer to
C.250:	they're the only connection with life
K.251:	mm
C.252:	yeh/their last connection with life

As the discussion continues, the group are occupied with looking at individual images and phrases, creating meaning from them and attempting to fit them into their overall perception of the pattern. Occasionally, they step back from this process in an attempt to articulate some kind of evaluation of the text, as in their discussion of the last line: 'And each slow dusk a drawing down of blinds'.

A.363:	like pull down the blinds and that kind of thing
K.364:	yeh
C.365:	oh yeh/that could be –
K.366:	like shutting out the light
C.367:	yeh
A.368:	I think some shops
C.369:	and the toll of death if you see what I mean/it's sort of shutting out/shutting out
A.370:	the light
C.371:	shutting out some people with the light
A.372:	yeh
C.373:	because you've died during the day and they've souls
K.374:	it makes you want to read that again/doesn't it/ because . . .
A.375:	mm
K.376:	. . . because (inaudible) has to read it
C.377:	you have to sort of concentrate on it to get it fully out
A.378:	there's a lot in there isn't there/it's not just something you can just –
K.379:	(inaudible) to get it rhyming as well
C.380:	mm
A.381:	yeh/doesn't
C.382:	oh hey it does/yeh its a good poem actually
A.383:	it must have taken ages
K.384:	he gets (inaudible) to say in it and he doesn't alter any of the things/and it might have not much rhythm but that doesn't matter really
C.385:	mm
A.386:	it's nothing you say with rhythm anyway/is it/it's something
K.387:	yeh

A.388: you wouldn't go la da di da di da dia
(laughter)

It is comforting to see that the students, here, admire the text, are not content with cursory reading and are able to recognize that certain kinds of rhythm would be inappropriate to the subject of the text. They are, at least, not prone to what Richards termed 'technical presuppositions'.[7] But, on the other hand, they have very limited notion of 'rhythm' as an obvious and banal stress pattern and they do not seem capable of describing any emotional effects which result from their creation of the form of the text.

The students are aware that some emotional response is being evoked in them, however, even though they ignore the contribution which the rhythm may have made to this. Towards the end of their tape, they announce that they will now discuss 'feelings':

K.621: it makes you feel weird, doesn't it? It makes *me* feel weird.
C.622: it's sad, it's like, you know like a wail, it's like a wailing song really
K.623: there's so much death, as well, it just makes you –
C.624: ˙ it sort of comes over you, are –
A.625: it's mysterious I think towards that bit
C.626: yeh
A.627: yeh
C.628: mysterious, the candles part
A.629: yeh
K.630: and it's described so well/I mean –
A.631: and it's sort of melancholy
K.632: mm you can/I mean it's described so well that it's so (inaudible) –
A.633: a big imagination/image in your mind kind of thing
K.634: it's so vivid that/it's like a vision
C.635: it's more sad and peaceful at the end
K.636: it is peaceful
C.637: than scary/but I think the last line isn't/ . . . it doesn't/it's not intended to frighten you I don't think
A.638: no
C.639: it's just intended to leave you in peace
A.640: in a thought/ . . . to think about it all you know
C.641: pardon
K.642: it's nice because/it's about the war which is so vicious/it's just like a small –
A.643: summary
K.644: summary/like gentle
C.645: just the patient

A.646:   you know its not very bitter either
C.647:   like a dying/dying away/just fading
K.648:   mm/that's why I like the end/it just sort of fades out
C.649:   yeh, and the rest of the poem's/the rest of the poem's
more angry and vicious
K.650:   it's more bitter towards it
A.651:   yes
K.652:   and the church part is more peaceful
A.653:   makes it more peaceful/yeh
C.654:   yeh
K.655:   and makes it more symbolic
A.656:   I was going to say that/I was going to say that/symbolic
(pause 5 secs)
C.657:   it's a poem that makes you think
A.658:   yeh
C.659:   (inaudible) the thought
K.660:   yeh
A.661:   yeh/you have a more open mind towards everything
else/you know
C.662:   makes you think about the war and realise that –
A.663:   yeh not just battles and killing
K.664:   it makes you aware of all the –
A.665:   it was, what actually happened there/their fears and
emotions
K.666:   the word kill/it doesn't really mean much when you just
say it but when it's like this
A.667:   yeh
C.668:   it's almost like you're seeing it
A.669:   yeh
C.670:   you're certainly feeling it in your mind

Two important questions emerge from this, and from the fact
that, in the research data as a whole, very few students make any
kind of reference to *the way the form of a text works in conjunction
with their emotional response to it*.

First, there is the question of whether it is necessary or desirable
to expect such references. Many teachers subscribe to the idea that
poems demonstrate the magic and music of words; there is even still
some support for the notion of 'pure' poetry. I wonder, however,
whether the same teachers would not accept the need for
discriminating reading, by their students, of newspaper and
television reports which may be just as emotive. I would rather
speak of the power of words, and the need for students to perceive
the nature of such power, and be able to take their share of it.

Second, and if one does want to see clear, articulate interpretations, there is the question of how to equip students with the vocabulary required, and what this vocabulary should be. The old labels, the lexicon of practical criticism, may be of some use, as may be the terms provided by recent literary theorists. But, surely, responses and interpretations should be creative: students should be encouraged to find *their* way of explaining and describing their responses, or of demonstrating that they have power.

Chapter 5

Conclusions

Michael Benton

A   Towards a response-centred methodology

We have called our book *Young Readers Responding to Poems* to indicate that 'response' is a process not a product, or even a series of products. Readers come to terms with poems over time; and, with those poems we come to feel are worth reading, the process remains open-ended; we never finish with such poems. The tremor of unease English teachers often feel when they hear themselves say that they have 'done' this or that poem with a class signals the mismatch between the process of reading and responding and what usually happens to poems within the constraints of the classroom where the stress is usually upon pinning the meaning down. In fact, we know that meaning cannot be fixed; that poems – like paintings or sculptures – are infinitely renewable; and that in good poems we will discover fresh things each time we read them and enjoy being reminded of old things.

Chapters 2, 3 and 4 all show young readers making such discoveries. While their emphases are different, they do share certain principles, notably, that aesthetic reading is a more circuitous process than reading for information. The traceries of individuals' initial responses (Chapter 2) and the meanderings of group exploration (Chapters 3 and 4) show that unfashionable (or, at least under-rated) qualities of ruminativeness, tentativeness, speculativeness are characteristic of response to poetry. All the evidence supports Rosenblatt's view that a poem is 'an event in time'; conversely, readers require time to come to terms with the event. Reflection is thus the key. Responses need time and space in which to grow. A methodology for teaching has to be built upon these principles.

John Teasey's work illustrates Rosenblatt's transactional theory most powerfully. Here we eavesdrop on two readers, Elizabeth and Kristina, bringing a poem into existence and simultaneously being aware of the experience of this 'event'. This data gives the hard evidence of 'evocation' that several recent researchers (Rosenblatt, Purves, Kintgen, in Cooper (ed.), 1985) have asked for but not themselves provided. The diagrammatic studies which map how readers initially move in and around a text lend substance to the common poetry-reading metaphor of 'taking a mental walk' around a poem and, indeed, to the sculptural analogy we drew in Chapter 1. They demonstrate clearly that every reading is a unique performance, that entry into the text is idiosyncratic. Each of us makes his own map. The 'first draft' reading is selective; its purpose is apprehension rather than comprehension. (A similar orientation is shown in the group work below.) Apprehension entails the reader in reaching out to the experiences that lie behind the words on the page. Subsequently, processes of editing and reshaping may take place as the reader continues to move in and around the text. This is consistent with Rosenblatt's view that 'We respond to the work that we are evoking'.[1] A measure of the successful evocation of a poem is that the reader explores and evaluates both the world behind the words on the page and the world within him brought to life by the words on the page. John Teasey's research thus deepens the concepts of evocation and response through meticulous, descriptive analyses of aesthetic reading.

The orientation of Ray Bell's enquiries is different. Transactional theory is again the starting-point and there is interesting evidence of several pupils' first, independent impressions of Blake's poems, monitored in writing or on tape. However, the main concern is to do with practical methodology. His evidence enables us to observe how pupils develop from the first encounter with a poem, through the phase of coming to terms with it by setting their own responses against those of others in a group, to finally making a considered written response. The tentativeness or assertiveness of the first phase, the thoughts that are edited out or developed in the second phase, and the character of the final statement are all displayed. We can observe what in mathematics is called 'the working' – the slow evolution over time and in different contexts of how readers make meaning. The teacher's role is also explored so that the main sources of variation in reader-response studies – among texts, among readers, among contexts – are all considered and cross-hatched, as it were, with the main means of monitoring – individual writing, group discussion, and individual tape-recording. The ramifications of this complexity can only be partially explored through the two or three examples discussed but, clearly, there are many opportunities suggested here for further enquiries. Moreover, the evidence has direct pedagogical implications: both in exploring responses and in striving for good practices in teaching 'the medium is the message'. The decisions that both researchers and teachers make about procedures dictate the nature of the reponses elicited and the learning that takes place. Here, particularly, the teacher-researcher role is properly hyphenated.

Keith Hurst's research originated in a different but complementary way as we have seen (p. 158). Whereas the other two enquiries had been built upon pilot studies with individuals within a small group, Hurst started at the other end, as it were, with the problem of achieving good practice with a whole class. Group work became the focus, and the analysis enables us to reflect upon the conceptual model he offers and upon the issue of the classroom management of learning that it implies. Diagrams of linguistic interaction are always reductive but as aids to thinking they can help us hold in the mind the elusive data of readers' responses. Hurst's model of three frames, developed from Barnes's and Todd's notion of the 'cycles of utterances' that characterise group talk, is a means of mapping the episodes of a group's engagement with a poem. It complements John Teasey's individual response diagrams. In both cases it is necessary to remind ourselves that we are dealing with manifestations of 'the world in the head'. Representations of three-dimensional concepts on one-dimensional sheets of paper are always awkward. Perhaps the best we can do is to think of these maps as transparent globes – at least this allows for both the spatial and the temporal dimensions of poem-reading. Hurst's model, in particular, provokes some crucial questions about classroom activity. If the 'story frame' is so important, what implications does this have for the choice of material at particular ages? If the 'poet frame' is also significant, why do we not encourage the social rapport between reader and writer (as in fiction-reading) by using more collections by individual poets? If the 'form frame' is relatively weak, should we not be employing more strategies (sequencing? group cloze?) that engage pupils with the formal patterns of poetry?

Taken together, the elements of responding to poems that these three enquiries illustrate encourage the tentative formulation of a methodological framework that can serve as the poetry-teacher's covert rationale for classroom activity. The caveats voiced above about the reductionist nature of diagrams of linguistic interaction apply equally to those which purport to define classroom methods. Nonetheless, the framework shown in figure 5.1 is offered as a way of translating some of the principal points to emerge from the enquiries into a methodology.

The exit arrows on the right of the diagram indicate the flexibility that poetry-teaching needs: sometimes the first encounter with a poem may be the last; at other times a series of lessons can be given over to all the phases. Frequently, we will not know the extent of the activities that the poem(s) will bear until we are actually busy doing the work with the class. The multiple exit points allow for a

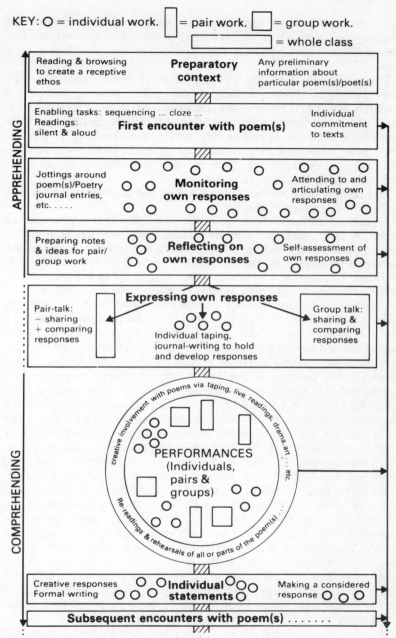

Figure 5.1   Reading and responding to poems –
a flexible methodology

due sense of praxis – our self-awareness, during the course of teaching, to know when to make further demands, when to cut our losses, when to change direction, and when to bring work to a close.

The continuum down the left side of the diagram signals the shift from individual apprehension of the poem through successive activities towards a fuller comprehension. At its most explicit, this entails a movement from evocation to critical evaluation. The distinction between apprehending and comprehending is crucial. They both form part of a continuous process. Would we want to talk, even to ourselves, if we were only permitted to do so when comprehension was complete?

The central spine of the diagram shows the successive phases in a response-centred methodology.

Figure 5.1 attempts to honour the principles that a poem is 'an event in time' and that the individual evocation needs room to develop prior to the sharing of responses. Approaches to poems are governed by a range of factors, not least by the attitude of the class and their familiarity with poetry. *Browsing* and *reading out* poems, *finding out* about particular poems or poets, *enabling tasks* such as sequencing and cloze (see pp. 215 and 216) may all have a part to play at different times to prepare pupils for the particular poem(s) a teacher wants to introduce. After any preparatory lead-in to the poem(s) and the initial readings, the framework allows for the fact that there are certain activities a pupil can and must undertake by himself. *Articulating* and *reflecting* upon personal responses are fundamental to the reader's early apprehension of a poem. Jotting around a text or in a journal aids the reader in attending to his own responses. At first, pupils may be reluctant to believe that their contributions are as important as those of the teacher, but it is foolish to underestimate how powerfully most areas of the curriculum appear to value memorisation and the passive reception of second-hand knowledge. There is a need to convey the fact that, in aesthetic reading, the pleasure lies in the richness of the personal responses that occur, and the challenge in the idiosyncrasy of the process of responding. Similarly, the reader must have the opportunity to reflect on his own responses before participating in group discussion. It is in the private talking to oneself and in the spaces behind public talk that the poem will be evoked and at this stage, the demands of group work may well push aside what the reader is trying to grasp. Reflecting on tape, for example, about a text the pupil has chosen to introduce to the class would be a useful and enjoyable task to be carried out at home.

Reading poetry is especially rich in opportunities for independent and peer-group work and for the teacher to develop strategies which will enable readers and texts to work on each other. Hence, the phase when pupils are *expressing their responses* might include a whole-class discussion controlled by the teacher but it is here that pairs and groups can most usefully share and develop their initial responses with each other. There will always be occasions when it is appropriate for some individuals to continue to work independently and this is allowed for. Many of the activities for individuals, pairs and groups suggested below (p. 212) are suitable during this phase.

The central part of the diagram emphasizes performance. Learning by doing is particularly apt with poems since, as we have already seen, much of their appeal and meaning derives from sound and rhythm. Activities which lift the words off the page are not only enjoyable in themselves but valuable aids to understanding. A special attraction of presentation is that the English teacher can turn for resources to other areas of the curriculum. Music, drama and art are areas from which poetry lessons have become unnecessarily distanced, either through an institutional tendency to separate subjects off, or in a misguided attempt to safeguard the supposed 'academic respectability' that education rarely grants to the arts. Preparing a performance takes the pupils back inside the poem(s). Re-readings and rehearsals involve discussion about pace, intonation, thought and feeling which, at its best, can engage pupils in the closest form of textual analysis without them really realizing it. There is no shortage of ideas for this phase: the ubiquitous 'Thirty-Six Things to do with a Poem'[2] and *Teaching Literature 9–14*[3] are useful starting-points.

The individual pieces of writing that might follow the performances are likely to be more sensitive and detailed for having been preceded by such activities. The importance of this phase is that the whole attention of the pupil is brought to bear upon the whole text from which each pupil is evoking, or has evoked, his own poem. A creative response (see p. 216), demanding cognitive and affective skills, is as revealing of the nature of the pupil's engagement with the text as any critical statement.

One significant change of emphasis that is highlighted by this methodology lies within the conventional three-part guidelines often given to pupils in studying and writing about a particular poem. As an aid to thinking and writing, pupils are commonly urged[4] to ask themselves three questions and to frame their written work upon the basis of their answers: what sort of poem is it? How does it work? What do I feel about it? These are text-oriented questions with a concern for efficient evaluation. Once the reader's responses are let in on the act of critical writing then, as Elizabeth's work shows (p. 42), the emphasis alters. The three-part guidelines become:

- an opening statement of the reader's experience of the poem 'as an event'; what the reader thinks the writer is looking at;
- a discussion of the text as blueprint; how the poem works for the reader – that is, which cues guided the evocation of the poem.
- an evaluation of the two worlds brought to life during the event, those of the reader and the text.

At the heart of this methodology is the uniqueness of the reading event. Comprehension and criticism are thus rooted in the processes of reading and responding.

B Classroom Implications

(i) A shift of priorities

First, a reprise of the propositions which these enquiries have led us to make. It is more important for young readers to experience poetry and to express that experience to themselves and others than it is to analyse it. Properly handled, literary understanding and critical evaluation develop *as the result of* reflective reading and responding: the 2Cs are parts of the 2Rs and are the stronger for being so. If they cease to be parts of the whole reading/responding experience, then comprehension degenerates into inquisition, criticism into mechanical analysis, and a gap opens up between the reader and the poem which reduces the latter to fodder for just another sort of textbook exercise. Poems, as we said at the outset, need to be given back to readers. It is the job of our methodology to see that this happens. For poetry is not about experience; it *is* experience.

The shift in priorities from the traditional, literary critical approach to poems to the one we advocate based upon reading and responding is sharply indicated if we contrast the way our young readers have operated with the advice James Reeves gives to students on how to read poetry.

First, shut out of your mind everything that is not on the printed page. Then, when you have mastered the poet's *meaning*, consider his *method*. . . . Finally, open your mind to all the *impressions and ideas*, more closely or less closely related to the text on the page, which come into it[5] (our italics).

It is doubtful if many human activities – and certainly not reading – are susceptible to the neatness of 'first', 'then', and 'finally'. Clearly, too, this is at odds with the ways in which our young readers functioned. To adopt such an approach in the classroom would be to reduce the activity of reading poetry to yet another exercise in efferent reading. What in practice happens in poetry lessons predicated on this principle is that the teacher desperately attempts to delay discussion of 'meaning' in order to discourage any premature or immature judgements. Most of the time is taken up in a question-and-answer session on those features of language and form determined by the teacher to be of importance. Whatever time is left is not, of course, given over to the final activity, which appears to be too chaotic and diverse to oversee, but in collecting information in preparation for the inevitable written homework.

However compelling the enthusiasm of the teacher, however inspired the choice of text, however genuine the intention to explore the text in partnership with the pupils, this approach is irrelevant to the needs of the good reader, inhibiting to the average reader, and inimical to the development of a personal response to literature. As argued above, it puts the cart of criticism and comprehension before the horse of reading and responding.

The model of reading proposed by Rosenblatt, illustrated by our young readers, and translated into a methodology in our diagram above, suggests that a very different classroom experience ought to be on offer. Talk about the *meaning* would be accepted as an initial approximation, to be edited and re-shaped. Talk about the *methods* would be delayed until the readers had had the opportunity to explore and share their own responses. When introduced, its purpose would be to help the reader to evoke the poem. All the impressions and ideas, which Reeves would have us delay or postpone, would be the very materials with which the pupil would work: from the beginning, to fashion the poem from the text; and at the end, if the poem has been of personal significance, when he engages in a dialogue with the implied author.

It is not the business of the teacher to instruct the reader on how best to attend an autopsy; rather, it is his business to enable the reader to bring his poem into being.

It follows that teachers must develop a clearer understanding of what is meant by the reader's interaction with a text. What constitutes a valuable reader-response? Where are the growth-points in what a pupil says about a poem? Will individual jotting or talking in pairs/groups or some other activity be the best way in for the class with this particular poem? These and similar sorts of questions arise naturally from a methodology that is based upon what individual readers do. They can easily lead to an English department deciding to monitor its own activities in literature lessons. Initiating workshop activities, listening to transcript extracts, monitoring the way individuals negotiate poems and so on are all easy to incorporate into day-by-day teaching. The space that has to be fought for is the teacher's room to respond to this material and to discuss it with colleagues. Given that space, the evaluation of readers' responses and the lessons to be learned from attending closely to what pupils say and write follow naturally. Teachers have an often unrecognised expertise in evaluation. Because they are evaluating for most of their professional lives, it is a skill that can easily be overlooked. Where, perhaps, a connection can be missed is in relating this evaluative skill to teaching method. Through the processes of teaching ourselves to recognize reader-text interactions, of learning to make judgements about which responses are more defensible than others, and of realizing the relationship between pupils' stated responses and the means that elicited them, we begin to bridge any gap that exists between our abilities to evaluate and to teach and we learn to relate what we discover about responses to our classroom actions.

(ii) Creating a receptive ethos: a checklist

The strictly practical business of what can be achieved with poems in the classroom depends very much upon the attitude of the English teachers, the importance poetry is seen to have within the school and the status it is given in the ongoing work of the English Department. A checklist of things teachers could do to improve the environment for poetry is given below. It makes no claims to originality; indeed, rather the opposite is the case since the suggestions are all based upon current practices in particular schools. It is often salutary, however, to remind ourselves of what we already know but do not necessarily do.

Resource box
The single most useful resource for poetry teaching is a collection of 40 or 50 slim volumes of poetry *by author*. There is a rich bibliography of books addressed to the young reader (see Appendix 1). Initially, the purpose of this mini-library is to encourage teachers to read and talk about poems; but, housed in two LP record cases, it becomes a portable classroom resource.

Anthology-making
The best anthologies grow out of lively classroom practice. It is also useful to have a goal. Staff and pupils could collect their own favourite poems over the period of a term or two with the idea of making a school anthology or, more specifically, compiling a collection for next year's class.

Poets in school
You may well be able to arrange for a poet to visit your school to read and talk about his work. Your local arts association will help; or write to The Poetry Society, National Poetry Centre, 21 Earls Court Square, London, SW5.

Creative writing
There is a danger that this becomes institutionalised on the timetable; or that it arises from a habitual three-phase lesson plan, viz. 'read – discuss – now write a poem yourselves'; or that it becomes a perfunctory exercise in stimulus-response work. Keep yourself and your colleagues up to date with ideas for writing. Some books to help you: Ted Hughes, *Poetry in the Making* (Faber, 1967); Sandy Brownjohn, *Does It Have to Rhyme?* (Hodder and Stoughton, 1980) and *What Rhymes With Secret?* (Hodder & Stoughton, 1982); Michael Rosen, *I See A Voice* (Hutchinson, 1981).

Classroom method
If readers apprehend poems differently from stories – 'walking round' them, finding varied points of entry, approaching them obliquely, as we have suggested – then variety in method is essential. The teacher who gives a class a 'guided tour' through a poem line by line is at odds with the reading process. Therefore, discuss with your colleagues at school, at the local teachers' centre or at your professional association, the *details* of classroom practice in the light of the ideas in this chapter.

Books about teaching
Make a collection of books and articles about poetry in school. Some of the older publications by George Sampson and David Holbrook are well worth inclusion, even if the schools have changed since the books were conceived. *New Directions in English Teaching* A. Adams (ed.) (Falmer Press) reprints pieces by me on creative writing and by Geoff Fox and Brian Merrick on 'Thirty-Six Things to do with a Poem'. The single most useful source of information is *Children, Language and Literature* (The Open University Press, 1982). Look at *The English Magazine*, especially numbers 4, 10 and 17. Also M. Benton and G. Fox, *Teaching Literature 9–14* (Oxford University Press, 1985); S. Tunnicliffe, *Poetry Experience* (Methuen, 1984); P. Benton, *Pupil, Teacher, Poem* (Hodder & Stoughton, 1986); M and P. Benton, *Examining Poetry* (Hodder & Stoughton, 1986).

Michael Benton

Poetry reading

It may be feasible to start a poetry reading group in your area. It might begin with a few local teachers, perhaps involve your local NATE branch, or library, or staff and students from nearby higher education institutions.

Library

Reappraise your library provision for poetry. Is the stock of slim volumes and anthologies up-to-date? Are the titles the most appropriate ones for your pupils? Basically, children up to the age of about fourteen prefer poems that are amusing, that tell them a story and that have a strongly marked rhythm. Current favourites appear to be Michael Rosen, Gareth Owen, Roger McGough and Kit Wright; with the older age group, Charles Causley, Ted Hughes, and D.H. Lawrence seem to keep their appeal. Also, in recent years, many excellent slim volumes by Afro-Caribbean poets and women poets have been published. Note especially the work of James Berry, Grace Nichols, John Agard, Fleur Adcock, Elizabeth Jennings – all of whom have a ready appeal to young readers.

Poetry festival

Organize a school poetry festival. The school play makes its routine appearance in many a school's year. An alternative event could be an evening of 'poetry in performance'. The production of a long poem (George MacBeth's 'Noah's Journey'?) could be preceded by several smaller items (children reciting their own verse, a brief talk/reading from a local writer, etc.) to provide an enjoyable entertainment. Around this set piece, displays, publications, competitions could be arranged as part of a poetry week.

Poetry magazine

Reassess the nature and role of children's published poetry in your school. Have you got the right sort of outlet for pupils' writing? Could you start a writers' workshop with a view to stimulating the children to talk more, write more and publish more? The establishment of a small-scale publication which appears regularly can be a useful focus for poetry writing.

(iii) Teaching ideas

Our purpose here is not to list 101 things to do in poetry lessons but to show what we have found to be examples of good practice.

212

Jottings

Pupils often need help to develop 'writing to think with' in order to capture initial responses, fleeting impressions and feelings. Notes or jottings around the text are an essential technique and should become a frequent practice. Properly used, they quickly develop into a means through which pupils formulate questions, indicate difficulties and areas of interest, construct hypotheses and so on. The numbering of initial responses around a text (see p. 68) can easily be adapted as a teaching device[6].

Journal

The poetry-reader's commonplace book. The handout shown in Figure 5.2 works well and helps pupils to focus all their poetry experience in one place.

You'll be spending two or three hours on your own, in the company of a large number of poetry books. At the end of this time we'll be sharing what has happened. Here are some ways to make use of your journal.

1 Sometimes a poem strikes you on first meeting. Jot down your thoughts and feelings as you read. Try to capture all that you experience.
2 Perhaps you've read a poem several times. Now, give yourself, say, five minutes, and write. Let your hand follow your pen – see where it takes you.
3 Copy out words or phrases or lines that you like, and try to explain why you like them.
4 If you like the whole poem, copy it out in the back of your book.
5 Make a list of the questions you have about a poem you like.
6 Sometimes we're very moved by a poem that reminds us of a personal experience. If you like, describe that personal association.
7 Sometimes words make pictures in our heads. Make a sketch of such a picture, and add the words which created the picture.
8 Perhaps a title, or a line, or a feeling gives you an idea for a short story, or a scene in a play, or a poem of your own. Write it.
9 If there's a poem you get to know really well, try to answer these questions:
   – What interests you about the poem? What does it 'say' to you?
   – As you reread it, how does your sense of the poem develop?
   – Does the whole poem work for you? Say what you like (and perhaps dislike) about it.
10 Look back through your entries. 'I like poems which . . .' Can you see any connections between the poems you've chosen to write about?

Figure 5.2   Keeping a Poetry Journal

Michael Benton

Room for response

Before the advent of GCSE, very few public examination questions gave primacy to the individual's responses to poetry. Among this minority are those of the Cambridge Plain Texts Paper. One rubric, typical of the house style, asks pupils to read Vernon Scannell's 'Incendiary' (*New and Collected Poems, 1950–1980*, Robson Books, 1980, p. 56) several times and then look at the following questions 'which are intended to help you to express freely your own reactions to the poem'. The questions read:

> This poem is about a small boy and a fire that he started deliberately. What impression of the fire does the poem create for you? Mention some of the details in the poem that contribute to this impression.
> Write about your impression of the small boy and the feeling towards him that the poem arouses. How far does the poem enable you to understand why he started the fire?
> The poet repeats the word 'frightening'. What things frighten him about this incident? Do you find that 'frightening' is the strongest, or the final, feeling that the poem expresses for you?

In formal examination conditions this is probably about as invitational as one can be. However, in the more informal circumstances of coursework, and with the impetus to the expression of personal responses given by GCSE, the readers can and should be more involved. We have found the following procedure most successful with this poem and these questions (NB the teacher reads the text aloud at the start of each activity):

- text given out; initial jottings around the poem;
- pupils write a paragraph to capture the experience of the poem and to explain what the writer is looking at;
- pupils underline words and phrases that caught their attention, for whatever reason;
- then, the questions are given out. Pupils asked either to answer the questions separately, or to incorporate answers into their own continuous response.

By intervening between the poem and the questions the teacher is 'making space' for the readers, providing time (the lead-in to the questions may take only fifteen minutes) for the poem to be evoked.

214

Making a poem for themselves is the most valuable experience readers can have. This carefully-paced approach provides that opportunity.

Helping the 'simple construction' of the text
The importance of pupils gaining a sense of the basic situation in a poem – what Keith Hurst calls the 'simple construction' – is self-evident. Tasks which demand this should be fun, not an inquisition. Hence, taking the example used in Chapter 4, in a poem like 'The Stag' where narrative and local geography are important, pupils could produce a film scenario, or a series of pictures or maps to plot the stag's progress; a taped radio commentary; or a written report of events from the viewpoint of one of the spectators who, at the end, return to their cars 'wet through and disappointed'. Creative activities take the pupils back inside the poem; they are another way pupils can make a poem their own.

Role play
Teaching strategies to enable pupils to engage with the implied poet of the poem could well make more use of role play in the form of writing, simulation or improvised drama. The 'experience gap' between poet and young reader in a poem like Seamus Heaney's 'Follower' can be bridged by role play. Youngsters can often grasp the idea of such a poem but find it difficult to connect with the underlying emotion. To role play a diary entry of the poet, or to improvise an encounter between the two characters can open up this affective dimension. Whether it is developed as a narrative reworking of the experience of the poem, or as an oblique commentary on it, such role play helps to make the reader's consciousness of the poet as a character in his own poem much more explicit.

Ways-in to language and form
Several strategies appropriated from the teaching of reading have become popular in poetry teaching in the 1980s and two, in particular, are helpful in heightening pupils' awareness of the language and structure of poems. It is essential that neither becomes a substitute for responding to the whole poem. They are enabling techniques, ways of making some poems more accessible. Both activities are most suited to work in pairs. *Cloze* deletion where specific words are blanked out from the text encourages plenty of talk about plausible alternatives. The teacher can direct attention to different aspects of the poem by deleting active verbs, or rhyming sounds, or descriptive adjectives and so on. There is an obvious connection between these choices and the choices poets make in

215

composition. It is a pity not to do some work on poets' early drafts of poems in tandem with cloze. For example, with a bit of judicious cloze deletion from the draft(s) of Owen's 'Anthem for Doomed Youth', pupils could compare their range of choices with the varied suggestions that both Owen and Sassoon tried during the sonnet's composition[7].

Sequencing entails slicing up a poem into single lines, couplets or stanzas and asking pupils to arrange the fragments into what seems to them to be the best order. Short poems with a regular form are the most appropriate, although elsewhere, as part of a teaching approach to *The Ancient Mariner*, I lay claim to inventing the biggest sequencing task yet devised![8] Pupil talk during sequencing focuses upon narrative structures, formulaic ways of beginning and ending poems, the logical development of ideas and feelings and so on. With both cloze and sequencing it is important to realize that they are just devices to help open up the poem to its readers: it is essential that pupils hear and see the complete poem and are encouraged to respond to the finished article as the poet wrote it.

Creative responses
Most of the foregoing suggestions are enabling activities, ways of helping pupils to express their personal responses in the process of coming to terms with poems. We have indicated, too, both in our methodology (pp. 207–8) and in *Keeping a Poetry Journal*, point 9, how this process leads into formal essay writing. Products, other than essays, are clearly desirable outcomes. There is nothing sacrosanct, or even particularly appropriate, about the essay as a means of response. It is a form descended from *belles-lettres*, appropriated by literary criticism, and bolstered by an examination system geared to assessing verbal chunks of timed virtuosity. In many respects it is a curiously inhibiting form of writing to impose upon the expression of personal responses to literature. Yet it is quite natural for readers to want to make some sort of 'final statement' in response to a text upon which they have been working. Unless the teacher has the limited aim of practice in timed examination answers to fulfil, it is important to encourage choice among different forms of responding. Pupils might make 'final statements' by presenting an annotated mini-anthology of a poet's work; by writing reflectively about coming to understand a particular poem; by making a short, taped radio programme of poems on a theme or as an introduction to a favourite writer; or by making a collage of words and images suggested by a poem. Reader and text can speak so powerfully to each other that pupils are moved to make their final responses through their own creative writing or illustration. In the course of

the work described in Chapter 2, Elizabeth and Kristina expressed their responses to Sylvia Plath's 'Mirror' and Andrey Vosnesensky's 'First Ice'[9] in ways that show a fine intelligence of feeling.

'A girl freezes in a telephone booth.
In her draughty overcoat she hides
A face all smeared
In tears and lipstick . . .'

First Ice
Kristina Nuttall

217

Lines

The human face
Is the individual's album;
Showing the joys, the heartaches
The sadness and the laughter.
Each line is a memory,
Happy or not,
Of a time long gone by
Of a person or a place.
Perhaps it is the sadness
Of these memories
That makes us hate these lines.

Perhaps it is the happiness
– of now, and years to come –
That makes us cry dry sobs and
Long
For days of youth
Into the mirror of our hearts.

Elizabeth Noble

Finally, it is worth reaffirming the truism that all our enquiries
show – that the teacher's attitude to poetry is crucial. Keeping up
our knowledge of what is available is a fundamental professional
requirement. In methodological terms, the trick is to allow the
uniqueness of each poem to dictate the strategies we adopt to
make it accessible to the pupils. Knowledge can be gained and
strategies learned relatively easily; but it is often more of a
personal challenge to adopt a changed attitude or role. For some,
giving literature back to its readers through the ways of working
we have outlined means divesting themselves of the role of expert
or critic; it may seem to undermine their habitual style of
teaching. Yet, paradoxically, to be a teacher is to be a learner, as
these enquiries demonstrate. In various ways, we see teacher-
researchers moving into unfamiliar territory alongside their
pupils. This brings benefits all round and facilitates the role of the
teacher as a sharing reader without a monopoly of knowledge. If
an exploratory attitude is adopted by the teacher then the chances
of educating 'keen readers', in both the senses described in the
Preface, are much greater. While we claim that our detailed
working-out of reader-response concepts is new, the issue of the

teacher-attitude necessary to sustain poetry in the classroom has long been familiar. Writing a few years before I.A. Richards's celebrated work, George Sampson (1921) eloquently reminds the English teacher that:

> If literature in schools is not a delight, if it is not, in all senses, a 're-creation', an experience in creative reception, it is a failure.[10]

C Enquiry methods and further research

(i) Refining enquiry techniques

We have seen how, in aesthetic reading, the reader makes his own meaning, building from the initial apprehension of the text, as reader and text interact. This same transactional model may be applied to the activity of the teacher-researcher, for it is through the interaction between the activity of teaching, and the interpretation of that activity, that effective classroom strategies can be developed. Sensing a problem, he will attend both to the area of his investigation and to his own teaching practice as he carries out his enquiry.

When 'reading' the 'texts' of the poetry experiences described in earlier chapters of this book, several points emerge which may be of use to others researching in this area. First, there is a marked advantage in working with children who are known. This familiarity is especially important when monitoring individual responses. The willingness to reflect on tape, the openness with which personal responses are offered, and the perseverance to tease out a poem alone, as evidenced in Chapters 2 and 3, all require time and trust. The pilot studies not only help to clarify procedures, they also establish the rapport that is as necessary to this sort of research as it is to teaching. By contrast, much of Keith Hurst's work was done at one remove from the action. His own class was one among many that he used but most of the data discussed in Chapter 4 is the result of working through other teachers acting as his assistants. Clearly, while it would be difficult to investigate detailed individual responses in this way, it does have the advantage of allowing the researcher to compare how different groups negotiate the same text and to construct an interactional model. Inevitably, if there is distance between the researcher and the pupils, there is a great deal of support and training needed to ensure that the co-operating teachers are in tune with the orientation and procedures of the enquiry. In such circumstances, if the children are not known, it helps if the teacher-assistants are.

Second, there is a certain amount of evidence, especially in Chapter 2, that, by involving children in an intensely focused experience of poetry-reading, we see the emergence of the pupil-researcher alongside the teacher-researcher. It should not surprise us. After all, there is ample evidence from elsewhere in the curriculum – from pupil astronomers monitoring space satellites to countless children engaged in field work activities in Geography or Science – that when teachers negotiate learning with pupils and encourage them to take on responsibility for their own enquiries then the pupils can come up with some remarkable discoveries and insights. There is no reason why the teacher-researcher into literary responses should not regard his pupils as research assistants. Practical ways in which this relationship might be developed could include both teacher and pupils keeping journals or diaries of the work. These might begin with all participants raising questions they want answered, followed by the logging of individual accounts of the activities undertaken. By these means ethnographies can become more subtle and sensitive instruments of enquiry.

Third, subsequent enquiries have had the benefit of being able to build upon the techniques and findings described here and advances are being made both conceptually and technically in the way analyses are conducted and presented. For example, Alec Roberts' (1987) study which explores how five teenage readers, individually and in groups, read and respond to poems and stories by D.H. Lawrence, offers a fascinating account, summarised vividly in diagrammatic form, of readings of 'Snake', 'Humming-Bird' and 'Bat'. What is particularly significant here is that Alec Roberts detects, in the shape of a group's responses, how the character of the text and the characters in the discussion come together and operate upon each other. To give the flavour of the work:

> 'Snake' is a story poem, 'Humming-Bird' is reflective and 'Bat' hangs somewhere between the two. The way students respond to these different kinds of poems needs exploring. The long and winding 'Snake' lends itself to a long and winding response; the short and fluttering 'Humming-Bird' evokes a spiral or cyclical kind of response, as does the staccato looping of 'Bat'.
> Such frameworks are the result of my interpretation of the data collected . . .[11]

The advances here are not only in the diagrams and summaries of the data ('Snake' pp. 23–5; 'Humming-Bird' pp. 69–71; 'Bat' pp.96–7) but in the way the concepts of Keith Hurst's work have been developed and refined (pp. 66–9).

A more theoretical enquiry by Pat Lynn-Macrae (1987) attempts to construct a conceptual model of Rosenblatt's transactional theory by recourse to Watson and Crick's account of the structure of DNA in *The Double Helix* (Penguin, 1970). The discussion is elaborate, sophisticated and daring, bringing together the double-stranded helix and its spiral structure with the 'cycles of utterance' (Barnes and Todd, 1977, *passim*) and the 'circular process' (Rosenblatt, 1978, p. 43) in an effort to describe a metaphor for the process of response. These and other enquiries are listed in the Selected Bibliography.

Fourth, work in this area can benefit from not being too doctrinaire about enquiry approaches. There is room, as suggested initially (p. 35), for both the content analysis of responses elicited in predetermined ways and for the descriptive interpretations of free-ranging responses that we have tended to concentrate on. Again, some advances are being made in this direction. Audrey Atter's (1987) work, in particular, deliberately sets out to explore the different effects of systematic and ethnographic investigations. It concludes that the former can be useful preliminary to the latter in making the enquirer attend closely to the data and describe what is there. Ethnographical analysis poses the problem of handling complexity: systematic analysis at least, offers a way-in and indicates general trends in the response data.

Some guidelines emerged which acknowledge both the relationships between the assumptions implicit in the conduct of the work and its results, and between these results and the means of assessing them. They are given below. They reflect the exploratory nature of the work, the need to give it direction and coherence as it is developing, and the need to assess it on completion.

First, it is essential to keep a log or diary of the method adopted, noting decisions made and the reasons for them as the work develops. The more informal writing is used as a means of reflecting upon the enquiry the better, both to sharpen the perceptions of the researcher at the time and to provide a record from which to draw when writing up the study in its final form.

Second, since many enquiries will involve tape-recording children, it is best to start with the process of transcribing tapes. This discipline gives a sense of the richness of the responses and makes the transcriber more attentive to content, implications, assumptions, tone, and so on than a mere listener is inclined to be. This area of the enquiry is laborious, time-consuming, and essential. It is the beginning of the disciplined process of using the response-data to think with.

Third, in keeping with the ethnographic approach, we prefer to rely on the teacher-researcher's assessment of the responses rather than the use of ready-made systems of content analysis. This is not to say that the two are mutually exclusive and there may be occasions when it is enlightening to apply both to the same material (see Atter, 1987). The 'attraction' of the classificatory approaches, usually derived from the early work of Squire and Purves and Rippere, is that they provide a detailed scheme for handling the stated responses of readers with all the reductive neatness of a multiple choice comprehension paper. A freer approach to interpreting what readers say, while lacking the satisfying tidiness of content analysis, is both more subtle and more flexible and, through being concerned primarily with what a reader means rather than with how a response should be labelled, it can claim greater accuracy and insight. Here the researcher relies principally upon sensitivity and understanding (a response to the response) without the support of a prescribed system. Yet the teacher-researcher is not alone, for James Britton (1971) and Douglas Barnes (1976) have shown how much can be achieved through this approach in the study of language and literature; and the interpretive freedom, first expressed in Stubbs and Delamont's (1976) explorations in classroom observation, is now accepted as a valuable element in ethnographic enquiries (Hammersley (ed), 1986). The process of interpretation is best served again by the use of informal note-making alongside the transcriptions or written responses. Patterns emerge and, through this intimate knowledge of the data, the most appropriate ways to reflect their nature appear. At the level of ideas, decisions have to be taken about how far to draw upon the categories and labels of others. At the level of practicalities, decisions have to be made about, for example, the punctuation and presentation of transcript material and, in particular, whether to use selected extracts for discussion, analysis and illustration or to opt for landscape pages with utterances and commentary in parallel.

(ii)   Further research

There are many avenues for further research already suggested in, or implied by, our enquiries. The more important ones appear to be:

- enquiries with different age groups, especially with primary and middle school children, to complement our secondary school emphasis;
- longitudinal studies in order to construct a developmental model of aesthetic reading;

– widening the focus of enquiries from the individual/group to take account more explicitly of the whole-class dimension; this will entail much more data gathering and analysis.

– studies of the teacher's role in the reader-response process with individuals, groups and whole classes;

– studies of 'pair-talk'. In initial literacy, paired reading has been a recent development but in literary response it is relatively unexplored. Pair work could well offer more on the insubstantial, fleeting responses than either individual work or small group talk. It maintains the strength of oracy as the medium and provides a continuous demand on the two participants for both initiation and response in a way that discussion groups with four or five children cannot do; the tendency to create 'surrogate teachers', 'passengers' and similar roles often observed in the dynamics of a group, is largely avoided;

– studies which map varieties of texts against varieties of readers.

There are, of course, many other possibilities. Louise Rosenblatt emphasises one above all others and it is fitting that she has the last word:

One factor deserves particular study: the effect of the teacher's own understanding of the theoretical basis for the fact that – although there is no single 'correct' interpretation – there can be developed criteria of validity of interpretation[12].

References

Chapter One

1 L. Rosenblatt, 'The Transactional Theory of the Literary Work: Implications for Research', *Researching Response to Literature and the Teaching of Literature* ed. C.R. Cooper, New Jersey, Ablex Publishing Corporation, 1985, p. 34.
2 A.C. Purves and R. Beach, *Literature and the Reader*, Urbana, Illinois, National Council of Teachers of English, 1972, p. 1.
  S.R. Suleiman and I. Crosman, *The Reader in The Text*, New Jersey, Princeton University Press, 1980, p. 45.
3 I.A. Richards, *How To Read A Page*, London, Kegan Paul, Trench & Trubner & Co., 1943, p. 94.
  For an interesting account of the conventional view that Richards's theories underwent a sudden and radical transformation in the 1930s see, 'I.A. Richards; Emotive Autonomy', Chapter 2 of Gerald Graff, *Poetic Statement and Critical Dogma*, Chicago University Press, 1970.
4 I.A. Richards, *Practical Criticism*, London, Routledge & Kegan Paul, 1929, p. 13.
5 Ibid., p. 3.
6 Ibid., p. 11.
7 I.A. Richards, *Principles of Literary Criticism*, London, Routledge & Kegan Paul, 1924, p. 25.
8 Richards, 1929, op. cit., p. 12.
9 T. Eagleton, *Literary Theory: An Introduction*, Oxford, Basil Blackwell, 1983, pp. 10–16.
10 Richards, 1929, op. cit. pp. 13–14.
11 Ibid., p. 181 ff.
12 W. Empson, *Seven Types of Ambiguity*, London, Chatto and Windus, 1930, p. 238.
13 Richards, 1929, op. cit., p.13.
14 Ibid., p. 14.
15 Ibid., p. 15.
16 Stephen Spender, 'The Making of a Poem', *The Creative Process*, ed. B. Ghiselin, New York and London, Mentor, 1952, p. 121.
17 Richards, 1929, op. cit., p. 237.
18 Barrett taxonomy in A. Melnik and J. Merritt, *Reading: Today and*

Tomorrow, London, University of London/Open University Press, 1972.
19 D.W. Harding, *Experience into Words*, Harmondsworth, Penguin, 1974.
N.N. Holland, *Five Readers Reading*, New Haven and London, Yale University Press, 1975.
20 Richards, 1929, op. cit., p. 15.
21 Ibid., p. 16.
22 Ibid., p. 16.
23 Ibid., pp. 274–8.
24 Ibid., p. 16.
25 Ibid., p. 17.
26 Ibid., p. 300.
27 Richards, 1924, op. cit., pp. 225–6.
28 Ibid., p. 36.
29 W.J. Slatoff, *With Respect to Readers: Dimensions of Literary Response*, Ithaca and London, Cornell University Press, 1970, p. 187.
30 G. Wilson Knight, *The Wheel of Fire* (rev. edn.) London, Methuen, 1949, p. 3.
31 Wolfgang Iser, *The Act of Reading*, London, Routledge & Kegan Paul, 1978, p. 9.
32 Ibid., p. 20.
33 A.C. Purves and R. Beach, 1972, op. cit. *passim*.
34 A. Jefferson and D. Robey (eds.), *Modern Literary Theory* (2nd edn), London, Batsford, 1986, p. 142.
35 For example, W.K. Wimsatt, *The Verbal Icon* (1958), London, Methuen, 1970; C. Brooks, *The Well-Wrought Urn* (1949), London, Dobson, 1968.
36 A. Easthope, 'Poetry and the Politics of Reading', *Re-reading English*, ed. P. Widdowson, London, Methuen, 1982, p. 141.
37 S. Fish, 'How To Recognise A Poem When You See One', *Is There a Text in This Class?*, Cambridge, Mass., Harvard University Press, 1980, p. 327.
38 S. Fish, 'Interpreting the *Variorum*' op. cit., 1980, p. 152.
39 L. Lerner (ed.), *Reconstructing Literature*, Oxford, Blackwell, 1983, p. 6.
40 L. Rosenblatt, *The Reader, The Text, The Poem*, Carbondale, Southern Illinois University Press, 1978, p. 151.
41 L. Rosenblatt, *Literature as Exploration*, London, Heinemann, 1970, p. 25.
42 Ibid., pp. 30–1.
43 W.C. Booth, *The Rhetoric of Fiction*, Chicago and London, The University of Chicago Press, 1961, pp. 137–138.
44 N.N. Holland, *The Dynamics of Literary Response*, New York, W.W. Norton and Co., 1975, *passim*.
45 Rosenblatt, 1970, op. cit., p. 38.
46 Ibid., pp. 34–5.
47 Ibid., p. 81.
48 Ibid., p. 113.
49 Rosenblatt, 1978, op. cit., p. 12.
50 Ibid., p. 7.

51 Rosenblatt, 1985, op. cit., p. 39.
52 Ibid., p. 39.
53 S.T. Coleridge, *Biographia Literaria* (1817), London, Dent, 1949, p. 150. I. Calvino, *If On A Winter's Night A Traveller*, London, Picador, 1982.
54 J. Britton, *et al.*, *The Development of Writing Abilities (11–18)*, London, Macmillan, 1975, p. 81 ff.
55 W. Blake, 'The Tyger', *Songs of Innocence and Experience*, London, Oxford University Press, 1970, p. 42.
56 R. Graves, 'The Cool Web', *Robert Graves: Poems Selected by Himself*, Harmondsworth, Penguin, 1961, p. 52.
57 N. Frye, *The Anatomy of Criticism*, Princeton, New Jersey, Princeton University Press, 1957, p. 263.
58 R. Weir, *Language in the Crib* (1962), The Hague, Mouton & Co., 1970.
59 W.H. Auden 'Words', *Collected Shorter Poems, 1927–1957*, London, Faber, 1969, p. 320.
60 A. MacLeish, 'Ars Poetica', *Collected Poems*, New York, Houghton Mifflin, 1963, pp. 50–1.
61 T. Hughes, 'The Thought-Fox', *Hawk in the Rain*, London, Faber, 1957, p. 14.
62 T. Hughes, 'Capturing Animals', *Poetry in the Making*, London, Faber, 1967, p. 20.
63 Coleridge, 1949, op. cit., p. 150.
64 T.S. Eliot, 'Matthew Arnold', *The Use of Poetry and the Use of Criticism*, Cambridge, Mass., Harvard University Press, 1933, p. 111.
65 D.W. Harding, 'Psychological Processes in the Reading of Fiction', *The British Journal of Aesthetics*, 1962, 2(2) pp. 140–4.
66 G. Josipovici, *The Modern English Novel: the Reader, the Writer and the Work*, London, Open Books, 1976, p. 8.
67 A.N. Applebee, *The Child's Concept of Story: Ages Two to Seventeen*, Chicago and London, University of Chicago Press, 1978, p. 91.
68 Iser, 1978, op. cit., p. 10.
69 W. Stevens, 'The House Was Quiet . . .', *Selected Poems*, London, Faber, 1965, p. 90.
70 Iser, 1978, op. cit., p. 10.
71 Rosenblatt, 1985, op. cit., p. 50.
72 M. Hammersley and P. Atkinson, *Ethnography: Principles in Practice*, London, Tavistock Publications, 1983, pp. 14–15.
73 Ibid., p. 24.
74 Ibid., p. 24.
75 G. Yarlott and W.S. Harpin, '1000 Responses to English Literature', *Educational Research*, 1972/73, 13.1 and 13.2.
76 Tony Oakley, 'A Survey of the Teaching of Poetry to Children Between the ages of 10–13 in 43 Primary, Middle and Secondary Schools in the E. Dorset Area'. Unpublished MA (Ed) dissertation, University of Southampton, 1981.
77 P. Benton, *Pupil, Teacher, Poem*, London, Hodder and Stoughton, 1986.

78 APU, '*Language Performance in School: Secondary Survey Report No. 1*'., London, HMSO, 1982.
79 P. Benton, 1986, op. cit., p. 8.
80 E.R. Kintgen, 'Studying the Perception of Poetry', Cooper (ed.), 1985, p. 128.
81 Ibid., p. 142.
82 Ibid., p. 134.
83 P. Benton, 1986, op. cit., p. 36.
84 P. Dias, 'Making Sense of Poetry. Patterns of Response Among Canadian and British Secondary School Pupils', *English in Education*, 1986, 20(2), p. 45.
85 T. Hughes, 'Capturing Animals', *Poetry in the Making*, London, Faber, 1967, p. 23.

Chapter Two

1 Eagleton, 1983, op. cit., p. 31.
2 Ibid., p. 33.
3 J. Mulford, 'Comments on Traditions of Literature Teaching', *Literature and Learning*, ed. E. Grugeon and P. Walden, London, Ward Lock Educational, 1978, p. 155.
4 Rosenblatt, 1978, op. cit., p. 11.

Chapter Three

1 D. Swanger, *The Poem as Process*, N.Y. Harcourt, Brace, Jovanovich, 1974, p. 63.
2 D. Jackson, *Encounters With Books*, London, Methuen, 1983, p. 22–3.
3 Ibid., p. 23.
4 J.S. Mill, 'On Bentham and Coleridge', *Autobiography* (1873), Oxford University Press, 1924.
5 H. Rosen, 'The Professional Education of the Teacher of English', *Classroom Encounters – Language and English Teaching*, eds, M. Torbe and R. Protherough, London, Ward Lock, 1976, p. 148.
6 Ibid., p. 148.
7 P. Williams, 'Talk and Discussion', Torbe and Protherough eds, 1976, op. cit., pp. 46–53.
8 D. Barnes, *From Communication to Curriculum*, Harmondsworth, Penguin, 1976, pp. 77–8.
9 D. Barnes, 'Bernstein in the Classroom', *Times Educational Supplement*, Nov. 1971.
10 J. Alcock, 'Students' Questions and Teachers' Questions', in Torbe M. and Protherough, eds, op. cit., 1976, p. 58.
11 Ibid., p. 75.

References

Chapter Four

1 B. Wade, 'Assessing Pupils' Contributions in Appreciating a Poem', *Journal of Education for Teaching*, 7(1), 1981.
2 D. Barnes and F. Todd, *Communication and Learning in Small Groups*, London, Routledge & Kegan Paul, 1977, p. 21.
3 Richards, 1929, op. cit., p. 13.
4 G. Genette, *Narrative Discourse*, Oxford, Blackwell, 1980.
5 Booth, 1961, op. cit., pp. 137–138.
6 M. Rosen, *I See A Voice*, London, Hutchinson/Thames Television, 1981, p. 7.
7 Richards, 1929, op. cit., p. 16.

Chapter Five

1 Rosenblatt, 1985 op. cit., p. 46.
2 G. Fox and B. Merrick, 'Thirty-Six Things To Do With a Poem', *The Times Educational Supplement*, 20.2.81
3 M. Benton and G. Fox, *Teaching Literature 9–14*, London, Oxford University Press, 1985.
4 M. and P. Benton, *Examining Poetry*, London, Hodder & Stoughton, 1986.
5 J. Reeves and M.S. Smith, *Inside Poetry*, London, Heinemann, 1970, p. 3.
6 M. and P. Benton, *Touchstones 4*, London, Hodder & Stoughton, rev. edn 1988.
7 Ibid.
8 Benton and Fox, 1985, op. cit., p. 90.
9 M. and P. Benton, *Poetry Workshop*, London, Hodder & Stoughton, 1975, pp. 40 and 104.
10 G. Sampson, *English for the English*, London, Cambridge University Press, 1921, p.106.
11 A. Roberts, 'A Study of Five Adolescents' Reading and Responding to Selected Writings of D.H. Lawrence', Unpublished MA (Ed) dissertation, University of Southampton, 1987, p. 66.
12 Rosenblatt, 1985, op. cit., p. 49.

Selected Bibliography

Full details of all the books and articles mentioned in the text are given in our chapter references. The aim here is to recommend particular publications which will be of help to others working in this area.

Agee H. and Galda, L. (eds), 1983, 'Response to Literature: Empirical and Theoretical Studies', *Journal of Research and Development In Education*, 16(3).

Applebee, A.N., 1978, *The Child's Concept of Story: Ages Two to Seventeen*, Chicago & London, Chicago University Press.

Atkinson, J. 1985, 'How Children Read Poems at Different Ages', *English in Education*, NATE, 19(1).

Barnes, D., 1976, *From Communication to Curriculum*, Harmondsworth, Penguin.

Barnes, D. and Todd, F., 1977, *Communication and Learning in Small Groups*, London, Routledge & Kegan Paul.

Barthes, R., 1975, *S/Z*, London, Jonathan Cape.

Benton, M.G., 1984, 'The Methodology Vacuum in Teaching Literature', *Language Arts*, 61(3).

Benton, M.G. and Fox, G., 1985, *Teaching Literature, 9–14*, London, Oxford University Press.

Benton, P., 1986, *Pupil, Teacher, Poem*, London, Hodder & Stoughton.

Bleich, D., 1978, *Subjective Criticism*, Baltimore & London, John Hopkins University Press.

Britton, J., 1971, *Language and Learning*, Harmondsworth, Penguin.

Cooper, C.R. (ed), 1985, *Researching Response to Literature and the Teaching of Literature*, New Jersey, Ablex Publishing Corporation.

Culler, J., 1975, *Structuralist Poetics: Structuralism, Linguistics and the Study of Literature*, London, Routledge & Kegan Paul.

D'Arcy, P., 1973, 'The Reader's Response', *Reading For Meaning, Vol. 2*, London, Hutchinson.

Dias, P., 1986, 'Making Sense of Poetry', *English in Education*, NATE, 20(2).

Dixon, J. and Brown, J., 1984, *Responses to Literature – What Is Being Assessed?* London, Schools Council Publications.

Eagleton, T., 1983, *Literary Theory: An Introduction*, Oxford, Basil Blackwell.

Empson, W., 1930, *Seven Types of Ambiguity*, London, Chatto & Windus.

Selected Bibliography

Fish, S., 1980, *Is There a Text in this Class?*, Cambridge, Mass., Harvard University Press.

Fox, G. and Merrick, B., 1981, 'Thirty-Six Things to Do With a Poem', *The Times Educational Supplement*, 20 February.

Genette, G., 1980, *Narrative Discourse*, Oxford, Blackwell.

Ghiselin, B. (ed.), 1952, *The Creative Process*, London, Mentor.

Hackman, Susan, 1987, *Responding in Writing: the use of exploratory writing in the literature classroom*, NATE.

Hammersley, M. and Atkinson, P. 1983, *Ethnography: Principles in Practice*, London, Tavistock Publications.

Hammersley, M. (ed), 1986, *Controversies in Classroom Research*, Milton Keynes, Open University Press.

Harding, D.W., 1974, *Experience Into Words*, Harmondsworth, Penguin.

Holland, N.N., 1968, *The Dynamics of Literary Response*, N.Y., Norton.

Holland, N.N., 1973, *Poems in Persons*, N.Y., Norton.

Holland, N.N. 1975, *Five Readers Reading*, New Haven & London, Yale University Press.

Holub, R.C., 1984, *Reception Theory*, London, Methuen.

Iser, W., 1978, *The Act of Reading*, London, Routledge & Kegan Paul.

Jefferson, A. and Robey, D., (eds), 1986, *Modern Literary Theory* (2nd edn.) London, Batsford.

Langer, S.K. 1953, *Feeling and Form*, London, Routledge and Kegan Paul.

Lerner, L. (ed.), 1983, *Reconstructing Literature*, Oxford, Blackwell.

Lewis, C.S., 1961, *An Experiment in Criticism*, London, Cambridge University Press.

Meek, M., *et al*, 1977, *The Cool Web*, London, Bodley Head.

Miller, J. (ed.), 1984, *Eccentric Propositions*, London, Routledge & Kegan Paul, 1984.

Purves, A.C. and Rippere, V., 1968, *Elements of Writing About a Literary Work*, Research Report No. 9, Champaign, Illinois, NCTE.,

Purves, A.C. and Beach, R., 1972, *Literature and the Reader*, Urbana, Illinois, National Council of Teachers of English.

Purves, A.C. (ed.), 1972, *How Porcupines Make Love: Notes on a Response-Centred Curriculum*, Lexington, Mass., Xerox Publishing Co.

Richards, I.A., 1924, *Principles of Literary Criticism*, London, Routledge & Kegan Paul.

Richards, I.A., 1929, *Practical Criticism*, London, Routledge & Kegan Paul.

Rosenblatt, L., 1970, *Literature as Exploration*, London, Heinemann.

Rosenblatt, L., 1978, *The Reader, The Text, The Poem*, Carbondale, Southern Illinois University Press.

Rosenblatt, L., 1985, 'The Transactional Theory of the Literary Work: Implications for Research', in C.R. Cooper (ed.), *Researching Response to Literature and the Teaching of Literature*, New Jersey, Ablex Publishing Corporation.

Ryle, G., 1960, *The Concept of Mind*, Harmondsworth, Penguin.

Sampson, G., 1921, *English For the English*, London, Cambridge University Press.

Slatoff, W.J., 1970, *With Respect to Readers: Dimensions of Literary*

Response, Ithaca and London, Cornell University Press.

Squire, J.R., 1964, *The Responses of Adolescents While Reading Four Short Stories*, Research Report No. 2, Champaign, Illinois, NCTE.

Squire, J.R. (ed.),1968, *Response to Literature*, Champaign, Illinois, NCTE.

Stubbs, M. and Delamont, S. (eds), 1976, *Explorations in Classroom Observation*, London, Wiley.

Suleiman, S.R. and Crosman, I., 1980, *The Reader in the Text*, New Jersey, Princeton University Press.

Tompkins, J.P. (ed.), 1980, *Reader Response Criticism: From Formalism to Post-Structuralism*, Baltimore and London, John Hopkins University Press.

Tunnicliffe, S., 1984, *Poetry Experience*, London, Methuen.

Valentine, E., 1978, 'Perchings and Flights: Introspection', in A. Burton, and J. Radford, (eds), *Thinking in Perspective*, London, Methuen.

Wade, B., 1981, 'Assessing Pupils' Contributions in Appreciating a Poem', *Journal of Education for Teaching*, 7(1).

Widdowson, P. (ed.), 1982, *Re-Reading English*, London, Methuen.

Witkin, R., 1974, *The Intelligence of Feeling*, London, Heinemann.

Unpublished Studies

The following dissertations and theses have all been carried out in the Faculty of Education, University of Southampton.

Atter, A., 1987, *A Reader-Response Study: Four Readings of a Poem by Edwin Morgan*.

Roberts, A., 1987, *A Study of Five Adolescents' Reading and Responding to Poems*.

Hackman, S. (nee Newton), 1986, *Responding in Writing: The Use of Exploratory Writing in the Literature Classroom*.

Hurst, K.E., 1984, *Teaching and Reading Poetry*.

Lynn-Macrae, P., 1987, *A Transactional Theory of the Literary Work: A Conceptual Model*.

Oakley, A.J., 1981, *A Survey of the Teaching of Poetry to Children between the ages of 10–13 in 43 . . . schools*.

Roberts, A., 1987, *A Study of Five Adolescents' Reading and Responding to Selected Writings of D.H. Lawrence*.

Teasey, J., 1986, *Close Readings*.

Appendix 1

Selected Bibliography of Poetry Written for Children

The intention here is to provide a limited selection of volumes that might form the nucleus of a small library of children's verse in a school or college staffroom, library or resources area. The emphasis is deliberately modern, one-third nineteenth and early twentieth century, two-thirds post-war, with a considerable number of poets represented who are still writing. The main criterion has been to list those books to which the reader might go with a reasonable expectation of finding a number of poems that he or she can share with groups of young readers.

For ease of reference, the paperback editions are listed below, preceded, when appropriate, by the date of the original publication in brackets. Where only the hardback edition exists this is indicated by an asterisk.

Poets from the nineteenth and early twentieth centuries

William Blake: *Songs of Innocence and Experience* (1789 and 1794) Illuminated edition, Oxford University Press, 1970
Edward Lear: *The Complete Nonsense of Edward Lear*, Holbrook Jackson (ed.) Faber, 1947*
  A Book of Bosh, chosen by Brian Alderson, Puffin, 1975
Heinrich Hoffman: *Struwwelpeter* (1848), Pan Books 1972
Lewis Carroll: *The Humorous Verse of Lewis Carroll*, Dover, 1960
Christina Rossetti: *Goblin Market* (1862). Illustrated edition, Harrap 1939*
  Sing-Song (1872). Illustrated edition, Dover 1968
Robert Louis Stevenson: *A Child's Garden of Verses* (1885) Puffin, 1952
Harry Graham: *Ruthless Rhymes for Heartless Homes*, Edward Arnold, 1910*
Hilaire Belloc: *Cautionary Verses*, collected illustrated album edition, Duckworth, 1940*
A.A. Milne: *When We Were Very Young* (1924), Magnet, 1965

Now We Are Six (1927), Magnet 1965. Also *The Christopher Robin Verse Book*, illustrated edition, Methuen, 1965
Eleanor Farjeon: *The Children's Bells*, Oxford, 1960*
  Invitation to a Mouse, Pelham Books, 1981*
Walter de la Mare: *Collected Rhymes and Verses* (1944) Faber, 1978
T.S. Eliot: *Old Possum's Book of Practical Cats* (1939) Illustrated edition, Faber, 1974

Poets published since 1945, listed alphabetically by author

John Agard: *I Din Do Nuttin*, Bodley Head, 1983
Allan Ahlberg: *Please Mrs. Butler* (1983), Puffin, 1984.
Alan Brownjohn: *Brownjohn's Beasts*, Macmillan, 1970*
Charles Causley: *Collected Poems, 1951–75* (1975) Macmillan, 1983
  Figgie Hobbin (1970) Puffin 1979
  The Tail of the Trinosaur (1973) Beaver Books, 1976
Roald Dahl: *Revolting Rhymes* (1982), Puffin, 1984
  Dirty Beasts J. Cape, 1984*
Roy Fuller: *Seen Grandpa Lately?*, Andre Deutsch, 1972*
  Poor Roy, Andre Deutsch, 1977*
Robert Graves: *The Penny Fiddle: Poems For Children*, Cassell, 1960*
  The Poor Boy Who Followed His Star and Children's Poetry, Cassell, 1968*
Gregory Harrison: *Posting Letters*, Oxford, 1968*
John Heath-Stubbs: *A Parliament of Birds*, Chatto & Windus, 1975*
Phoebe Hesketh: *A Song of Sunlight*, Chatto & Windus, 1975*
Ted Hughes: *Meet My Folks* (1961) Puffin, 1977
  The Earth-Owl, Faber, 1963*
  Season Songs (1976) Faber, 1986
  Moon-Bells and Other Poems, Chatto & Windus, 1978*
  Under the North Star, Faber, 1981*
  What is the Truth? Faber, 1984*
Brian Jones: *The Spitfire on the Northern Line*, Chatto & Windus, 1975*
Brian Lee: *Late Home*, Kestrel, 1976*
George MacBeth: 'Noah's Journey' in *Collected Poems 1958–1970*, Macmillan, 1971
Roger McGough: *In the Glassroom*, Cape, 1976
  You Tell Me (with Michael Rosen) (1979) Puffin, 1981
  Sky in the Pie (1984) Puffin, 1985
Spike Milligan: *Silly Verse for Kids*, Puffin, 1968
  Unspun Socks from a Chicken's Laundry (1981), Puffin 1982
Adrian Mitchell: *Nothingmas Day*, Allison & Busby, 1984*
Ogden Nash: *Custard and Company*, selected and illustrated by Quentin Blake, Puffin, 1981
Gareth Owen: *Song of the City*, Fontana Lions, 1985
  Salford Road, Kestrel, 1979*
Brian Patten: *The Sly Cormorant and the Fishes*, Kestrel, 1977*
  Gargling With Jelly, Viking Kestrel 1985*
Sylvia Plath: *The Bed Book*, Faber, 1976*

James Reeves: *Complete Poems for Children*, Heinemann, 1973*
Michael Rosen: *Mind Your Own Business* (1974), Collins Lions 1975
  Wouldn't You Like to Know (1977), Puffin, 1981
  You Can't Catch Me (1981), Puffin 1983
  Quick, Let's Get Out of Here (1983), Puffin 1985
  (See also under R. McGough)
Clive Sansom: *An English Year*, Chatto & Windus, 1975*
Vernon Scannell: *After the Apple-Raid and Other Poems*, Chatto & Windus, 1972*
Kit Wright: *Rabbiting On*, Fontana Lions, 1978
  Hot Dog and Other Poems, Puffin, 1981

Note:

In recent years there have been two hardbacks series of contemporary children's poets – Chatto & Windus's single author series, *Chatto Poets For the Young*, edited by Leonard Clark and Oxford University Press's series *Three Poets*, edited by Michael Harrison. The former series is now out of print but many of the books are still available in libraries; several are listed above. The OUP series began with four titles published in 1984/85:

Catch the Light: Vernon Scannell, Gregory Harrison, Laurence Smith
Upright Downfall: Roy Fuller, Barbara Giles, Adrian Rumble
The Candy-Floss Tree: Gerda Mayer, Frank Flynn, Norman Nicholson.
The Crystal Zoo: U.A. Fanthorpe, John Cotton, L.J. Anderson

Appendix 2

Poems used in the enquiries but not quoted in the text.

Days

What are days for?
Days are where we live.
They come, they wake us
Time and time over.
They are to be happy in:
Where can we live but days?
Ah, solving that question
Brings the priest and the doctor
In their long coats
Running over the fields.

Philip Larkin

Frogs in the Wood

How good it would be to be lost again,
Night falling on the compass and the map
Turning to improbable flames,
Bright ashes going out in the ponds.

And how good it would be
To stand bewildered in a strange wood
Where you are the loudest thing
Your heart making a deafening noise.

And how strange when your fear of being lost has subsided
To stand listening to the frogs holding
Their arguments in the streams,
Condemning the barbarous herons.

And how right it is
To shrug off real and invented grief
As of no importance
To this moment of your life.

When being lost seems
So much more like being found,
And you find all that is lost
Is what weighed you down.

Brian Patten

Epitaph in Lydford Churchyard

Here lies in a horizontal position the outside case of
GEORGE ROUTLEDGE, WATCHMAKER
Integrity was the mainspring and prudence
the regulator of all the actions of his life;
humane, generous and liberal,
His hand never stopped till he had relieved distress.

So nicely regulated were his movements that
he never went wrong, except when set going by
people who did not know his key.
Even then he was easily set right again.
He had the art of disposing his time so well,
till his hours glided away, his pulse
stopped beating.

He ran down November 14, 1801 aged 57,
In hopes of being taken in hand by his Maker,
Thoroughly cleaned, repaired, wound up, and set
going in the world to come, when time shall be no
more.

Anon.

'I share my bedroom with my brother'

I share my bedroom with my brother
and I don't like it.
His bed's by the window
under my map of England's railways
that has a hole in just above Leicester
where Tony Sanders, he says,
killed a Roman centurion
with the Radio Times.

My bed's in the corner
and the paint on the skirting board
wrinkles when I push it with my thumb
which I do sometimes when I go to bed
sometimes when I wake up
but mostly on Sundays
when we stay in bed all morning.

That's when he makes pillow dens
under the blankets
so that only his left eye shows
and when I go deep-bed mining
for elastoplast spools
that I scatter with my feet
the night before,
and I jump on to his bed
shouting: eeyoueeyoueeyouee
heaping pillows on his head:
'Now breathe, now breathe'
and then there's quiet and silence
so I pull it away quick
and he's there laughing all over
sucking fresh air along his breathing-tube fingers.

Actually, sharing's all right.

Michael Rosen

Follower

My father worked with a horse-plough
His shoulders globed like a full sail strung
Between the shafts and the furrow.
The horses strained at his clicking tongue.

An expert. He would set the wing
And fit the bright steel-pointed sock.
The sod rolled over without breaking.
At the headrig, with a single pluck

Of reins, the sweating team turned round
And back into the land. His eye
Narrowed and angled at the ground,
Mapping the furrow exactly.

I stumbled in his hob-nailed wake,
Fell sometimes on the polished sod;
Sometimes he rode me on his back
Dipping and rising to his plod.

I wanted to grow up and plough,
To close one eye, stiffen my arm.
All I ever did was follow
In his broad shadow round the farm.

I was a nuisance, tripping, falling,
Yapping always. But today
It is my father who keeps stumbling
Behind me, and will not go away.

                  Seamus Heaney

Anthem for Doomed Youth

What passing-bells for these who die as cattle?
   Only the monstrous anger of the guns.
   Only the stuttering rifles' rapid rattle
Can patter out their hasty orisons.
No mockeries now for them; no prayers nor bells,
   Nor any voice of mourning save the choirs, –
The shrill, demented choirs of wailing shells;
   And bugles calling for them from sad shires.

What candles may be held to speed them all?
   Not in the hands of boys, but in their eyes
Shall shine the holy glimmers of good-byes.
   The pallor of girls' brows shall be their pall;
Their flowers the tenderness of patient minds,
And each slow dusk a drawing-down of blinds.

                  Wilfred Owen

Index

Index